High Praise ̣
YIPPIE GIRL
by Judy Gumbo

GUMBO DELIVERS A sharp-edged memoir of years of protest and resistance . . . A welcome addition to the literature of radical activism in the age of Johnson, Nixon, and beyond.

KIRKUS REVIEWS

YIPPIE GIRL LEAVES much unsaid. But it's the best account in existence of what life was like for a woman in the theatrical, goofy, messianic world of the Yippie boys . . . A fun read and a valuable political document, long overdue. It's cause for celebration.

COUNTERPUNCH

JUDY GUMBO WAS a friend and ally of the Black Panther Party back in the day—she is my friend and ally now. Like me, Judy believes in All Power to the People—Black people, white people, brown people, yellow people, blue, red, green and polka dot people. The theater that Yippies and the left radical protest groups pulled—it was great: To be satirical about everything! I loved it. People's Park was about land equity against the power structure. It was democratic and socialized. Then I was put on trial at the great Chicago Conspiracy Trial of which I was the eighth defendant. I heard Bill Kunstler tell the other defendants, "If you're not going to rise for Judge Hoffman you're going to jail." I told the defendants, "You're my buddies. I don't want you dudes in jail. I want you out on the streets speaking up, saying 'Free Bobby!'" But the FBI repressed all those great moments that we were involved in. We have to get our history right. So young folks can see where we were coming from. These stories have got to be told. And *Yippie Girl* tells it like it is.

BOBBY SEALE, founding chairman and national organizer, Black Panther Party

THERE ARE THOSE who were anti-war activists in the '60s and '70s—and then there is Judy Gumbo. She lived it, 24/7. Always a powerful life force, Judy has turned into a powerful writer—about herself, about the movement, and about life as a target of the FBI. Her own FBI file serves as a grand reminder of how activists were spied on back then. In *Yippie Girl*, Judy's remarkable memoir of her life events, she takes us back to an era that redefined the country, and redefined the lives of so many (then young) Americans.

BILL RITTER, news anchor, WABC-TV New York

JUDY GUMBO WAS and is quite a dame. Her new book is splendid. Hurrah for her.

SUSAN BROWNMILLER, feminist, activist, author, *Against Our Will, Men, Women and Rape*

JUDY GUMBO HAS written an irreverent, yet intimate, insider's romp through the most dramatic events of the late '60s and early '70s. Yippies, Black Panthers, Chicago 8 defendants, the Capitol bombing, and FBI agents populate this politically important, feminist work that also provides the setting for a passionately powerful love story. A fantastic trip that the reader will delight in taking.

ROBERT MEEROPOL, son of Ethel and Julius Rosenberg; founder, the Rosenberg Fund for Children; author, *An Execution in the Family*

IN JUDY GUMBO'S *Yippie Girl*, she shares her adventures as one of very few Yippie girls with her fellow travelers including my father Phil Ochs. The Yippies' unending creativity and courage provided the sardonic wit, wisdom, insight, and brutal honesty in the form of political music and theater needed for the revolution of the '60s. Judy's stories effortlessly dance between playful and profound and always deeply personal. With the world fractured by orchestrated divisiveness, *Yippie Girl* is a healing balm.

MEEGAN LEE OCHS, daughter of Phil Ochs; Artist Relations Manager, ACLU of Southern California

JUDY GUMBO WAS, and is, a badass. *Yippie Girl* chronicles, with passion and charm, her years on the front lines of the '60s resistance movement. There's so much to know and learn about in these pages. My advice to every young revolutionary, young feminist, future badass out there looking to heal this troubled world? STEAL THIS BOOK!

ALEXANDRA STYRON, author, *Steal This Country: A Handbook for Resistance, Persistence and Fixing Almost Everything* and *Reading My Father: A Memoir*

A TOUR DE force of a memoir from an activist and idealist, who made her mark in the '60s, '70s, and '80s and continues to live a life deeply committed to social justice and political action. A primer on how to stand up and be counted and have a good time doing it.

MARGARET KUNSTLER, civil rights attorney; co-author, *Hell No: Your Right to Dissent in Twenty-first-century America*

JUDY GUMBO IS a great storyteller, though it helps that she has a great story to tell. Her tales of Yippie (and Yippie-inspired) political theater should be on the shelf of anyone interested in activism.

CRAIG PEARISO, Associate Professor of Art History, Boise State University; author, *Radical Theatrics: Put-Ons, Politics, and the Sixties*

I FIRST MET Judy Gumbo at the Chicago Conspiracy Trial where I provided legal assistance to Bill Kunstler and Lenny Weinglass. I'm proud that Sorkin's movie portrays Fred Hampton as doing my job at the trial, but Judy's *Yippie Girl* tells it as it actually was. And it ain't over yet. Read this book!

MARIE "MICKI" LEANER, activist, Jane, Chicago-based underground abortion service; co-founder, Women's Prison Project and The China Group

WE'VE ALL READ about the counter-cultural adventures of the Yippie Boys—Abbie Hoffman, Jerry Rubin, Paul Krassner and Ed Sanders. Now we finally get to hear the real deal stories from the other side of the cisgender divide. And who better to deliver them than Judy Gumbo, activist extraordinaire? Her memoir is a rollicking ride through the '60s and '70s and an honest appraisal of the some of our youthful excesses. All I can say is "Yippie!"

LARRY "RATSO" SLOMAN, author, *Steal This Dream: Abbie Hoffman & the Countercultural Revolution in America*

VIVID, SEXY, HEARTBREAKING, jubilant; Judy Gumbo's *Yippie Girl* tells a story of living the '60s: changing your life, adopting new values and fighting the Man. She broke from her Canadian upbringing and Communist parents while embracing liberation. Judy and her Berkeley boyfriend and eventual husband Stew Albert followed the Black Panthers while trying to politicize the hippie movement. A founding member of the Youth International Party, she fought to overcome Yippie's male-dominated culture. And her love affair with the Vietnamese Revolution—literally—is all here, told realistically and without apology.

JEFF JONES, Consulting for Good Causes; and
ELEANOR STEIN, JD, LLM in Climate Change Law

NO ONE HAS told Judy Gumbo's story before. No one has recreated the '60s more vividly, more compassionately or with a more delicious sense of humor. *Yippie Girl* traces Gumbo's marriages, her lovers and her friends and does it without blowing anyone's cover. Gumbo includes portions from FBI documents that describe her adventures in the counterculture and the movement. Abbie Hoffman would say "Steal This Book." Jerry Rubin would say "Do It!" I say buy *Yippie Girl*, read it and let it blow your mind the way it did mine.

JONAH RASKIN, author, *Beat Blues: San Francisco, 1955*

A ROLLICKING TALE of the radical '60s, finally told by one of the women who made it all happen. Judy Gumbo's insightful, sexy, often-funny memoir of the Yippies is a wild ride through Berkeley, Chicago, Hanoi, and other hot spots of an era that reshaped America.

LAWRENCE ROBERTS, author of *Mayday 1971: A White House at War, a Revolt in the Streets, and the Untold History of America's Biggest Mass Arrest*

LOVE THE WRITING: *Very* live, immediate—this does not feel like ancient history, it's living and breathing in our lives right now. It's part of our power, people power.

KRIS WELCH, host, *The Talkies*, KPFA-FM

AT LAST! WE so need to hear more voices of women involved in the '60s youth and anti-war movement. Zelig-like, Judy Gumbo seemed to be everywhere, with an insider's vantage point on key protest events and personages of the late '60s and early '70s. More importantly, she brings a clear-eyed but unjaundiced feminist perspective on the blithe misogyny of the movement's male "heavies." Nevertheless, Gumbo's fun-loving Yippie ethos continues to burn bright in the pages of her memoir: *Yippie Girl* provides a rollicking read, entertaining as well as instructive to a new generation of youthful social change activists. As a '60s historian, I learned much I didn't know—and can't wait to introduce Judy Gumbo to my students. I think they'll love her as much as the FBI loathed her.

ANIKO BODROGHKOZY, Professor of Media Studies, University of Virginia; author, *Equal Time: Television and the Civil Rights Movement*

RED-DIAPER BABY-DOCTORAL STUDENT turned *Yippie Girl*, Judy Gumbo— so named by Panther leader Eldridge Cleaver—engagingly recounts her revolutionary travails, including tussles with the FBI and other police operatives, during the long '60s. A peripatetic quest lures Gumbo from her native Canada to Berkeley, NYC, the 1968 Democratic Party Convention in Chicago, Hanoi, Havana, and innumerable sites in-between. Her captivating memoir proves most illuminating as a feminist corrective to the male-centric antics of and accounts by fellow Jewish Yippies Jerry Rubin, Abbie Hoffman, and the author's sometimes partner-later beloved husband Stew Albert, among others. Running the gamut of emotions, Gumbo's story, which she deems "narrative or creative non-fiction," sparkles with its revelatory honesty, particularly as she moves "out of girlhood into womanhood." Absolutely indispensable for its insights into the anti-war, counter-culture, and women's liberation movements.

ROBERT C. COTTRELL, Professor Emeritus, History and American Studies, California State University, Chico

JUDY GUMBO STOOD where the Black Power and Anti-Vietnam War movements intersected. She participated in the Chicago '68 protests. You've read of her infamous comrades: Jerry Rubin and Abbie Hoffman. Now comes the first-ever female Yippie memoir—and it's a scorcher! Her words hit hard—yet she's reflective and insightful—which male autobiographies lack. Gumbo tramples through the war torn jungles of Vietnam and emerges to push women's rights of the '70s and beyond. Read this, then start your own movement.

PAT THOMAS, author, *Jerry Rubin: An American Revolutionary* and *Listen Whitey: Sounds of Black Power*

GUMBO HAS WRITTEN a romp—breathless, amazing, and terrifying all at the same time—through an equally divisive time in American history with a "you are there" energy. Even if you weren't there, you will want to know about this and what youth, sexism, and political commitment can, and cannot, do. Don't miss this.

SUSAN M. REVERBY, PhD, Marion Butler McLean Professor Emerita in the History of Ideas, Professor Emerita of Women's and Gender Studies, Wellesley College

WRITTEN AS NARRATIVE nonfiction with the smooth contours of a novel, *Yippie Girl* provides a comprehensive insider history of early Yippie days. For those of us that arrived late to the revolution, Gumbo gives us a joyous and intimate guide to our roots, bringing us into the lives and homes of countercultural icons. At the same time, she revisits living amidst sweaty hippie machismo and Yippie sarcasm through the lens of a 21st-century feminist, giving us a badly needed window into a time of hopeful chaos and cultural transformation.

MICHAEL I. NIMAN, Professor of Journalism, SUNY Buffalo State; author, *People of the Rainbow: A Nomadic Utopia*

THE MOVEMENT AGAINST the war in Vietnam was not known for laughs. Except for the Yippies, a band of activists who were determined to combine the counterculture of the hippies, the politics of the radical left and a sense of humor. As Yippie Judy Gumbo reminds us in her important new book, *Yippie Girl*, the Yippies were Marxists—a mix of Karl Marx and Groucho Marx. Exhibit A: they nominated a pig, Pigasus, for president of the United States as they gathered in Chicago in 1968 for the Democratic National Convention—an event that otherwise was decidedly not funny and was marked by police riots against Yippies and other anti-war protesters. Lacking a sense of humor, FBI Director J. Edgar Hoover regarded Yippies as terrorists. In fact, an FBI file on Gumbo declared she was "the most vicious . . . and the most dangerous to the internal security of the United States." For nearly a decade, the FBI tapped her phones, attached tracking devices to her car, and broke into her homes, including a very isolated cabin in the Catskill Mountains where agents often secretly schlepped and illegally broke in. Like many women then, Judy faced a confounding situation: at the same time she strongly opposed the war in Vietnam and injustice at home she also fought the sexist behavior of the men she loved and worked with in the anti-war movement. Her clear-eyed history of those years is evidence not only that she did survive. It also is evidence of the important role she and other women played despite the efforts of the FBI to silence them and the efforts of movement men to either use or ignore them.

BETTY MEDSGER, author, *The Burglary: The Discover of J. Edgar Hoover's Secret FBI*

YIPPIE GIRL IS one hell of a good read. Serious, but never sanctimonious, Judy Gumbo takes us into her '60s world, and what a world it was! A Canadian red-diaper baby, she joined up with the politicized hippies who formed Yippie, was an ally of the Black Panther Party, became a women's liberationist, and, through her anti-war work, had a clandestine affair with a high-ranking North Vietnamese official. Throughout, she was relentlessly surveilled by the FBI, whose role in subverting the '60s she usefully highlights..

ALICE ECHOLS, Professor of History, The University of Southern California

BEHIND EVERY SUCCESSFUL man is a woman—and behind every prominent Yippie guy was an unsung Yippie girl. One of the most fascinating is Judy Gumbo, a Canadian communist who found herself at the epicenter of various seminal events in counterculture history. Her chock-full-of-details memoir offers a rare, behind-the-headlines look at the characters, conflicts, and craziness that helped drive the anti-war movement.

ROY RIVENBURG, journalist and humor writer

IN THIS RIVETING, intimate memoir, Judy Gumbo, takes her readers on a magical mystery tour with the Yippies, Black Panthers, Weather Underground, Women's Liberation, and the FBI agents who relentlessly pursued them. Written with candor, humor, and page-turning suspense, Gumbo transports us to the barricades of the late '60s and early '70s social and political revolutions. From anti-war protests and the Chicago 8 trial, to a lesbian commune in Texas and a peace conference in Hanoi, Gumbo brilliantly brings the passion of the time alive and pulsing on the page. A must read for students of the '60s and anyone who wants a blueprint for how to challenge the patriarchy.

CLARA BINGHAM, author, *Witness to the Revolution: Radicals, Resisters, Vets, Hippies, and the Year America Lost its Mind and Found its Soul*

JUDY GUMBO IS a badass, and *Yippie Girl* is a badass book. Intersectional before the term existed, Judy, born Clavir and later dubbed Gumbo, has led a life shaped by her opposition to racism, sexism, imperialism, and war and by her commitment, as she puts it, to being where the action is. *Yippie Girl* chronicles that life, setting the author's quest to define herself and the growth of her capacity to love in the context of her activism in the anti-war and feminist movements of the '60s and beyond. Bearing witness to the many ways that the personal is political, *Yippie Girl* is an important addition to the archive of twentieth-century protest movements and a crucial document in the history of American feminism.

LOUISE YELIN, Professor Emerita, Literature and Gender Studies, Purchase College SUNY, feminist and anti-war activist

IN THIS MEMOIR, Judy Gumbo, a principal figure in the Youth International Party from the late 60s through early and mid 70s, establishes her place among those she dubs winners of "the Academy Award of Protest." We see how she and her closest comrades negotiated all the contradictions, personal and political, that living as a revolutionary in the United States during those years entailed. Gumbo is revelatory about self, deeply respectful of others (and their privacy, as appropriate), and proudly radical to this day. The 'happy ferocity' that guided Yippie rebellion via theatrical satire stands out vividly. And from those recollections Gumbo leads us to a moving elegy for the dissenters of that period that we have now lost.

   HOWARD BRICK, Louis Evans Professor of History, University of Michigan

YIPPIE GIRL IS the book that future historians will turn to for the real, true story of women revolutionaries in the '60s. Literary, rollicking and color splashed, this engrossing book tells the story of a complicated, bold Canadian heroine at the heart of the '60s counterculture and anti-Vietnam war movement; whose rebellion and triumphant feats of defiance, made her push harder and dare more. Written in a vibrant, deeply observant style, Gumbo's thrilling treasury of tales recalls the ecstasy, perils and possibilities of those now mythic days. Judy Gumbo is a legend; her book, *Yippie Girl* lets the sun shine in.

   LESLIE BRODY, author, *Sometimes You Have to Lie: The Life and Times of Louise Fitzhugh, Renegade Author of Harriet the Spy*

JUDY GUMBO'S MEMOIR is a rollicking tour-de-force. Few books so vividly convey the idealism, excitement, and devil-may-care recklessness that inspired some people who were caught up in the maelstrom of radical politics and countercultural experimentation in the late 60s and early 70s. It's an absolute delight to read, full of fascinating anecdotes, populated by a virtual *Who's Who* of the '60s countercultural left, and narrated with a verve that sometimes elicits the sensation of time-travel. Offering the much-needed perspective of a woman on events that have been largely told from the perspective of famous men, *Yippie Girl* will delight—and surprise—young readers as well as grizzled veterans of the "movement."

   CHARLES L. PONCE LEON, Professor of History and American Studies, Long Beach State University

YIPPIE
GIRL

YIPPIE GIRL

EXPLOITS IN PROTEST
AND
DEFEATING THE FBI

JUDY GUMBO

THREE ROOMS PRESS
New York, NY

Yippie Girl: Exploits in Protest and Defeating the FBI
by Judy Gumbo

This is a work of creative nonfiction. The events are portrayed to the best of the author memory. Some parts of this book, including dialog, characters and their characteristics, locations and time, may not be entirely factual.

ISBN 978-1-953103-18-5 (trade paperback original)
ISBN 978-1-953103-19-2 (Epub)
Library of Congress Control Number: 2021947721

TRP-095

First Edition

Publication Date: May 3, 2022

BISAC category code
BIO032000 BIOGRAPHY & AUTOBIOGRAPHY / Social Activists
BIO022000 BIOGRAPHY & AUTOBIOGRAPHY / Women
BIO026000 BIOGRAPHY & AUTOBIOGRAPHY / Personal Memoirs
BIO010000 BIOGRAPHY & AUTOBIOGRAPHY / Political

COVER AND INTERIOR DESIGN:
KG Design International, www.katgeorges.com

COVER PHOTO:
Judy Gumbo leading the Women's March, Miami Beach 1972. Photo © Jean Raiser, from the personal archives of Judy Gumbo Albert

MORE INFORMATION ON JUDY GUMBO:
www.yippiegirl.com

DISTRIBUTED INTERNATIONALLY BY:
Publishers Group West: www.pgw.com

Three Rooms Press
New York, NY
www.threeroomspress.com
info@threeroomspress.com

"*Judy Gumbo is a hero of the movement. Her story includes a compelling and intimate narrative of the unwarranted government intrusion experienced by dissidents in America who attempted to halt the war in Vietnam.*"
DANIEL ELLSBERG, "LEAKER," *PENTAGON PAPERS*

"*I too have great respect for Judy Gumbo. She's an excellent thinker . . . her thinking is many times more advanced than my own which is patently naive at times.*"
ABBIE TO ANITA HOFFMAN, DECEMBER 10, 1974,
LETTERS FROM UNDERGROUND

"*Be good to friends who are good to you, also be good to friends who are bad to you, for only friends will go with you on the long road to revolution.*"
DO XUAN OANH, VIETNAMESE POET AND DIPLOMAT

"*One is not born but rather becomes a woman.*"
SIMONE DE BEAUVOIR

TABLE OF CONTENTS

PROLOGUE

I AM AN ORIGINAL YIPPIE. YIPPIE is a state of mind.

In the late 1960s, when Yippies were briefly darlings of the media, those of us who "dropped out," who rejected mainstream values, were called hippies; a Yippie is a *politicized hippie*, a protestor who has been hit over the head by a cop—and woke up. Satire was our primary organizing strategy. Yippies made fun of all things serious and used humor to hold evildoers up to ridicule—a president, murderous cops, misogynist men, an uncaring polluter, capitalist profit seekers, and/or anyone who practices any form of injustice.

I first bonded with my lover Stew Albert based on his Yippie politics, his personal network in the protest movement, and his blue eyes, and curly blond hair which I found incredibly sexy. I was also lucky: Stew's two best friends were Yippie founder Jerry Rubin and Eldridge Cleaver, Minister of Information for the Black Panther Party.

Thanks to Stew, when I first moved to Berkeley I met Kathleen and Eldridge Cleaver. For me, Kathleen and Eldridge represented the most influential of 1960s protest movement power couples. Plus, in 1968, the Black Panther Party was the only Black radical group who welcomed white support. Kathleen and Eldridge would visit our Berkeley home to talk and smoke pot. Eldridge also invited me to attend a Black Panther Party study group, where I'd raise my fist and chant along with Panther Chairman Bobby Seale:

Power to the People,
Black Power to Black People
Panther Power to the Vanguard

Panther Power to the Vanguard means that, in any resistance movement of color with white supporters, people of color must lead.

Our most memorable Yippie protest also took place in 1968 at the iconic Democratic Convention in Chicago. To satirize greed, my lover Stew, me, and the Yippie inner core ran a live pig named Pigasus for President of the United States. 1968 was the year before what I'd named the Great Chicago Conspiracy Trial. In 1969, the U.S. government charged eight male leaders of that demonstration—including Yippies Abbie Hoffman and Jerry Rubin, plus Black Panther Bobby Seale—with conspiracy to incite a riot. In the game of who got to scale the highest peak of Yippiedom, Jerry boasted that, as a defendant, he'd won "The Academy Award of Protest." Abbie told me I would have "done nicely" as a defendant had any women been indicted. No women were. Abbie's praise did not mollify me. I was not named a defendant or even an unindicted co-conspirator as Stew was. I was crushed.

And the Trial of the Chicago 8 became the show trial of my generation.

Early on in the Trial, lead attorney William Kunstler appointed me manager of the Conspiracy Trial office. Mine was a traditional woman's job—I answered phones and handed out mail. Later, I went on to type, copy, and then snail-mail transcripts of the Trial's dramatics to underground and mainstream media across America and Europe—scenes such as Bobby Seale being chained and gagged like a slave in the courtroom of an old white man judge. But I got it—she who disseminates history can rule worlds.

In January 1970, a clandestine message arrived at the Trial office. A delegation from America's enemy—North Vietnam—wanted to meet the Conspiracy defendants in a town outside Montreal. For peace activists like me to meet North Vietnamese—who our protest movement considered heroes—was the crown jewel in the pantheon of anti-war privilege. Our visitors wanted to update the defendants on the progress of the Vietnam War and to be themselves updated on the progress of the Trial. The defendants quarreled; they fantasized about leaving the country. But crossing the Canadian border would have violated their bail. Saner lawyers prevailed. The Chicago 8 defendants did not go. I, a Canadian citizen, did.

A brief twenty-four hours after I first met the delegation's leader, a dark-eyed North Vietnamese poet nationally known in Vietnam, we became lovers.

On occasion I still ask myself—what the hell was I thinking? How could I have slept with an enemy of the United States when my adopted country was at war with his? Did my strong attraction to this man make me unpatriotic? But if I time-travel back to early 1970, to Washington D.C., to the spot where Honest Abe sits on his democratic throne, I can see myself now, with my brown curls spilling down my back, a National Liberation Front (NLF) flag painted on one cheek, and an orange Women's Movement symbol on the other. A green marijuana leaf decorates my chin and I've painted a Weather Underground lightning bolt on my forehead. I speak into a microphone in my best take-no-prisoners voice:

> *"President Richard Nixon and his arrogant pig generals are the traitors to America. They betray the American people by invading and bombing Vietnam. Vietnam has a 1000-year history of defeating foreign aggressors. The Vietnamese will win. And we will help them stop that evil war. All the Nixon war machine does is condemn young people like us—and millions of Vietnamese—to death. I belong to a New Yippie Nation. We believe in peace, justice, sex, drugs, and rock and roll. Youth will make the revolution! Yippie!"*

By 1972, both Republican and Democratic Conventions were to take place in Miami. By then, more than 50,000 Americans had died in Vietnam, and more than three million Indochinese had been poisoned, burned, maimed, or killed. In Miami, Conspiramania reigned. I have a photo that shows me in the front lines of an anti-rape/anti-war march. I'm wearing short shorts and beating a drum. A banner behind me reads Women in Revolt. But who was that tall, blond, well-dressed woman marching on my left who stuck to me like glue then disappeared? What would I have thought had I known my name appeared on a secret FBI Security Index of over 11,000 people to be incarcerated as subversives in the event of a national emergency? Or that an operative of President Richard Nixon planned to kidnap dissident leaders in Miami and imprison us in Mexico until after the conventions, claiming,

> *Of the individuals connected with the anti-war movement going on in Miami Beach, Florida, the subject JUDY GUMBO is considered to be the most vicious, the most anti-American, the most anti-establishment, and the most dangerous to the internal security of the United States.*

I celebrated when I read this in my FBI files. I'd won my personal Academy Award of Protest.

By 1973, Stew and I decided it was time to take a break both from our public lives and from the FBI. We moved to an isolated cabin in the Catskill Mountains. But our plan to escape intense FBI surveillance turned out to be magical thinking. FBI harassment of me did not end. Nonetheless, I ended up a total winner against them.

YIPPIE
GIRL

CHAPTER 1:
"KILL YOUR PARENTS"

WHEN I FIRST HEARD JERRY RUBIN use the slogan "Kill Your Parents," the phrase appalled me. But Jerry did not claim with any serious intent that I murder both my parents. He meant let go of the dysfunctional conditioning we absorb growing up. A Yippie uses satire and ridicule to confront evildoers. I am a Red Diaper Yippie—a child of parents who were members of the Communist Party. Many 1960s activists were Red Diaper babies, but I've met only a few who joined the Yippies. Communists are far too serious for us.

Jerry Rubin was no Red Diaper baby. He did, however, epitomize the communist ideal of a working-class hero—Jerry's mother was a secretary; his father drove a bread delivery truck then became an organizer in the Bakery Drivers Union. Abbie Hoffman's mother was what in the 1940s we called a homemaker while his father was a distributor of legal, wholesale prescription drugs.

I began at a young age to call my parents by their given names. My mother was no "mom" or "mommy" to me; I addressed her as Harriet, as if formal speech could keep her at a distance. I called my father Leo, rather than by his function as my biological parent. Although I could not have articulated this at the time, I believe I did this both to create intellectual distance and to make real my childhood version of the communist equality I was taught.

My father Leo Clavir was a communist; my mother Harriet Clavir was a communist—and an alcoholic. When I was growing up in Canada, Leo held a prestigious job in the global communist entertainment industry—he was for a time the only importer and distributor of films to the entire North American continent from what was then the Union of Soviet Socialist Republics. In my adult opinion, Leo must have been a Russian asset.

I suspect that my parents were clandestine Party members. For business purposes, it would benefit the Russians to give their North American film franchise to someone they could completely trust, but who was not publicly identified with the Party. But the Party was my parents' community—all their close friends were Party members. Canadian Party Chairman Tim Buck and other communist notables were frequent visitors to our home. Early on, my parents had let my younger sister and I in on it. Yes, they were members of the communist Party, but this information was not to be broadcast. Or even spoken aloud.

I grew up short for my age but possessed of an intense lifelong curiosity which prompted me to make a dash toward anything I found compelling, especially the world of nature, flowers, and dogs. Curiosity was my entry to seeking great adventure. But my curiosity did not extend to communism. I was so immersed in communism that for me it was just there. I learned the word "comrade" as an expression of minimalist endearment; I came to accept as a comrade anyone with whom I shared an acquaintance-ship and a similar political outlook.

By the time I was seven, the Red Scare of the 1950s had taken hold in the United States. communism, specifically Soviet communism, inspired fear and loathing in American hearts and minds—initially with those on the right. But hating communism rapidly became normalized for the majority of "patriotic" Americans. The evil doings of Reds like my parents— "communists controlled by Russia"—were promoted by mainstream media outlets across the United States. Reds were to be found everywhere—programmed like robots to carry out their evil agenda, corrupting children in schools, professors in academia, Hollywood screenwriters, and government bureaucrats. Together with fellow travelers and closeted gay people, to be labelled a Red meant you dedicated your life to subverting the American—i.e. Capitalist—Way of Life. This same ideology applied in Canada. With brutal consequences. The Canadian Communist Party was outlawed by the Canadian government in 1940, since the Party's support of the Hitler-Stalin Pact meant it opposed helping Britain in World War II. Around 130 prominent Canadian communists were interned in camps under harsh conditions and without trial—acquaintances of my parents among them. The communism I learned from my parents would, in the gendered language of my day, create a new "socialist man," an ideal which, once achieved, would unify the world. Our entire planet would be committed to *"mir i druzbah"*—world peace and friendship—with equality and justice for all. This vision of a better world as my parents, my younger sister Miriam, and I defined it was collectivist, anti-racist, and committed to the power of the working class.

All my superheroes as a child were communists, as portrayed in Soviet cinema. By the time I was eight or nine, I'd perch upstairs on my grandmother's green sofa in my hometown of Toronto, as my father Leo gave me, his eldest daughter, first-run private screenings of Soviet films that became classics. I still recall director Sergei Eisenstein's images from his film *Battleship Potemkin* of sailors rebelling against a repressive Tzarist regime, and a wild-eyed Ivan the Terrible, a dictator who got things done. No cartoon *Sleeping Beauty* for this girl. Galina Ulanova—internationally acclaimed ballerina and my primary female superhero—floated across my father's screen with a single-minded seriousness that created both art and beauty.

I'd watch expectantly as Leo extracted two circular brown metal reels—one empty and one full—out of his battered square case covered with stickers in incomprehensible Cyrillic. He'd click a reel wound with celluloid into the top arm of his film projector, thread the film carefully through the projector's sprockets, attach the film onto the empty bottom reel, then ask:

"Ya ready?"

* * *

MY FATHER'S JOB IMPORTING SOVIET FILMS to North America came with perks—specifically trips to the Soviet Union. In September 1953, motivated perhaps by a fear of persecution by Canadian authorities similar to that faced by communists in the United States, my father diversified his business. He identified himself publicly with the mainstream. He called himself an impresario; he organized trips of artists who just happened to be communists or fellow travelers to visit Moscow, Tashkent, and Samarkand. My mother Harriet, my sister Miriam, and I stayed home.

Like most children, however, I was an instinctive convert to capitalist acquisition. "What did ya bring me?" were the first words I spoke each time my father returned home with a treasure: a black sheepskin Cossack hat, a set of wooden nesting peasant dolls painted in multicolored enamel, and my favorite, a Soviet Barbie doll with slim, un-Soviet-like proportions. She wore a peasant blouse, green vest, and hand-made, brown leather ballet slippers that laced up to her knees. My father also gave me a witch puppet. Her name was Baba Yaga—a lead character in Russian folktales. She arrived at my house complete with black cape and oversize peasant stomping boots made of gray and yellow plaster. My younger sister Miriam lusted after Baba Yaga; I, the older, more competitive sibling, refused to allow my sister to play with her.

I had internalized a kiddie version of the communist mantra: "From each according to their ability, to each according to their need." You put in what you are able, and you get back what you need. Simple. Equal. No discrimination based on wealth or class. Or age. Or race. Or privilege. Or even gender. But I also understood that ownership of private property gives you power. I refused to put in according to my ability. I did not allow my sister to play with either my Soviet Barbie or my Baba Yaga puppet. And I got back what I needed. I made my sister jealous—an early lesson for me in the power of owning property.

* * *

LED BY LEO, THE CLAVIR FAMILY loved to deconstruct our world while at our family's dinner table. We were both Jewish and "godless" communists as the far right likes to claim. Instead of synagogue, our rituals took place in front of bookshelves, my atheistic family's holy of holies. The shelves contained, among other titles, the complete works of Lenin and a blue and white Volume I of Karl Marx's *Capital* printed in the USSR.

From my seat at the family table I'd stare longingly at one book, third shelf from the top, titled in blood-red capital letters *Seduction of the Innocent*. A subhead followed: "the influence of comic books on today's youth."

If my mother Harriet caught me looking wistfully at *Seduction* she invariably announced, "You are not allowed to touch that book."

I disobeyed. I'd tiptoe to that bookshelf after bedtime, extract *Seduction* from its shelf, crawl under my sheet, turn on my flashlight, and read it. I understood only a portion of Fredric Wertham, M.D.'s claims—that Wonder Woman was an S&M lesbian, Superman was a fascist, Batman and Robin had sex with each other inside the Batmobile—but Wertham also gave me my first experience with misogynist violence. I can still picture in my mind Wertham's illustration of a dagger being plunged into the eye of a screaming woman. Whether such an image promotes actual violence remains controversial—at least for me. And Wertham used this illustration as an agitational tool. My mother bought in. But she overdid Wertham's insight. After I was caught reading *Seduction*, I was not allowed to read or own *any* comic book.

I admit it now, Wertham's title was in part correct; I had been seduced. Not by his anti-queer prejudice or violent anti-woman imagery, but by that which was forbidden.

By the time I became a Yippie I had benefited from my childhood insurgencies; I knew how to combine anarchy with discipline—an effective strategy for resistance.

* * *

MINE WAS A FAMILY OF IMMIGRANT Jews. Meyer Lionel, my mother's great grandfather, born in 1864, was given his last name "Willinsky" when he answered, "I'm from Vilna" to the question "What's your name?" put to him in incomprehensible English at Ellis Island. He later moved his family to Toronto. My father's family, the Clavirs, obtained passage from a piano-maker who died before he boarded the boat, passing on to my great-grandfather both steerage tickets and the last name Clavir from the German word "Klavier" for piano.

When Leo first met Harriet, she was a 1930s beauty: a tall, slim, blue-eyed blond. Both my parents were students at the University of Toronto. Leo majored in economics, political science, and history; he graduated in 1933. But Harriet's scholarship, funded by leading Toronto hoteliers—also communists—lasted only two years. My mother, who considered herself an intellectual, never graduated college. But Leo and Harriet did embrace both each other and the Canadian Communist Party.

My parents married in 1940. I was born on June 25, 1943. I grew up in a white three-story house at 9 Kendal Avenue just north of Toronto's original Jewish enclave. Ours was more a matriarchal than a communist dwelling. My mother, father, younger sister Miriam, and I laid claim to Kendal's middle floor— and the most progressive politics. My mother's older sister,

Florence Kamman, or "Kammie," lived with her husband Peter Skinner in Kendal's studio basement. I adored my Uncle Peter. He was a kind and gentle man who staggered from cerebral palsy when he walked and earned a pittance doing menial work inappropriate to his intelligence. He found solace playing classical music on his upright piano. After Peter was fired from the Parker Pen Company, he committed suicide in his car which he had parked deliberately in the company parking lot.

Kammie and my mother were the two surviving daughters of my grandmother Ida Willinsky and my grandfather M. J. (Morris Jacob) Kamman. Zelda, my mother's middle sister, a brown curly-haired beauty, had died of a brain tumor before I was born. My grandmother and my mother rarely talked about Zelda; only her photo informed me of her existence. I was left explaining Zelda's death to myself as the reason why Ida and M. J. occupied separate bedrooms on Kendal's top floor.

To grieve a personal death was minimized for us Clavir children; death by ideology was honored. I turned ten in 1953, six days after Ethel and Julius Rosenberg, accused "atomic spies" for the villainous Soviets but good guys of my childhood, were executed.

Most likely at my parents' urging, in the week before the Rosenberg execution I climbed onto a kitchen chair, picked up our yellow wall phone, dialed "0" then asked the operator to call the White House. My mission was to ask President Eisenhower to grant the Rosenbergs clemency—a word I had just learned. I consider this my first act of opposing government injustice. But my telephone call, and a world-wide protest movement on the Rosenbergs's behalf, went unrewarded. The "Atom Spies" had to die.

Shortly after the execution, at our family table, her voice tight with rage, my mother read out loud Ethel's and Julius's final message:

We were comforted in the sure knowledge that others would carry on after us.

7

That I can recall so clearly climbing on that kitchen chair means my communist parents had imprinted on me that I must both fear and at the same time resist the power of the state. From the day of the Rosenberg execution on, I have done as Ethel and my mother demanded: I carry on. I have also never violated a prime communist directive—*never talk to the FBI, and do not name names to government officials.*

* * *

1956 WAS A HARSH YEAR—FOR THE communist world, the Clavir family, and for me. By 1956 I was 13 and busy at my public high school flirting with a tall, gangly boy with pimples so he would ask me on a date. He never did. At home, my surging teenage hormones allowed the anger I had so long repressed to surface. I quit apologizing to Harriet. I gave up my fear of siding against her. Instead, I became the ambusher, waiting for my mother to make a mistake. I did my best to trip her up. It registered on me that when my mother said "I love you," she always followed it with a "but" which contained what I experienced as a harsh critique. And impacted my self-confidence. To be good was not good enough for Harriet; to be good was the enemy of the perfect human my mother expected me to be. Even today I can't help but second guess myself after completing a major project or an innocuous email. I always check; it's always fine.

To demonstrate his affection, Leo gave me gifts of stuff and money. My father's largess made me happy. I learned that gifts of money equaled love. I'm grateful to my father for such early conditioning since, as an adult, I became a very successful fundraiser for progressive causes.

One day in 1956, a senior functionary who oversaw Toronto's communist newspaper arrived at 9 Kendal. He informed my mother that she must throw out her just completed layout of the Party newspaper, with its now grossly incorrect, pro-Stalinist line. In those days, laying out a newspaper was a tedious job involving columns of various sized type that had to be cut and pasted by hand to fit onto sheets of paper to print. An enraged Harriet picked up our largest knife and chased the man from kitchen to living room and back to kitchen before my father subdued her. My mother's act was not a pro-Stalin protest. She was rebelling against being taken for granted. Harriet adhered to boundaries only if she could justify them politically or set them for herself. With such a sudden change in political line over which my mother had no control, she could no longer repress her rage at what arbitrary authority demanded of her.

It's a truism that gaps emerge between your ideals and your ability to implement them. It is in that gap that disillusion lies. In 1956, Soviet Premier Nikita Khrushchev publicly denounced Joseph Stalin's cult of personality, creating pain and disillusionment in the global communist movement. In Canada, J. B. Salsberg, a friend of my parents who was a trusted, high-level Jewish functionary in the Canadian Party, returned from a trip to the Soviet Union, appalled by the anti-Semitism he encountered there.

The personal intersected bitterly with the political after Khrushchev's and Salsberg's revelations. One third of Jewish Canadian Party members quit the Communist Party. Including Harriet. My mother struggled her entire life with the dissonance between her communist ideals of equality and her perfectionism, a battle which she covered up by drinking and chain-smoking. She was helped along by the frustration I know she felt about the limits of her life as my father's helpmate. It took decades for me to see my mother as a woman who dealt with her oppression by railing drunkenly against the hypocrisy of others but who, in 1956 was brave enough to face herself and quit the Party—but escalate her drinking. Not so my father, who I looked to as a paragon of virtue. While the communist commandment to keep secrets likely added to my mother's disillusion, Leo kept his Party affiliation secret until the day he died.

To grow up a Red Diaper Canadian made me an idealist for life, even though, in the majority of cases, communism turned out to be the opposite of what was advertised. I also understood that, to succeed, communist ideology is sustained by authoritarian practice. I was encouraged to read a book titled *The Road to Life* by Anton Semyonovich Makarenko. This novel gave my intellectual mother Harriet an ideological justification to crack down on my behavior. I was trained to abide by Makarenko values: work diligently, act responsibly, and happily accept, for the greater socialist good, limits set by others on my independence. I now jokingly call this trio of commandments Stalinist Discipline. They are not as negative as they appear: I still work diligently, I stick to a task with obstinacy and tenacity—but rather than conform to restrictions set by others, I negotiate from strength. And win. Or leave.

Surprisingly, my immersion in Stalinist discipline served me well—especially in the anarchic world of Yippie.

CHAPTER 2:
FROM COMMUNIST PARTY TO HIPPIE PAD

IDEALISM OFFERS YIPPIES THE FREEDOM TO make foolhardy choices. My first was to get married. I was 20. I assumed my ideal of a traditional marriage would give me everything I wanted—sex, security, and the freedom to pursue a career of my own. Yes, my college pal Dierdre had moved in with her ideal lover and ended up pregnant with no mate; Toby, my best friend from high school and a budding classical pianist, had married a man with money and given up her career. I was arrogant enough to believe such a future could never apply to me.

I was a graduate student in Sociology at the University of Toronto when I met a student actor named David Hugh Milner Hemblen. I was attracted to the superficial: his British lineage, his well-trained Shakespearian voice, his straight blond hair that set off a wide-set boxer's nose and a penis so large—to my inexperienced but no longer virginal eye—I had named it "The Man." I saw Hemblen as my personal Prince Charming who I could count on for financial stability and reassurance—and sex. Had I been honest with myself, my motivation was not so much to enter bourgeois wedded bliss but to escape Clavir family drama.

I married Hemblen in October 1963. Ours was a non-religious ceremony at a Unitarian Church, followed by a reception at a prominent Toronto hotel, owned by two members of the Party. My father Leo oversaw my wedding as if he were a Hollywood mogul. To curry favor with my Scottish in-laws, Leo hired a bagpiper; to impress his Communist Party pals and business cronies he hired two almost-famous, progressive Canadian folksingers. Harriet, by then financial manager to our family's ever fluctuating fortunes, bought for herself, as mother of the bride, a green velvet dress with a bejeweled gold lamé jacket. Jealous, I decided her attire must have cost double what she allocated for my white organza wedding gown and bridesmaids' green sateen dresses with matching hair bows six inches tall. When I realized Leo must have spent $10,000 (Canadian) on my wedding, my jealousy evaporated. Communist ethics triumphed; Leo had put in according to his at the time wealthier ability and I got back what I needed— I won a round in my family's money equals love battles.

Mine was a minor victory. Overall I felt powerless. My parents' display of bourgeois wealth did not cut it for me; I was given no say in planning my own wedding.

Three years later, I walked into catastrophe. I had climbed two flights of stairs that led into Hemblen's and my three-room central Toronto apartment, unlocked our door, and entered. I had, that day, completed my Ph.D. oral exams under the gaze of Elsie the Cow, the sole remaining wooden remnant of the former Borden's Dairy, now home to the Sociology Department at the University of Toronto. I ought to have been happy, but I was not. Instead I undermined myself by second guessing mistakes I decided that I had made in arguing for a divine truth favored by conservative sociologists—that functional systems are those in which people happily maintain social equilibrium.

I sat down in my orange chair under the eaves. White cowrie shell eyes in an elongated head of ebony such as those sculptures Picasso admired in his African period stared at me. I hated that sculpture for its uncompromising gaze, but I could not discard it. No dutiful daughter returns a wedding gift from an important business associate of her father's. Next to the head I'd placed a 12-inch black and white TV on which, a month after my wedding, I'd watched television announcer Walter Cronkite make an announcement that defined my generation—that President John F. Kennedy had been assassinated. My mother was not shocked. The Kennedy assassination only confirmed Harriet's opinion that Americans were uncouth, uncultured, and ungovernable, off-spring of that furious rabble who threw out civility along with the British in 1776. For her, communist though she was, the Thirteen Colonies should never have rebelled against the British.

I heard a noise. It sounded like a wounded animal occupying my bedroom at the far end of my flat. I did not feel afraid, merely curious. Toronto was an innocent place. Home invasions were unheard of, burglaries rare. I wondered if a stray raccoon had found its way inside. Still, no animal but human could give off the odor of perfume I picked up as I approached my bedroom door—a sweetish, cloying scent, nothing I would ever wear.

I pushed my bedroom door open. Two heads popped up from under my flowered comforter. Both heads were blond. One belonged to Hemblen—he stared at me, his eyes a gla-cial blue. I recognized the other. Hemblen had introduced me to her at a party he and I had attended the previous week. Like anyone who suddenly discovers infidelity, I went into shock, the jagged scar that ran the length of the woman's right cheek lashed out to inflict its pain on me. I could hear nothing in that instant beyond a voice that resembled mine raise itself in agony.

"David, what the fuck is going on?"

I'd never said the word fuck out loud before. Now it felt appropriate.

I still remember the woman's name—Angela. Angela grabbed her clothes and vanished. I turned my back on Hemblen and ran out of a bedroom that was no longer mine.

My marriage to Hemblen had ended. Like women often do, I blamed the victim—me. Marriage even to the wrong person necessitates reciprocity. I asked myself if I had been so self-absorbed, so blind to anything but my own needs, so caught up in my anxiety over the demands of my Ph.D. program that I had denied the obvious—my marriage was disintegrating. I berated myself for misinterpreting as enthusiasm the hard stomp of Hemblen's right foot as Mick Jagger sang, "Look at that stupid gu-urrl."

Hoping to cheer me up, my father bought me an airplane ticket to Europe. In London, I did what I knew best at the time: I sought solace through shopping. In the newly hip neighborhood of Carnaby Street, I bought a mini-skirt constructed entirely of foot-long silver zippers. Black piping attached the zippers side-by-side into a complete garment, so, in theory, I could seduce a new fantasy Prince Charming to come un-zip me. I next took a train across Europe with a college chum and his young brother, where, in the sanctity of an empty rail car, I initiated the younger man into sex while the older brother waited patiently in our assigned seats, I returned to Toronto to have a brief affair with a lonely professor of classical music, then moved into a modern almost bare apartment of a pot dealer, the son of Communist Party friends of my parents. This young man, a dark-haired marijuana dealer-in-training (having never met a dealer, I failed to recognize the syndrome) inhaled all profits from his sales. I helped. One afternoon, as an anemic Canadian sun forced its way through the dirt on the apartment's bare windows, I opened his refrigerator to discover only a single item—a pound of butter. I ate it. The entire pound. One luscious, yellow, salty spoonful after the next. Even my pot-addled friend was shocked.

As it was, I got off easy. I did not get pregnant. Or contract a sexually transmitted disease. Still, I found no stability in the social disequilibrium of my life's chaos. I woke up one morning in the pot dealer's rumpled bed and realized I'd had enough. I had listened over and over to the rock band Procol Harum's "Whiter Shade of Pale," with its dirge-like chorus of sixteen vestal virgins leaving for the coast. I was no virgin; but I was determined to reject Canadian stodginess in favor of adventure. I'd quit Toronto—on my own—to free myself from all its negative associations.

I once believed John Lennon had it right when Lennon sang that love is all you need. I'm now convinced the Cuban freedom fighter Che Guevara said it better: the true revolutionary is guided by great feelings of love—and hate.

* * *

IN AUGUST 1967, TWO MONTHS AFTER my 24th birthday, I decided I'd attend the 62nd annual meeting of the American Sociological Association in San Francisco.

I arrived in California not as an impoverished Dust Bowl refugee but as a privileged young woman in a prosperous 1960s. San Francisco stopped me cold—or warm, since sunshine warmed my face, trees bore fruit in winter, cable cars clattered down steep hills, a street vendor hawked orange and blue glass pot pipes. In a Macy's window I caught a glimpse of a multicolored paisley jacket I lusted after. Twenty-four-year-old rejected Judy Hemblen had found a Shangri-La for shoppers in San Francisco.

I also found a line of protesters picketing the San Francisco Hilton where my conference was being held. I noticed a man who carried a handwritten sign that read:

"To oppose evil is the moral obligation of a true scholar."

I believe today, as I did when I entered that Hilton Hotel in August 1967, that human beings are born to serve not just their own self-interest, but the greater good. I agreed. My professors at the University of Toronto seemed like bland, suit-jacketed conformists, not activists. But now in front of me I saw a picket line of protesting professors. Unable to process such an inconsistency, I stopped instead under a gold speckled mirror at the Hilton bar and debated whether or not to order myself a drink—unwittingly repeating my mother's pattern while pretending to myself that I was different.

A stranger from the picket line approached. I did not know him, but I recognized his dress—grey jacket, white shirt, tie, dark, horn-rimmed glasses, and goatee—a 1960s version of my parent's hero, the Russian revolutionary Vladimir Illyich Lenin. He introduced himself as Jack then handed me a leaflet covered in a forest of single-space type. I found Jack's surface familiarity reassuring, I shook his hand, thanked him, and moved on.

My courageous but last-minute decision to attend the conference meant I'd failed to register. I marched directly into a room, arriving to hear a red-haired woman who looked young enough to be a graduate student like me declare, "Free love is the politics of sexual pleasure and personal happiness."

I was an aspiring Ph.D. The only route I knew to understand myself was to ask theoretical questions and read books. But free love sounded eons better than anything I'd had with Hemblen. I asked myself—did free love mean I could satisfy my bodily needs with whomever I chose, without asking anyone's permission? I'd not yet learned that to act politically based only on abstract principle results in highly negative consequences.

I met up with Jack again on the final day of the conference, in front of that same gold-speckled mirror in Hilton's bar. I told him I had decided to move to California. At age 24, to move from repressive Toronto to a college town where I knew only Jack did not faze me. My desire to break free had overwhelmed all caution. I had no idea that moving to Berkeley in late 1967 meant I'd be adopting as my hometown an epicenter of hippie counter-culture, free love, and anti-war protest. Or that an entity called the State of California had a history of turning the dreams of immigrants like me into reality.

Jack's reply was hesitant but warm.

"Well, Judy, when you do, you can stay with me."

* * *

JACK TURNED OUT TO LIVE IN a guy apartment for intellectuals, so stacked with books with thick paragraphs of type and pamphlets on Marxist revolution that they made me claustrophobic. I also discovered Jack belonged to the International Socialists, a neo-Trotskyite group. Communists like my parents who idolized Lenin and Stalin hated Trotskyites; for them the expression "Trots" was a swear word that magnified ideological differences. I could not tell if Jack was interested in me sexually or in recruiting me to his faction. But it rapidly became apparent to Jack that I was too needy, emotional, and chaotic to co-exist in close proximity to his straight-arrow personality. In December 1967, Jack relocated me to the home of a graduate student friend of his at 1049 Keith Street in the Berkeley hills. For that, I am forever grateful to Jack.

I pushed open Keith Street's two intricately carved redwood entry doors to find myself in Wonderland. At first, I could not absorb what I saw. In one corner of a gigantic living room, a figure of a naked woman made from pink and off-white alabaster reclined on the mantelpiece of a rococo fireplace. She fed purple alabaster grapes into the mouth of an alabaster cherub. Across the vast expanse of living room opposite the fireplace, a flock of yellow finches chirped and hopped in a floor-to-ceiling birdcage. The ceiling itself boasted a pattern of identical rosettes, painted gold, each centered in an alabaster square decorated with vines. It looked to me as if the pleasure-seeking Greek god Dionysus also inhabited this place.

I followed my about-to-be housemates—Jack's friend David Minkus and a married couple, Miche Beaudoin and Walter Hittleman—up a set of narrow wooden stairs. An open door led to an outdoor balcony with an incomparable view of three bridges crossing San Francisco Bay. I'd adopt that balcony as a place to lose myself—to watch a glowing California sun fall behind the

Golden Gate Bridge into the Pacific Ocean, to be replaced by San Francisco's twinkling lights.

Miche opened a second hand-carved wood door and invited me into a master bedroom. In its center, six columns rose in a circle, each ten or twelve feet tall, joined at their apex into a dome made of glass. Miche's name for this was solarium—a word I'd never heard but a setting in which, if I chose, I could pay obeisance to some hippie deity and find my way to true enlightenment. Michie said the Floating Lotus Magic Opera Company had just staged a fake prom in this solarium; naked young people had wound themselves around the columns in a Martha Graham-esque modern dance.

It wasn't just Keith Street's hippie and artistic architecture that drew me in; it was the higgly-piggly freedom of the house itself. By the time I walked into the room that would become my bedroom, I was undone. Tiny, deep-blue flowers with curlicues of gold adorned the bedroom's ceiling; a double bed mounted on a platform rose five feet above the floor. Three more alabaster cherubs cavorted on the top of the room's corner fireplace—a fireplace which, I'd discover through direct experience, warmed my bedroom only slightly during Northern California winters. 1049 Keith had no central heat. I didn't care. I'd live in a house that embodied the essence of 1960s counter-culture—a counter-culture whose adherents opposed all that mainstream America and its profit-making ethic had to offer.

"When can I move in?"

"Anytime you like," came a chorus.

I lived at 1049 Keith Street for more than two years. I admit: the house had its flaws in addition to its lack of central heat. To enter Keith Street through its double front doors, I or any visitor, including the FBI, had to climb a zig-zag concrete path whose steep incline left me panting. An enameled Westinghouse kitchen stove made clear that Keith Street's kitchen had not been remodeled since the 1930s; its windows never fully shut against the cold California winds. To me no defect mattered. To live at Keith Street meant I resided in the midst of an artistic, counter-cultural community that defined Bay Area life and politics. I had not merely stumbled into Wonderland; I was immersed in it. I was not surprised to learn that Allen Ginsberg had penned his epic poem *Howl* in a Berkeley bungalow less than a mile away.

David Minkus occupied the room across the hall from me. With David's help, for one semester, I obtained an adjunct teaching position in the Sociology Department at the nearby University of California, Berkeley. I was relieved; I needed more income than my parents deigned to provide. I had no reason to suspect that, after I was hired, the San Francisco office of the FBI inquired about me at the University of California. The University in turn **advised this office that JUDITH LEE HEMBLEN would have a Teaching Associate position with UCB at $4,000 per annum.**

Had I known the FBI was watching, or that I would shortly reject the caution that permeates academic life, I might not have been so quick to spend down what I considered a generous $1000 salary I received for teaching one University quarter.

It's obvious to me now that immigrating to a new country, to an unfamiliar city, to a house that both Alice and the Red Queen would have envied, saved my life. I woke up one morning to see the California sun stream through my bedroom window as if to coax its ceiling flowers into bloom. The flowers stayed blue, but I did not. Keith Street became my hippie haven, a protective shell in which to discover myself and take on a new identity.

* * *

I BEGAN MY BRAVE NEW LIFE in Berkeley looking for love in all the wrong places. I arrived by myself at the University of California campus to be handed a flyer that advertised a meeting sponsored by the Revolutionary Union aka the R.U.

The FBI claims that, in early 1968, they caught sight of me at an R.U. meeting in Palo Alto. This memo marks the first occasion where I come to the attention of the FBI:

> *(BLACKED OUT) advised that Judy Hemblen was one of approximately 20 individuals in attendance at a meeting of the Revolutionary Union (RU) held in Palo Alto, California. He had no current information as to Judy Hemblen's status in the Revolutionary Union (RU). (BLACKED OUT) pointed out that while prospective members of the RU are permitted to attend the educational classes, only members are permitted to attend meetings.*

An FBI agent, or in this case more likely a civilian informant, had provided incorrect information—I never joined that scurrilous organization. The R.U. was neo-communist; I had convinced myself I would feel at home in any communist party—the social or the socialist kind. Compared to my future dealings with the Bureau, the mistakes the FBI made here are bush-league: I don't recall attending meetings but I *did* attend an R.U. party which, predictably, took place in a nondescript house in a run-down working-class neighborhood, since that's where workers were. Mostly men but a few women argued with each other, their voices serious but fierce. I heard no music. I had learned early from my parents that proper protocol at a Communist party is to get drunk. I chose vodka, though I have never been able to hold hard liquor. Bored, dizzy, and nauseous, I retreated to a nearby bedroom, nestled fully clothed onto a stack of coats, and passed out.

I woke up in a room bathed only in the yellow glow of a streetlight that shone through a dirty side window. I lay on my stomach, but I could not move. At first, I thought my paralysis came from being drunk, but soon realized I was pinned down by a weight, heavy and hot. I felt wet lips close over my right ear. I inhaled the bitter reek of beer on breath that was not mine. I was too drunk to form coherent words; I do remember how painful it was to turn my head to escape those marauding lips. I tried to shriek; no sound emerged. My head was held down by what felt like an out-sized arm, my voice was muffled by coats. I found it almost impossible to draw a breath. A warm, large body pressed on my back; its lower half began a thrusting motion; a hand attempted to wiggle under me, headed toward my crotch. I did my best to raise myself up on one elbow, to push off the weight on top of my body, but the weight pushed back. I did not scream, my panic had left me with no voice. Yet that same panic caused me to squirm my tiny body with such ferocity that—and to this day I do not know exactly how—I managed to hoist myself up on my right side, use my back and butt to push mightily against my attacker, and roll out from under his oppressive, stinking drunken weight. I landed hard on the bedroom floor.

Fear breeds weakness but also extraordinary strength. From my position on the floor, I watched my attacker lift his head and turn his fat face toward me, bemused, as if I had done this man some great wrong by rejecting his precious gift. My flight response kicked in. Drunk but grateful still to be clothed, I scrambled to my feet. I saw a knob on what I hoped would be the bedroom door and not a closet. I yanked the door open. In the haze from a bare bulb in the hallway, I turned my head, caught sight of my attacker on the bed, a foot away from my brand-new red leather purse which I must have dropped. As my attacker tried to rise, I clenched my fists, re-entered, grabbed my purse, and ran to the end of the hall where I pushed open a screen door. I fumbled for the keys to my VW Bug and took off—drunk driving laws be damned.

This was no rape attempt by a stranger. I escaped what I now call acquaintance rape. I recognized the man, who was an R.U. member. His name was Tuna. He was well named; he was a giant, ugly creature like the fish. I did not reveal Tuna's assault to anyone. I blamed myself for choosing to attend that party and getting drunk. I hated to think of myself as victim even though I almost was one.

At first, I felt as if I were a winner for escaping being raped, but my sense of triumph devolved quickly into numbness—a numbness that ensured I'd keep Tuna's attack a secret. Still a convert to academic conceits, I gave Tuna's assault an abstract label. I created emotional distance—I named the attempted rape "My Incident."

In keeping with the misogyny of the late 1960s and my heritage as a British colonial subject, I put on a stiff upper lip and soldiered on. But being attacked and almost raped did sow a seed of rage inside my psyche that would one day help me reap what had been planted—I vowed never to let Tuna's attack sour my determination to become a sexually free woman. I'd study martial arts and the skills of self-defense. And do it for myself.

* * *

I'D READ IN THE *BERKELEY BARB*, Berkeley's pre-eminent underground newspaper, about a meeting to support the Oakland 7—seven draft-age men who faced jail for attempting to shut down the Oakland Induction Center to oppose the Vietnam War. I hoped to find a community of folks as passionate as I was about my Red Diaper legacy of fighting injustice. But I had not yet let go of my need to make my inner Harriet proud. I put on my favorite outfit: black fishnet stockings and a light brown suede miniskirt that matched my hair. My commitment to the theater of dress originated in that dysfunctional feedback loop my mother Harriet had implanted inside my head: "You may be short, but you must always look your best when you go out in public. Hold your head high. You are, after all, a proud subject of Her Majesty the Queen."

Neither my mother's condescending tone nor her telling me to subject myself to Her Majesty's authority affirmed my sense of self-worth. None the less, Harriet taught me well: the way you dress in public sends a message that identifies you—especially if you are a protester and a Yippie.

In 2016, the feminist icon Gloria Steinem, a supporter of then-presidential candidate Hillary Clinton, made an offhand remark about Hillary's spotty support among young women—a remark that generated a brief firestorm for its non-feminist implication.

"When you're young, you're thinking: Where are the boys?" Steinem opined. "The boys are with Bernie."

Fifty years earlier, Gloria Steinem might have asserted the same—that women joined the anti-Vietnam war movement because protest was where the cute guys were. Individual motives to take part in protest vary. Idealism dominates, but Steinem's remark, which she quickly retracted, was, in my experience, a partial truth. I went to that Oakland 7 meeting hoping to find like-minded political compatriots, but at the same time, as women of my generation often did, I used dress to impress. Gloria Steinem knows as well as I do that the late 1960s were a both/and—at least for politics and sex. For me, politics dominated, romance just happened.

I trekked downhill from Keith Street telling myself it was no big deal to go to unfamiliar places by myself. I arrived at Ludwig's Fountain, in front of the Student Union near the Telegraph Avenue entrance to the U.C. Berkeley campus. I caught a glimpse of a man perched on the rim of Ludwig's Fountain, named by Cal students after Ludwig, a dog. Geysers of water shot up from the fountain's center, then cascaded down behind the man's curly blond hair into a circular blue pool. The man looked to me like a golden eagle in a beige and brown paisley shirt. As the man moved out of my peripheral vision, I imagined he glanced back at me.

Inside Cal's Student Union, I found tables crammed with leaflets printed not like stodgy communist pamphlets but in cheerful reds, oranges, and blues. Young women towered above me as if they had materialized out of "California Girls," a popular—and sexist—Beach Boys song. The women argued intensely with each other—about politics! I began to sing; aware of my height limitations but knowing that, like the song said, I wished I too would be a California Girl. I identified equally with the long-haired young men, mostly white but also of color, some in green army jackets, who argued in raised voices with short haired men I decided must be professors or graduate students. For me, the righteousness of their arguments felt more convincing than any doctrinaire conflicts I had suffered through thanks to my parents, and certainly the R.U.

Romance and idealism can reinforce each other—at least they do for me. Which explains why I remember now what came next as if I were the director of a major motion picture; a Yippie fantasy I've appropriated from the title of Abbie Hoffman's 1980 book *Soon to be a Major Motion Picture.* I spied my golden eagle standing next to a card table. His blue jeans and light brown boots with fringes assured me he was cool. A second man stood next to him. This man's hair was equally blond, but straight. With his white shirt and tie, this second man looked more mainstream—but equally attractive. As Dylan's "Times They Are A-Changin" predicted a momentous future, the State of California lived up to its reputation for abundance—it offered me progressive politics and a twofer of blonds.

I approached the boys and introduced myself, mumbling that I was a Canadian new in town. In tandem, the boys looked me up and down.

"Stew," said the blond with curly hair.

"Steve," said the blond with straight hair.

In a courtly gesture that had a lasting outcome, Stew reached out with his long right arm and touched me on the tip of my nose with his little finger.

The next day, Stew and I walked to Strawberry Creek on the University of California campus. We sat side by side on the ground inside a grove of Eucalyptus trees—trees which I had never seen before. Each time I'd move my leg, I'd inhale their mild and menthol-like perfume.

I was 24. Stew was 29. I was separated. Stew was divorced. Stew's divorce story went like this: one year earlier, Stew's pal Jerry had asked Stew to come to New York City to help him organize a March on the Pentagon scheduled for November 1967. I was delighted to hear Stew tell me he'd agreed instantly. But once Stew had arrived in New York, he'd telephoned his then-wife Joanne in Berkeley, asking her to join him.

Joanne had told him, "I don't want to be married anymore. I don't want to be a revolutionary."

At that, I interrupted. "I came home and found my husband in bed with another woman."

I felt strangely triumphant to have won the game of "what's the worst thing that ever happened to you in a relationship" yet surprised I could so easily volunteer such intimate information to a stranger. Stew and I were the dumped. Our former spouses were the dumpers. It was the failure of our starter marriages as much as our attraction to each other that would cement our love of protest.

By early evening, when shadows cast by eucalyptus leaves resembled giant's fingers, Stew turned toward me, put his hand over mine, gazed at me out of those intense blue eyes of his and said, "You're pretty cute, you know."

"You're pretty cute yourself," I thought as my stomach went *flip*.

Judy Gumbo often acts first, then figures out later how to rationalize what she's done. Without a second thought, I invited Stew to spend that night with me at Keith Street. I felt no need to be cautious or to obsess over negative outcomes; I had already dropped my "Incident" into my denial bin and covered it with mental compost. I was instead determined to adopt the mandate of free love; but I'd be the one to choose. My clit tingled like a doorbell as the cherubs on my bedroom fireplace watched me watch Stew take off his fringed suede boots, unbutton his paisley shirt and drop his jeans to the floor. Since Stew wore no underwear, I got a terrific and welcome view of his long ballerina legs and an erect penis. We climbed together up a wooden ladder into my bed that stood five feet off the floor, me first, Stew following.

And so began our forty-year relationship.

I rated Stew a 10 on the sexy human scale. His Brooklyn accent turned me on, as did the blond curls on his head, barrel chest, back, and genitals. I found him charismatic, quick-witted, a master of the incisive, humorous quip and, judging from how much he appeared to know about the world, highly intelligent. The sexual electricity between us could have powered a Prius had Priuses been invented in 1968. Stew's Yippie politics, of which I knew little, both confounded and intrigued me. Born in 1939, five years too early for the draft, Stew was never called up. He had the freedom to become a Yippie, a revolutionary—and the first great love of my life.

Stew often called me a naïve optimist. Which I was and remain. I look for positives even in difficult times—a trait which to this day can get me into trouble but can also lead to great adventure. Two weeks after Stew and I spent our first night together, I asked him to move into Keith Street with me. By the end of my first quarter teaching, I lost any interest I once had in becoming a Sociology professor. Teaching at a university was too respectable, too conformist, too distant from the action. A revolution beckoned.

CHAPTER 3:
WHITE GIRL MEETS BLACK PANTHERS

STEW HAD TWO BEST FRIENDS: ONE was Yippie founder Jerry Rubin. The other was Eldridge Cleaver, Minister of Information for the Black Panther Party.

Every immigrant needs a road map which shows them how to live in their adopted country. I was no exception. In 1968, I began my education about how to assimilate into the United States with Eldridge Cleaver—author of a best-selling prison memoir *Soul On Ice*, a man whom literary critics had anointed a revolutionary prophet.

On February 2, 1968, I watched a TV broadcast, filmed the previous day, that showed a South Vietnamese police commander point his pistol at the forehead of a barefoot civilian in a checked shirt, extend his arm, and fire. Just as the civilian toppled to the ground, I heard a knock. I opened the carved wooden front doors of our Keith Street house to find a 6'2", well-built, well-dressed Black man illuminated in the porch light. Stew and the man embraced in the universal language of their gender: chests touching, palms slap-slap on backs, air space between the genitals.

Stew announced, "Hey, Rage. Come on in."

The man Stew addressed as Rage had broad shoulders, a skin color between ebony and coffee and a carefully manicured goatee. He surveilled our living room, his magnetic almost-green eyes taking in the finches in my roommate Miche's birdcage, the alabaster lady with her boy companion reclining on the fireplace, and the lights of San Francisco that twinkled outside our living room window.

"Man, this crib is outta sight," were the first words I ever heard Eldridge Cleaver speak. "It's like a palace . . . a hippie palace."

I subsequently discovered in my FBI files an agent who referred to 1049 Keith as a **typical hippie pad.** For Eldridge Cleaver and for me, there was nothing typical about Keith Street. Eldridge and I first bonded over home decor: we both appreciated high-end hippie when we saw it.

Growing up, I was raised with an understated Canadian racism—abominable underneath but genteel on the surface. Toronto's Black community was almost invisible to me. My communist parents saw no contradiction between hiring a Black housekeeper as "the help" and a treasured photograph of them, smiling up at an equally Black Paul Robeson—celebrity actor, singer, film star, concert performer, and Rhodes scholar boycotted for refusing to denounce the Soviet Union. In high school I had an Afro-Canadian boyfriend. I thought of him as "just a person," not as a young Black man. His name was Norman Cook. I called him Normie. To Canada's credit, Normie's great-great-grandparents had escaped slavery on the Underground Railroad and found sanctuary there. My mother disapproved of Normie—especially after she interrupted the two of us, high-schoolers, making out in my bedroom. My mother's well-honed, withering glare at Normie was enough to do the trick—nothing "serious" happened. I believe that Harriet's dislike of Normie was motivated not so much by my sexual experimentation or by her covert racism—it was my mother's disapproval of any friend of mine who happened to be a boy.

When I first arrived in the United States, I was amazed to find explicit and overt racism—and equally explicit resistance to it. Which prompted me, rebellious child of communists that I am, to fall in love with Stew for being both a Yippie and profoundly anti-racist, a man trusted by many in the leadership of the Black Panther Party.

I stared up at the world-famous Eldridge Cleaver for the first time and heard Stew say, "Eldridge, I'd like you to meet Judy."

"Judy? She's your rib? Mrs. Stew? Hello, Mrs. Stew," Eldridge replied.

"Hey," I sputtered, unfamiliar with Eldridge's rhetoric and too nervous to attempt my usual grin. Eldridge bent down with genuine warmth to grasp my hand.

Stew guided Eldridge past the alabaster lady and her cherub, up a wooden staircase toward our bedroom. I've often wondered if the famous 1960s cartoon the Fabulous Furry Freak Brothers modeled Fat Freddie after Stew, given Freddie's blond hair, skinny legs, and belly hanging over his belt. If so, a cartoon Stew/Fat Freddie would be followed up the stairs by a tall handsome Black man in a turtleneck and black leather jacket, with diminutive, Jewish/Canadian Judy last in line.

I had wrapped both my hands vise-like around our four-foot-tall brass hookah so as not to embarrass myself by spilling its sacred contents of sake and hashish. Eldridge sat himself down in our beige upholstered chair in front of the two cherubs who decorated our bedroom fireplace. Stew and I occupied the floor at Eldridge's feet. I lit the hookah and passed its hose to Eldridge. I watched him stretch his legs, breathe in deep, then begin to recount what I soon came to recognize as a typical Eldridge Cleaver tale:

"I was a Muslim when I was first in the joint. I believed that the chicken was evolved from the snake. I don't remember why. Maybe some quote from the Bible or Quran. And so, I would never eat chicken. Other Muslims wouldn't eat pork, but I got to the point where I couldn't even look at a chicken."

Eldridge then asserted that everyone ought to recognize snake-to-chicken evolution as a natural part of the Darwinian order of things. With that, the three of us began to laugh. I felt as if I'd never stop.

* * *

I BESTOWED ON ELDRIDGE CLEAVER THAT level of awe celebrities enjoy. I was equally star-struck the first time Eldridge brought Kathleen to Keith Street. I found her as impressive as her husband. She had worked with Black Power advocates in the Student Non-Violent Coordinating Committee (SNCC), famous for organizing freedom rides and voter registration drives in the South. When I first met Kathleen she was the only woman member of the Central Committee of the Black Panther Party. Her title was Communications Secretary. Kathleen's passion for life, her glamour, and her Black Panther politics brought me out of fandom and cemented our friendship, yes, but above all it was her Yippie sense of the absurd. Kathleen could not prevent racist cops from murdering Black students in South Carolina, but she could take action—even if from 2,600 miles away. I watched her create, on our newly acquired color TV set, a monochromatic if temporary world in which no racist cop could kill people of color since everyone was equally bright green. In that moment Kathleen proved herself both an idealist and a Yippie; she had arranged an ideal future using 1968 technology.

At first, I had no clue how to relate to this tall Black woman with her throaty laugh, hazel eyes, a beauty mark on her forehead, and a medium-brown Afro at least six-inches high that framed her face as if she was the subject of a Botticelli painting. Before I got to know Kathleen as a friend, I objectified her. I focused on the superficial: her knee-length high-heeled boots, her three-quarters length black leather coat, and fluffed out, stylish Afro, which signaled to Black Americans but also to white activists like me that Black is Beautiful.

The Panthers popularized a unisex "uniform"—blue shirts, black berets, and black leather jackets signified Panther identity; it stood for Black defiance and struck fear into the hearts of white people. Kathleen Cleaver set the gold standard for what 1970s author Tom Wolfe and mainstream media had labeled "radical chic." I subsequently learned that some Black Panthers rejected that term as derogatory. To me, at least initially, to be radical plus chic seemed like a terrific combination.

Optics matter. I learned from Kathleen to dress for success as a revolutionary fashionista. I relegated my tie-dye blouses and suede miniskirt to my Keith Street closet. I appropriated money sent by my parents for my education to buy myself a pair of brown Frye stomping boots and a matching jacket and skirt made of fake brown leather. Tie-dye stood for hippie pacifism, suede is soft and fuzzy, while leather, even fake and especially in that time before PETA, connoted authority. For me to dress in black leather would have been inappropriate—black leather was the provenance of the Panthers. But fake brown leather advertised my support. And made me look tough.

Eldridge first brought Kathleen Cleaver to Keith Street on February 8, 1968, one full week after I saw the barefoot Vietnamese peasant get murdered on our hand-me-down but color TV. Kathleen, Eldridge, Stew, and I, plus my roommate, David Minkus, now watched our TV images morph from explosive Tet Offensive orange to grimy gray. White highway patrol officers in Orangeburg, South Carolina had shot directly into a crowd of Black students protesting segregation at a local bowling alley. Three Black protesters died; at least twenty-eight were wounded.

In 1968, the colors on TV's like ours could be manipulated by hand if I turned one of six round knobs—two large, four smaller. I stared at Kathleen as she rose from her seat, fiddled with the knobs, then used the smallest knob to make all human figures on the screen glow florescent green.

"All cops aren't pigs," she said,

Her statement startled me. Why would Kathleen Cleaver, Black Panther Party VIP, utter what I thought of as a pro-cop statement?

I had misjudged; I assumed every Black Panther considered every cop to be a pig.

"Only some cops are true pigs. The others are just number pigs." Kathleen spoke as if she were some imaginary police dispatcher, her voice loud and commanding,

"Got a One Eighty-Seven . . . Got a Five Two Five Zero hold at 26th Street . . . Got a Five Two Oh. They're number pigs. Number pigs don't decide anything. There are the true pigs and then there are the pigs who just take orders, the pigs who all they do is repeat numbers, you dig where I'm coming from?"

Kathleen ended her deconstruction of piggy authority with what I would come to recognize as a bitter version of her trademark, good-natured laugh.

I responded with a Panther slogan I had just learned: "I guess the pigs of the power structure are oinking at the people."

I felt as if my spouting Panther rhetoric was a lame response to Kathleen's insight. Just another of those situations where I felt ignorant and foreign. The way the Panthers talked came from a world unfamiliar to me. I did not yet understand that Black English has a unique history originating in slavery, or that when spoken by a person of color, a word can contain racial and class variations in meaning. I'd eventually absorb the rudiments of Panther-speak from Eldridge and Kathleen's frequent visits, from Panther education classes and by reading the Black Panther Party newspaper. But on this first occasion, after Kathleen and Eldridge left, I whined angrily at Stew.

"Half the time when Kathleen and Eldridge say stuff, I don't understand them. I don't get what they mean. I can't talk to them. I can't answer them. It really pisses me off."

Stew nodded.

"Just a sec," he said.

Stew climb upstairs past the hookah to our bedroom. He returned to hand me a wrinkled, dog-eared paperback book. Its black cover proclaimed in graffiti-like yellow letters, *The Wretched of the Earth, A Negro Psychoanalyst's Study of the Problems of Racism and Colonialism in the World Today* by a Black, anti-colonialist, West Indian psychoanalyst named Frantz Fanon.

* * *

AS FAR BACK AS I REMEMBER, colonialism has made me angry. Young children are small and powerless; as a young child I must have identified with colonial subjects. While Americans, or so I'd learn, had created one nation, under God, indivisible, with liberty and justice for all, all God did for me was Save the Queen. Bright, day-glow pink dominated my grade school maps, illuminating a British Empire that extended into India, Iraq, the Palestine Mandate, Nigeria, Sudan, Kuwait, Hong Kong, Burma, Rhodesia (now Zimbabwe), Kenya, Sierra Leone, Somalia, Honduras, the British East—and West—Indies, Australia, New Zealand, Scotland, Ireland, and Wales. White racism underpins colonialism. I never encountered the word racism or colonialism in any Toronto classroom.

In early March of 1968, Stew, Eldridge, and I sat as we often did on Keith Street's balcony, watching clouds shaped like dragons scutter above San Francisco's Golden Gate Bridge. Eldridge began to sing under his breath a line from what I knew to be his favorite Bob Dylan song: *"Something is happening here, but you don't know what it is, do you, Mr. Jones?"*

Then Eldridge, who had studied Frantz Fanon in prison, started in. His name for white America was mother country; America's Black community was an internal colony of the United States. The pigs were its occupying army.

Reading Fanon had changed me. I leaned on Keith Street's balcony, and without forethought, I jumped in. I followed up Eldridge's harangue with my own. I said I fully agreed with Eldridge's point of view. And that Frantz Fanon's advocacy of violent response to stop the violence of colonial oppressors was justifiable. To illustrate my deep hatred of colonialism in general and the vicious, racist occupation of its colonies by the British Empire specifically, I began to recite, out loud, word for word, the first verse of that racist Rudyard Kipling poem from 1900 I'd been forced to memorize in high school, "The White Man's Burden."

Act first, the saying goes, and ask forgiveness later. I must have recognized I was walking on the edge. I started to berate myself—how arrogant and insensitive could this white girl be? How fucking racist was I to recite to Eldridge Cleaver, Minister of Information of the Black Panther Party, a poem that defined Black slaves as devilish and childlike? Would Eldridge recognize that I wasn't supporting that racist asshole Kipling but opposing him?

To cover my embarrassment at the blunder I'd just made, I ended my peroration by declaring with all the forcefulness I could muster that I recognized my skin was *not* black, brown, yellow, or red. That I had *not* been exploited, enslaved, oppressed or murdered like people of color across the globe. But, I told my audience, to come of age in Canada, a country subjected to the racist British imperialists I hated, gave me, as I saw it, a partial understanding of what it meant to be a colonial subject.

Eldridge and Stew turned their heads—one black, one blond—and stared at me. I began to tremble, deciding I had given horrific offense. By now I get it: the problem lies not with all white folks but with any white person who believes in and supports, actively or passively, by word or by deed, overt or covert, any and all manifestations of white supremacy. Especially white privilege. Or, as I came to understand it after I memorized a definition of racism coming from Huey P. Newton, Black Panther Party Minister of Defense:

> *Racism is a system of social domination by which a group, seen as inferior or different, is exploited, controlled or oppressed, economically, socially or psychically by the super-ordinate group.*

Racism is a power relationship in which white people dominate people of color in one or all of life's aspects. I didn't know enough to make such a distinction then. I do now.

To my relief, Eldridge replied, "OK, Mrs. Stew. I dig where you're comin' from."

I took this as an affirmation. I would find my way in Panther World.

* * *

A PORTION OF MY EDUCATION IN the non-traditional world of the Black Panther Party came in traditional fashion: reading and classroom study. I was thrilled when Eldridge invited Stew and me to attend a Black Panther Party study group. It was March of 1968. Black separatist ideology was surging. Two years previously, Ron Karenga in Los Angeles had established Kwanzaa as an alternative holiday to Christmas for Black people. SNCC had expelled all its white members, allowing Black activists to make decisions for themselves. The Black Panther Party leadership, especially Eldridge and Party Chair Bobby Seale, disagreed. They wanted white allies, but under Black Panther terms.

Stew and I climbed two flights of stairs at Panther headquarters, a brick and stucco two-story building on Shattuck Avenue in Berkeley. "Excuse me," I'd say in my best apologetic Canadian way, as I tried, careful to give no offense, to make my way into a room crowded with the Party's rank and file, most folks younger than me. Elders called them Panther "cubs." Most wore their hair in Afros, but I noticed one teen had slicked his straightened hair back and dyed it bronze. He wore a white shirt open to the waist.

"Jackanape in training," Stew opined.

"Jackanape" was yet another code word for which I needed a translation. "Jackanape" or its diminutive "nape," turned out to be Panther Speak for individuals who engaged in behavior—"napery"—that led at times to a negative outcome. Jackanapes were known to practice "trickeration," drink to excess, behave in a self-destructive manner, engage in unauthorized activity or, occasionally, instigate acts of violence on their own. I decided it was not a compliment in Panther World to be singled out for napery—until I heard the affection in Eldridge's or Kathleen's voice when they discussed alleged misdeeds of some specific jackanape.

Huey P. Newton, the imprisoned Black Panther Party's Minister of Defense, glowered down at me from a poster at the front of the room. Huey holds a spear in his right hand, a rifle in his left while next to him two African shields lean against a wall. Eldridge told me he'd designed this poster to merge African and American symbols into a single iconic image that empowered Black people to resist. I had tacked that identical poster, a gift from Eldridge, next to the cherubs in Stew's and my bedroom.

Eldridge asserted that Black people were a colony internal to the United States. Since Black people were colonized by a white "mother country"—the United States—Eldridge and Party members approvingly called white people who supported the Panthers "white mother country radicals." We were white folks who helped subvert a racist system. As a White Mother Country Radical and a girl, I got it that the only thing I had to fear from Black America was fear itself.

I recall watching Bobby Seale, the Party's official spokesperson, take his seat upstairs in the front row of the room at Panther headquarters. A stocky man of greater than average height, Bobby's goatee reminded me of Eldridge; his black Cossack-style fur hat resembled those my father used to bring home from Russia. Stew, an amateur historian, began to whisper in my ear. In 1967, Stew said, his voice so loud it made me cringe, Bobby had led a group of Black Panthers carrying Magnums, shotguns, and .45-caliber pistols into Sacramento's state capitol building to demonstrate that, in accordance with California law at the time, members of the Black Panther Party could patrol Oakland's streets, law books at the ready, guns at open carry, to deter police abuse and advise Black people being arrested of their constitutional rights.

Bobby stood. The room quieted. Stew continued to whisper. A Black woman behind me glared. I shushed Stew. Our white mother country radical exemption went only so far.

Bobby began: "Say it loud! I am . . ."

"A revolutionary!"

In unison, the crowd shouted back:

"I am a revolutionary! I am a revolutionary!"

And so the formal portion of my informal education began.

"What is power?" Bobby asked and went on to answer his own question.

"Power is the ability to define phenomena and make them act in a desired manner."

My knowledge of philosophy is negligible; do not ask me to define the word "ontological." But when the chairman of the Black Panther Party explained that I can change my circumstances by force of human will, that strength resides not only in the downtrodden or the elite but also in me, I felt as if I had swallowed an imaginary pill whose logo was a raised Black fist. I took the inner rebelliousness I had lived with since my childhood and made it public. With an authenticity and determination I'd not previously known, I stood up along with the crowd, clenched my right hand into a fist, and raised my fist above my head to chant along with Chairman Bobby:

> Power to the People,
> Black Power to Black People
> Panther Power to the Vanguard
> I am a revolutionary! I am a revolutionary! I am a revolutionary!

Which means that, in any resistance movement of color with white supporters, people of color must lead.

* * *

STUDY GROUP ENDED. A PUDGY WHITE man turned and squinted at me from across the room. My euphoria vanished. I was staring at the pudgy, round face of Bob Avakian, the designated leader of the Revolutionary Union at whose party Tuna had attacked me. I despised that self-styled leader. He'd shown himself to be a woman-hating asshole who espoused authoritarian communism to support his true believer agenda. To this day, I refuse to let go of my hatred. And I had not yet confided my "Incident" to Stew; I continued to minimize it as a transitory but unpleasant episode.

Repressed anger has its uses. As a woman alone I felt powerless, but by the time I arrived back at Keith Street high on Panther Power, realizing that Stew and this asshole shared a toxically masculine rivalry over which of them could claim the title "Eldridge Cleaver's Best White Friend," I felt ready to use Stew as my instrument of revenge. I counted on Stew's quick temper and Brooklyn code of honor to prompt him to act.

Under the unwavering gaze of the alabaster lady, I confessed my "Incident" to Stew. I used the phrase "attempted rape," after which I inhaled a breath so deep it felt new to me. To speak aloud of hidden injury helps release inner turmoil. I could relax. Stew stayed briefly silent but then began to pace, cursing, the harshness of his voice setting Miche's finches all atwitter. To my knowledge, no Stew revenge scenario came to pass, but my usually warmhearted Stew never forgave that man. Or his hardline, authoritarian communist organization. Nor have I.

* * *

ON THURSDAY, APRIL 4, 1968, FOUR months after Kathleen and Eldridge had become Stew's and my friends and role models, a white man, James Earl Ray, assassinated Dr. Martin Luther King Jr. Across America, Black communities went up in flames.

Stew and I spent the evening of King's assassination on the top floor of a brown shingled house in West Berkeley, watching it all on TV. With Eldridge and Tricia.

Tricia was Eldridge's lover. She was petite, dark haired, and white. Tricia reminded me of a young Beverly Axelrod, that intense, dark-haired, freckle-faced white attorney who had compiled Eldridge's writings into his best-selling book, *Soul On Ice*. Eldridge had dedicated his book: *To Beverly, with whom I share the ultimate of love.* Beverly got Eldridge released from prison and secured a publisher for him. At which point Eldridge dumped Beverly to marry Kathleen Neal. Kathleen was twenty-two, Eldridge ten years her senior.

My friend Eldridge Cleaver was a charismatic, self-educated, intellectually powerful Black man, a former prisoner who articulated with passion the deep trauma racist imprisonment inflicts. For Stew and me, as well as audiences and readers numbering in the tens of thousands, no other late 1960s writer, revolutionary, or activist was as powerful or compelling.

Still, it is the written word that lasts.

I had begun to read Eldridge's *Soul On Ice* in February of 1968. At first, I could not connect the book's front cover of a stern but sad Black man inside a prison yard with the amiable, fun-loving Eldridge Cleaver I now knew. I asked Stew what Eldridge's title *Soul On Ice* meant.

"Soul stands for Black man," Stew informed me, "Ice means prison. San Quentin, Folsom, and Soledad. You know Eldridge did ten years in those hellholes, right? He'd been convicted of assault and rape. Eldridge is the Soul who is on Ice."

OK, I thought. I read on. Until I came to page 14, where Eldridge justifies raping first Black then white women because, as he wrote:

> *Rape was an insurrectionary act. It delighted me that I was defying and trampling on the white man's law, upon his system of values and that I was defiling his women—was the most satisfying to me because I was very resentful over the historical fact of how the white man has used the Black woman. I felt I was getting revenge.*

The more I read, the more I failed to grasp the depth of what today I'd label Eldridge's toxic masculinity. As in so many situations with one's heroes, I found myself unable to acknowledge flaws. And rape is not a flaw; it is a horrendous act of violence against women. Given my own "Incident," how could I accept Eldridge's affirmation of rape as an insurrectionary act? Unable to face my own ambivalence, I deflected. I took my confusion and my anger out on Stew. I started to berate him—he was an easy target. Stew urged me to read on. On the very next page, and with that soul-searching years of imprisonment can offer, Eldridge wrote that he could "no longer approve the act of rape," that he had "gone astray from being human."

"I started to write," Eldridge claimed, "to save myself."

In my gut, my first reaction to Eldridge's assertions of regret fell flat. I doubted his sincerity. But for Eldridge to reverse himself was, at the time, good enough for me. My commitment to the Panthers and the anti-racist cause dominated any nascent feminist consciousness I then possessed.

Still, only in the last line of the first chapter in *Soul On Ice* did I find Eldridge speaking with the honesty of the man I knew. He writes:

The price of hating other human beings is loving oneself less.

* * *

TWO DAYS AFTER DR. KING'S ASSASSINATION, on April 6, 1968, a fierce gun battle broke out between Panthers and the Oakland police. Eldridge ordered seventeen-year-old "Lil' Bobby" Hutton to take all his clothes off, so the police would see he did not have a gun. Eldridge himself stripped naked. Lil' Bobby, likely embarrassed at age 17, took off only his shirt—but not his pants. Oakland cops shot Lil' Bobby to death. This was an early, and by no means final, episode of Black Panther death by cop. Unlike Lil' Bobby, Eldridge had escaped death but faced being re-imprisoned. Shortly afterward, I visited Kathleen in her

Victorian home at 2777 Pine Street in San Francisco. I found her pacing between window and doorway in her upstairs study.

"Kathleen," I asked, "what the fuck is going on?"

Kathleen thrust a page of cream-colored stationary into my hand. On it was a message: "Your husband is having an affair with a white woman." A woman's address followed this single line of type. I couldn't make out whether or not the address belonged to Tricia. The letter was signed "Soul Sister." I glimpsed what I decided had to be a tear of rage run down Kathleen's cheek.

She asked, "Why would a sister say such a thing?"

I had no honest answer for Kathleen. But how could I know I held in my hand an insidious product of a still secret FBI program called COINTELPRO? In August 1967, FBI Director J. Edgar Hoover had directed his agents to **expose, disrupt, misdirect, discredit or otherwise neutralize and destroy** Black militant and other American dissident groups.

In FBI parlance, neutralize means stop—by any means necessary. The memo continues:

> **No opportunity should be missed to exploit through counterintelligence techniques the organizational and personal conflicts of the leadership of such groups.**

This letter is a prime example of Hoover's use of COINTELPRO to exacerbate interpersonal conflicts between Black Panthers. I did not know at the time whether or not Kathleen knew about Tricia, but I could tell by her demeanor that she found such a revelation—even to a friend—embarrassing. It was also embarrassing for me, a friend who was a witness but who did not speak up.

COINTELPRO itself was exposed in 1975 by a Senate committee; however, secret COINTELPRO-like operations like this continue into present time but under other names. But death by cop of Black Americans is now daylighted in both mainstream and alternative media—and is finally accompanied by widespread resistance.

* * *

I'M STILL GRATEFUL TO ELDRIDGE CLEAVER. He gave me my real name. It happened late one night in early Spring 1968, in San Francisco, in the rain. Stew, Eldridge and I were cruising in Eldridge's black and gold Pontiac. Eldridge drove; Stew sat beside him in the front seat with me in back. Kathleen was not with us. Neither was sleep. At 2 a.m. our gallant band of misfits walked upstairs into a dimly lit attic of a Victorian mansion in Pacific Heights, owned by a prominent physician who was also a dedicated Panther supporter. Ten Black men in black leather jackets had gathered in a circle around a red Formica table. In front of them, illuminated by a single bare bulb overhead, three bottles of what I came to know as Panther Piss (lemon juice in port) surrounded a shiny pistol that lay in the table's center. Stew and I were the only white people present.

A large man squinted at us, moving his bulk toward the table as if to grab either a drink or the gun. This was the only time I ever felt afraid in the company of a member of the Black Panther Party.

I heard the man say, "Hey Rage, this is a private Panther matter."

Eldridge scowled. He replied he was the Minister of Information; he could bring with him anyone he chose. Eldridge went on to declare that Stew was the only person in the room he, Eldridge Cleaver, trusted. With that the room went silent. I could not breathe; I found myself close to praying that Eldridge's statement that Panthers must have support of "white mother country radicals"—me included—had to count for something. Eldridge and the man circled each other, eyes directed toward the handgun, real-life panthers battling for dominance. I figured Stew and I would be red meat if the heavyset man won. Then I saw circles of sweat begin to stain the underarms of the man's powder blue shirt. He stepped back. As did Stew and I. We retreated to a corner of the attic as Eldridge concluded whatever secret business had brought us there. The three of us headed out.

I snuggled myself down as far as I could into the black vinyl upholstery of the Pontiac's back seat. I managed to exhale. I looked up to see Eldridge's eyes staring at me out of the rear-view mirror.

"Mrs. Stew?" he began.

A loud *brnng* interrupted. As an early adopter of what passed for mobile technology in 1968, Eldridge had a car phone. It was the size and shape of a land-line telephone; its handset attached to a black base by a curly black cord. The entire apparatus lay wedged between the Pontiac's two front seats. On previous occasions, I'd observe Eldridge place his calls by picking up the receiver and dialing "0," after which a live operator patched him into a land line. Now Eldridge picked up the handset and listened.

I heard him say, his tone friendly, "Hey man, no hard feelings. I was just fuckin' with your head."

It had to be the chubby man at the other end of the line. After he hung up, Eldridge tilted his head back toward me and began again, "Hey, Mrs. Stew. You know sometimes I like to test people. I . . ."

Perhaps my adrenaline had not yet given way to exhaustion, but I no longer cared if Eldridge Cleaver had been fucking with my head. I cut Eldridge off.

"Eldridge, I am not Mrs. Stew! I am not Mrs. Anybody! I'm me. I'm Judy. Judy Clavir."

I hated to use the name of my dysfunctional birth family, but I did not have another alternative.

"You are Stew's rib, ya know, Mrs. Stew," Eldridge retorted, as if to caution me that he, Eldridge Cleaver, would never cave. With that, the Minister of Information of the Black Panther Party had handed me one Mrs. Stew too many.

"I am a person in my own right!" I screeched.

Only the hum of the Pontiac's engine broke the silence. From my perch in the rear seat I saw Stew's broad shoulders scrunch up as if to block from his ears any negative outcome Eldridge's and my battle might provoke. By then my Panther education had taught me that words, when spoken by people of color, often come with variations in meaning unfamiliar to white people. I waited, my breath coming in ragged spurts, proud of myself for having made my declaration but unsure what lay ahead for me after this white girl's second-time all-too-rash verbal confrontation with the great Eldridge Cleaver.

Eldridge twisted his head to glare at me. I huddled in my seat. I hoped he was trying to find a way to end our argument that made a small concession to me. Eldridge turned out to be an exceptional diplomat. Gradually, in the rear-view mirror, I watched his expression soften.

He said, "Alright then, I'll call you Gumbo."

Eldridge named me Gumbo since for Eldridge, born in Arkansas, Gumbo was a spicy Stew.

Women come into this world with no last name of our own. The name that best suits our evolving identity arrives, I believe, during life's transformative moments. From that day on, Eldridge called me Gumbo, and on occasion just to rub it in, "Stew's rib, Gumbo." Kathleen called me Gumbo; all the Panthers I knew called me Gumbo. The Yippies soon came to call me Gumbo. My friends from that era *still* call me Gumbo. As does everyone who "likes" me on Facebook or castigates me on Twitter.

Like Eldridge said, Gumbo went with Stew.

I loved my new name. It separated me from my dysfunctional birth family and prompted me to divorce myself emotionally from Hemblen—unlike the FBI who, with typical bureaucratic rigidity, continued for decades to categorize me under that hateful name. Although at first my Gumbo name defined me as Stew's counterpart, it impelled me to create a new identity for myself, to re-make myself into whatever type of human being I wanted to become.

CHAPTER 4:
RISE UP AND ABANDON
THE CREEPING MEATBALL

As if "Kill Your Parents" didn't go far enough, Jerry Rubin borrowed a second slogan from Ed Sanders, a Woodstock poet, Yippie, and member of a rock band called the Fugs (a euphemism for "Fucks"). Jerry turned Ed's slogan "Rise Up and Abandon the Creeping Meatball" into a Yippie meme.

The first time I heard Jerry say it, I thought the slogan was ridiculous. I took it literally. No meatball in my life had crept. They had thundered down my psychic slopes in an avalanche of unfaithful husbands, my mother's hostility, and the passivity, fear, and self-hatred I'd absorbed growing up. To abandon creeping meatballism, I needed to act as if my life was theater, to become a fun-loving and non-serious Yippie who refused to let restrictions define her world. But back in the 20th century, before my 25th birthday, I had no idea how.

* * *

If, by the summer of 1968, I had taken on my later alternate persona of the fortune teller Mme. Gumbo, I might have foreseen in my Tarot cards these three earth-shattering events: On March 31, President Lyndon Johnson, beaten down by his war in Vietnam that eclipsed his civil rights accomplishments, announced he would not seek a second term. On April 4, Dr. Martin Luther King Jr. was murdered. On June 5, two months and a day after King's death, Robert Kennedy was assassinated. For me these events proved

SNCC leader H. Rap Brown—and my mother—right: violence is as American as cherry pie.

March 1968 began well. Keith Street's telephone rang. My father Leo ordered me back to Toronto. I had an appointment with a judge. To use my now least favorite girly word, I was thrilled. I'd have no problem proving adultery—the only legal grounds for divorce in Canada at the time. I'd acquired a method to take my revenge on Hemblen: I had found myself a new man who was blonder, sexier, more political—with famous friends—and he was infinitely more trustworthy than Hemblen could ever be. That British bitch Angela could have the despicable Hemblen for herself!

I found Stew outdoors on Keith Street's balcony contemplating fingers of grey fog above the Golden Gate Bridge. I blurted out, "Stew, I gotta go back to Toronto as quick as I can! I'm getting divorced!"

Our landline's *brrring* interrupted a second time. Jerry's voice came through the line so loud I overhead it. Jerry invited—more like commanded—that Stew come east to help him organize a protest at the 1968 Democratic Convention in Chicago. Stew must drop everything! Move to New York City! Right now! To help organize an anti-war extravaganza, a Festival of Life! This coming August! To resist the Democratic Party's Convention of Death and stop the pro-war Hubert Humphrey from seizing the party's presidential nomination! To be a Yippie with him and Abbie!

As a universe of adventure sparkled in Stew's blue eyes, he grinned at me and asked, "Will you come and live with me in New York? After you get divorced, I mean?"

There are experiences life offers that it is foolish to turn down. This was one. I chose to take Stew's invitation as an escalation in commitment. I did not hesitate; I kissed him on his dome-like forehead and said yes.

In Toronto, I suffered through my mother Harriet's critiques lobbed at me as gobs of sympathy, then faced a grim Canadian judge, and explained, with appropriate Canadian politeness, that I had discovered my husband in bed with another woman. The next day, Leo dropped me off at Toronto's airport so I could catch a plane to New York City. Leo hugged me, told me to take care of myself, handed me $300 in U.S. bills, then said, "Use this to make a little revolution for me, eh?"

Even in my communist Clavir family, a gift of money from either parent signaled love and approval. Leo's financial cushion may have contradicted our family's communist value of obtaining income equality through class struggle, but I was grateful. I took the money.

A Yellow Cab dropped me on a one-way street in New York City. This was my first time in that fabled metropolis. Like a turn of-the-century immigrant just landed at Ellis Island, I dropped my father's heavy Cordovan leather suitcase on the pavement then extracted from my pocket a piece of crumpled paper on which I had written *343-¼ Bleecker Street, Greenwich Village, New York City, USA.*

The sign in front of me hand-painted in black and green read "Liberty House." It surprised me that a riot of hand-made consumer goods filled the store's two windows. I knew that Stew was not an arts-and-crafts-y type. Of all the places I'd expected us to reunite in New York City, a crafts store named Liberty House in Greenwich Village was not it. Puzzled, I pushed the shop door open and heard a small bell tinkle. Behind the counter a short, dark-haired woman raised her head. She said, "Hi. I'm Ellen Maslow. Can I help you?"

Although we'd never met, Ellen looked familiar. It took a moment for me to put the puzzle together. I wondered if those wide-set penetrating eyes plus the name Maslow meant Ellen was related to Abraham Maslow, a world-renowned psychologist whose face I remembered from my college psychology textbooks. Maslow's concept of self-actualization had intrigued me—it was a way to strive for a higher stage of morality through insight, acceptance, and by focusing on others over myself. I turned out to be right; Ellen Maslow was Abraham Maslow's daughter. And the first person among many I would subsequently meet who demonstrated how deep the Yippie network spread among the famous.

"I'm . . . uh . . . Judy? I'm looking for Stew Albert? I was told to meet him here?"

As Canadians can, I turned the insecurity of my sentences into questions. Ellen looked straight at me, which wasn't difficult since we were both just five feet tall.

"Stew's at Jerry's. He wanted me to call him the moment you arrived. Can I get you anything?"

"A washroom would be nice, eh?"

"The restroom's over there," Ellen replied, and pointed to the rear of the store.

Language can be a barrier for any immigrant—even a Canadian. I was an immigrant of privilege in many ways, among them that English was my "native" tongue. But even so, my passive Canadian English marked me as an outsider with just a titch, as we Canadians say, of British arrogance. In the United States, what I called a washroom was a restroom. I decided as a first act in the United States to divorce myself from the Queen's English, to change the word "washroom" to "restroom" even though this made no sense to me since I found more to wash than rest in any restroom I'd been in.

As I waited for Stew, Ellen explained about Liberty House. Liberty House was a retail outlet for goods handmade by Black people in Mississippi. The display I'd spotted in Liberty House's front windows charmed me—coin purses, hip pouches, women's hats, and shoulder bags made from rust and orange leather, beeswax candles, yellow pillows in the shape of lion's heads, men's ties and girl's dresses, Raggedy Ann dolls with brown skin, instead of the white dolls I was used to. Ellen sent any profits Liberty House generated south to support the civil rights movement. The women and men who sewed hats for Liberty House made better money than they ever had as maids or sharecroppers. Civil rights tactics of local organizers against Southern racism combined with non-violent civil disobedience had, Ellen said, seeded all subsequent protest movements in the United States. Abbie Hoffman, Ellen went on to tell me, was a former civil rights worker who had just quit as Liberty House's acting manager to become a Yippie.

I've loved hats ever since I was twelve, when I worked my first ever job at my grandmother Ida's store, the Adele Hat Shoppe on Bloor Street in Toronto. The silver-haired Canadian ladies who bought Ida's creations at Easter preferred the chintzy look in hats—I never did. For me, Ida's hats did not compare in brilliance, style, or fabric to a neo-cowgirl, deep rust number of Ellen's that I lusted after. It matched my hair. Its price tag was $4. I did not hesitate. I used my father's cash to make my first purchase for the revolution. I figured Leo would approve.

Just, as I put my new—and glamorous—American hat on my head, I heard the store's bell tinkle. I felt Stew's arms around me. His lips landed on my mouth, his tongue made its way between my teeth, my new hat landed, crown first, on the floor. I might as well have stuck one leg up behind me like in a romantic 1940s wartime movie.

I heard Stew's voice murmur in my ear, "Hey Gumby, welcome to New York." He moved to yank open a trap door on Liberty House's floor.

"We'll live down here," Stew said, and started down a wooden ladder into shadows.

I followed.

The air around me felt cool and motionless. A sliver of natural light glowed through a six-inch opening. Beyond that, no daylight entered. A bare bulb at the end of a frayed black electric cord provided the cellar's sole illumination. Outside the bulb's arc, I noticed stacks of merchandise piled up ghost-like and unopened. Within that circle of light, I glimpsed a double bed with two paisley pillows; next to it stood a night table constructed from an upended wooden crate plastered with labels illustrated with oranges, next to that a grey Formica kitchen table and three metal chairs. On top of a wooden plank that connected two more empty orange crates, I made out an electric frying pan, a percolator for coffee, and a two-ring, cracked, white ceramic hotplate, all plugged by means of equally unsafe and frayed extension cords into that same outlet as the overhead bulb.

First things first. Having a place to pee is always a priority for me.

"Washroom?" I asked. Oops—there was that word again. "I mean restroom?"

Stew pointed to a metal faucet at the end of an exposed pipe. Beads of water from it dripped down into a wooden barrel two feet tall. No wine occupied this barrel. Stew explained that we'd shower at friends' homes, piss in the barrel at night, and climb upstairs to use the Liberty House facilities for anything solid.

"It's wonderful," I told Stew, inhaling deeply. I spoke the truth. Apart from Jerry's largess, Stew had little income. Our New York City cellar came rent-free. I knew Stew had done his best. For me, the cellar was transformative. It lives on in my memory as a cold-water love-nest that Stew created just for me. I could not have felt more wanted or adored.

* * *

I soon became familiar with Stew's morning ritual: he'd pull up his jeans, then climb up a set of metal stairs inside the cellar which led outside to Bleecker Street. Stew would reach out his long right arm, unlock a padlock between the two steel plates that closed our cellar off from Bleecker Street and, to what I assumed must have been the disgust of passers-by, I'd watch my lover, a blond, curly haired troll naked to his waist, stagger onto Bleecker Street and dump our night's barrel of piss water into the gutter.

Living in a counter-cultural cellar may seem bizarre, but bizarre experiences have advantages. I first met William Kunstler, a famous left-wing attorney, in our cellar. Stew had assured me that he and Bill, as he and everyone who knew Kunstler called him, were good friends. Bill's wife Lotte was Liberty House's owner.

One morning early in April of 1968, after Stew and I had occupied our cellar for a day or two at best, the famed attorney paid us a visit. Stew had just completed his ritual dumping of the piss water. He'd left open the metal plates on Bleecker Street that allowed in both our single sliver of light and direct access to our cellar. I heard a clang. A black loafer topped by a gray sock appeared on our top-most metal step. Above the sock a tailored trouser leg emerged. A second clang announced a second shoe, topped by its own gray sock and pant leg, until New York City's most eminent defender of the downtrodden stood upright on my cellar floor. It was as if a main-stream CEO had bungled his way into a Yippie convention.

I'd soon become familiar with Bill's trademark Shakespearian speech. Bill began to orate, as if he were in a courtroom, his voice clipped and formal.

"Stew, I regret to inform you . . . "

Why, I wondered, did this legendary attorney, who had defended the recently murdered Dr. Martin Luther King Jr., speak to his friend Stew Albert in such an uncompromising tone? Something was not right. I worried: my lover had a quick temper, he could be provoked. Stew placed his hands on his hips, a stance I knew Stew had honed beating back bullies as a teenager in Brooklyn. Kunstler studied Stew then surveilled the chaos of our cellar. I saw the shoulders of his impeccable jacket sag.

"Screw it. I'm not gonna do it."

"Do what?" Stew and I inquired in unison.

"Nothing. Never mind. You guys got a joint?"

Shortly after, Bill confessed he'd come to evict us. He blamed his wife Lotte for demanding he carry out this heinous act. I empathize with Lotte now; how could it be good for business if customers caught sight of a bare-chested, curly-haired denizen of a basement emerge to dump a barrel of piss water into the gutter in front of her store?

Bill and Lotte soon divorced.

Bill also conferred on Stew and me the nickname, "Jew and Stewdy," which Abbie, Jerry, and our inner Yippie circle used frequently and with delight. I did not. Except for the freedom festival of Passover, I did not identify as a Jew. Israel was to me neither an oppressor of Palestinians nor a beacon of enlightenment; it just was. I did identify with Jewish powerlessness—as a result I admired the Black Panthers who turned the powerlessness of the marginalized into power. And Stew had long since abandoned his Orthodox Jewish upbringing for Yippie atheism. By naming us Jew and Stewdy—or occasionally Stewdy and Jew—Bill, who was also Jewish but of elite German Jewish lineage, raised both Stew's and my immersion in each other and our Jewish roots to a level of public scrutiny I found embarrassing.

All of us in the Yippie inner circle—Bill, me, Stew, Anita, Abbie, Jerry, Nancy Kurshan, Paul Krassner, and Phil Ochs—were secular Jews who rejected and rebelled against Jewish orthodoxy. We also rejected the pious, non-ironic legacy of American Puritanism. We were influenced by Jewish culture and especially by 1950s Jewish-American male comedians like Mort Sahl and Lenny Bruce. On top of that, our Yippie commitment to liberation ran so deep that those of us who identified as Yippies supported a multitude of movements with the word "liberation" in their title—including organizing Yippie demonstrations in New York City to support the Palestine Liberation Organization (PLO).

A Yippie uses theater to lay bare what it means to be oppressed.

* * *

LET ME TELL YOU ABOUT HOW Yippies came to be:

One day in Berkeley in 1967, Stew and Jerry Rubin had an epiphany while smoking pot. They'd build a protest movement to politicize hippies while "turning on" young leftist protesters. Jerry and Stew were right: a political hippie like me differed from Students for a Democratic Society (SDS)'s earnest, demanding, and increasingly extremist activism, from the pacifist seriousness of an older David Dellinger—and especially from the absolutism of communists in all their dogmatic stripes. Jerry, Stew, Nancy, Anita, Abbie, and Paul Krassner were among the many who advocated fusing a rising youth culture with politics. As did the Diggers in San Francisco, the Motherfuckers in New York City, and the Provos in Amsterdam; singers Bob Dylan, Joan Baez, Arlo Guthrie, Judy Collins, Phil Ochs, and Country Joe McDonald energized a growing counter-culture with their music. The concept of a political hippie bubbled up the only way it could—from the grassroots of my generation.

On New Year's Eve of 1967/1968 in New York City, Jerry, along with his partner Nancy Kurshan, Anita and Abbie Hoffman, and Paul Krassner, got really stoned on pot. In their altered state of consciousness, they founded "Yippie"—the Youth International Party. "Y" stands for youth, meaning youth will make the revolution; "I" for International, which we always knew we would be; "P" means to *have* a party, not *be* one.

Yippies took our inspiration from Marshal McLuhan, a professor who taught at my alma mater, the University of Toronto. McLuhan had famously proclaimed that: "the medium is the message." Jerry and Abbie believed television could create myths. They'd use a newly popular medium—color television—to spread our satiric Yippie message. They'd expose establishment hypocrisy using theater of ridicule to sway even mainstream media. The Yippie spirit was also ultra-democratic: anyone who chose to could call themselves a Yippie and create whatever theater of protest they desired to further a counter-cultural revolution.

"We're not leaders; we're cheerleaders," Abbie often said.

One dark evening in the cellar as Stew rubbed his fingers over my butt, he recounted a story which he called the first famous act of Yippie theater. "It was late August 1967, before you and I even met. Abbie had booked a tour of the New York City Stock Exchange. Tours took place every fifteen minutes. Eighteen Yippies showed up, in addition to me, Abbie, and Jerry. Plus the requisite reporters and photographers. But the guard at the Stock Exchange informed us that the visitor's balcony was closed for repairs.

To which, Abbie retorted, "The only reason you won't let us in is because we're Jewish."

Abbie had turned the pain of anti-Semitism into a joke. A joke that in those days was a rebel stance but, as jokes can, covered up an inconvenient truth.

"The guard backed down," Stew went on. "And when we got upstairs to the visitor's gallery, we threw $1 and $5 bills over the railing. Hundreds of stockbrokers and clerks stopped their trading to grab at the cash. That's how the Yippies brought the New York City Stock Exchange to a halt."

Delighted and curious, I asked, "How much did you throw?"

"Abbie says at least $1,000, but I don't believe him. Abbie exaggerates. And everybody had to chip in. It couldn't have been more than $200. When we ran out of paper money, we threw coins. Quarters, dimes, and pennies. They jeered and booed at the tiny amounts. We got escorted out; got great media coverage, and no one was arrested."

If this was what the Yippies meant by exposing the capitalist system through satire, I told myself I'd convert in a New York minute to having fun with politics.

"You know what they did afterwards? The Exchange put a barrier up on the balcony. I guess we got to them, greedy capitalist pigs that they are!"

Stew went on to tell me about a second famous Yippie act that took place in November of 1967. A mainstream—in other words serious and traditional—protest organization called the MOBE organized a huge march in Washington, D.C. against the Vietnam War. The Yippies, by contrast, arranged an "Exorcism of the Pentagon," and led the crowd in an effort to levitate the giant building that was the center of the U.S. war machine. They got thousands of people to shout at the Pentagon "OUT DEMONS OUT!" The Levitation was successful; Stew always claimed the Yippies raised the Pentagon six feet off the ground! I guess how high the Pentagon rose depended on how much pot you'd smoked. That time, plenty of people were arrested.

I'd discover decades later that even the FBI acknowledged the worth of our Yippie strategy. In their 12-point plan to disrupt the anti-war movement dated in July 1968, an agent made this claim about the Yippies:

> **Ridicule is the most potent weapon we can use against them.**

The FBI, a truly serious, strait-laced organization, never tried it.

I was there in spirit but not in person when the Yippies brought the Stock Exchange to a halt and levitated the Pentagon. I chalk it up to my bad luck—and good. I missed the founding party, but I did hook up with Stew in time for the third—and greatest—Yippie action: the confrontation in Chicago at the August 1968 Democratic National Convention. Chicago 1968 became the crown-jewel of events in Yippie history. And I was there.

* * *

LIBERTY HOUSE WAS THE GATEWAY DRUG that led me to the Yippies.

I became a tourist in my own life, eager to absorb and learn from every new person, place, or thing around me. As a first day in New York treat, Stew had promised me an egg cream, so we headed toward the old-time Jewish enclave of the Lower East Side. Around me car horns honked. New York City was louder, faster, older, dirtier, and more exciting and exotic than stuffy old Toronto or even hippie Telegraph Avenue in Berkeley could ever be.

Consumerism is the engine of capitalist societies; letting go of it is neither swift nor easy. In the late 1960s, I was a de facto supporter of capitalism since, whenever I had access to money, I'd shop. I'd just decided that a pair of two-tiered silver filigree earrings I saw on display beneath an orange and yellow psychedelic poster of a naked woman fit my father Leo's criteria of "for the revolution." I dashed across St. Marks Place; Stew followed slowly and deliberately as was his way. I heard a nasal voice yell out:

"Stu! Stu, hey Stu, over he-ah. I'm over he-ah."

The man who shouted at us pronounced Stew's name as he would always spell it—not as a mixture of vegetables or meats but as if it ended with an outbreath of fresh air. The man who yelled was a little shorter than Stew; he had a leading man's cleft in his chin and a head of brown curls that barely hid the joint perched behind his left ear. He'd pinned a button bearing the word Yippie in pink psychedelic script onto a fringed brown suede jacket he'd slung over one shoulder.

"Stu, Stu, c'me-ah, it's almost time for Cronkite! Let's go!"

Such was my introduction to Abbie Hoffman.

My filigree earrings and first taste of the sweet foam that topped vanilla egg creams would have to wait. I followed Stew and Abbie down a short flight of stairs into a ground floor apartment at 30 St. Mark's Place. "War is Not Healthy for Children and Other Living Things," claimed a poster of orange sunflowers taped to the apartment's red brick walls. In a kitchen at the far end of narrow hallway, I spotted a teenager with stringy hair and a jean jacket frayed at the elbows staring off into space. I'd never met a runaway, but he fit my stereotype.

I found two people sitting side-by-side on a run-down living room couch. Stew draped one arm around my shoulder and pushed me gently forward. He introduced me first to Paul Krassner, editor of *The Realist*, a satiric magazine of small circulation but, Stew assured me, of profound impact. At that time, I formed the majority of my first impressions based on someone's physical appearance—the woman with her long black hair looked gorgeous to me; the man, his baby-like face scarred by adolescent acne, made him appear too young for what I imagined was such an exalted position.

"Hey," Paul Krassner said, and waved. I puffed up with self-importance. No matter its circulation, a magazine is, after all, a magazine.

Then Stew said, "Anita, this is my girlfriend, Judy."

Young women in their teens and early twenties fantasize about becoming movie stars. With her gray-green eyes and well-defined cheekbones, I decided Anita Hoffman might give it a shot. I used my most diffident Canadian smile to introduce myself. Anita stared back at me, then, without saying a word, returned to her embroidery. Already insecure in such a strange environment, I felt crushed. I later understood that Anita's unfriendliness was not about me—Anita was suspicious of any stranger who happened to be a woman. Anita Hoffman was no fool. She faced the traditional, patriarchal bind of a woman married to a charismatic man. Abbie came on to women; women came on to Abbie. When I understood that Anita may have viewed me as cute enough to be a threat, I decided to take her cold greeting as a compliment—as well as evidence of distrust.

Misogyny creates a multiplicity of harsh consequences—sowing discord between women is one. Anita and I kept each other at a cool but friendly distance that summer of 1968. Only after the rise of the women's movement did Anita and I become friends.

* * *

I'D LEARN THE ART OF SHAMELESS self-promotion from Jerry Rubin.

In May of 1968, the month before my 25th birthday, my third day in New York City and shortly after I'd met Anita, Abbie, and

Bill Kunstler, I met Jerry Rubin and his partner Nancy Kurshan for the first time. Nancy and Jerry lived at 5 St. Mark's Place, half a block west of Anita and Abbie. The location of these two apartments typified Jerry's relationship with Abbie—close, but on opposite sides of the flower child/politico street. To me, Abbie was charmingly funny, a politicized flower child who gave speeches and pulled pranks, while Jerry was a brilliant grassroots organizer. Together, they'd become, at first, a winning combination.

When Stew told me Nancy and Jerry's apartment was a walk-up, he wasn't kidding. Squares of dark-brown tin lined the hallway of this former tenement. The stairway's floor of black and white hexagonal tiles had long since lost its battle with grime. By the time Stew and I reached the fourth, top, floor, I decided the stairway must be furnished with an air freshener emitting marijuana fumes at top capacity. Stew knocked on the brown metal door of #16. I heard bolts squeak. An iron bar moved. A short, bearded man, just a little taller than I am with hair like a brown Brillo pad and dressed in a yellow crew-necked long-sleeved t-shirt with red stripes, smiled merrily at me.

"What atrocious taste in clothes!" was my first uncharitable thought on meeting Jerry Rubin.

Jerry hugged Stew then slapped him on his back in that universal greeting of the male gender. Jerry beckoned us into a flat crammed with hippies—hippies on the floor, hippies on the couch, hippies on the windowsill, hippies at the door. Female hippies, male hippies; long haired, short haired, no-haired hippies, hippies, hippies everywhere, as if the felines in *Millions of Cats*, my favorite childhood book of poetry, had shape-shifted into human form on St. Mark's Place in New York City.

Stew and I squeezed ourselves underneath a window propped open with a stick. Jerry began to address the hippies in what I would come to identify as trademark Jerry behavior—an excited voice emitting a staccato burst of words.

"Every rock band in the country will come to Chicago for the Festival of Life! Abbie knows Jefferson Airplane personally! The Festival will be free! For the people! In the streets and in the parks! Fifty-thousand people will arrive! Maybe half a million! We'll turn on everybody who can be turned on and turn off everybody else!"

Thanks to Stew, I knew by then that mainstream Democrats considered the young supporters of presidential candidate Senator Eugene McCarthy a "clean" alternative to us equally young but way more grungy hippies.

"Clean for Gene supporters of Senator McCarthy will join the Yippies in the park if only for the music," a woman's voice insisted.

"That's Nancy Kurshan, Jerry's pal," Stew confided, giving me Lesson #1 in how to navigate Yippie World—no matter how articulate or intelligent you are, to have a relationship with a Great Yippie Man gave a woman extra clout. I'd soon learn to assert myself in Yippie circles, but only after I felt I could add something impressive to what the guys said. I did wonder if there was any Yippie protocol for getting recognized. Did Yippie women have to follow men in speaking out? Should I raise my hand? If I did that, I'd look ridiculous. Besides, I had nothing to say. Since Stew was Jerry's best friend, I figured I was golden, but to comment first time out? Let Nancy do it!

Nancy and Jerry worked the room as if they were a tag-team of professional wrestlers. They insisted Senator Eugene McCarthy would be the Democratic Party's candidate for president, to oppose the pro-war Hubert Humphrey who the hippies in the room clearly hated. Nancy stood. I liked her long-sleeved, black lace top way more than Jerry's shirt.

"Pigasus, our Yippie candidate for President of the United States, will steal the Democratic Party's thunder. Pigasus will win . . ."

Jerry interrupted Nancy, "Why vote for half a pig when you can have the whole hog?"

Everyone laughed. Why indeed?

Spontaneity generates energy; acting "in the interests of caution" kills it. I watched a woman light a joint on the other side of the three-room flat, then, in a spirit of peaceful hippie communalism and before anyone cared about contracting a deadly virus, she passed the pot to a hippie seated next to her. I inhaled sweet fumes, hoping the marijuana would last long enough to make its way to me. It never did. Nancy began to hand out yellow mimeographed sheets stapled together into a booklet—our preferred medium for social messaging in 1968. On the booklet's cover, superimposed over a map of the Midwest with Chicago at its center, an arrow pointed to the dates August 25–30—along with a drawing of a naked couple having sex. Today I'd censure such a drawing as either exploitative of women or excluding LGBTQ+ folks—or both. But Spring of 1968 showed up less than a year after San Francisco's free-form sexual—and sexist—Summer of Love. Such an image of cis-gender coitus was considered as a liberating act to lure hippies into politics, at least by the Yippie men I'd come to know.

The woman who lit the joint piped up, "Now that's the politics of ecstasy, man!"

I disapproved, then felt disappointed in myself. I thought I'd let my puritanical Canadianism go! A thin blond male hippie seated next to her took over. I detected a hint of panic in his voice.

"So, what about Mayor Daley's shoot to kill order, huh? What about that?"

"It ain't gonna happen!" Jerry countered. "We've freaked Daley out! He'll grant permits. Everyone wants a peaceful protest. We've been negotiating for months. You'll see."

The long-haired blond hippie answered back, "Well, Jerry, if you don't put out a warning to tell people not to come, I will. I'll put a flyer out myself."

"Shut-up, Jim!" I heard a different male voice exclaim.

I watched Stew draw in his breath. Stew, on his way to becoming a skilled orator, believed that to wait before speaking gave what he had to say more weight. Stew's was not the usual Yippie way. Yippies like me are interrupters, too nervous or too ego-driven to wait to speak until others finish. I'd try my best to postpone speaking until that moment where words can influence or temper differences, but I was rarely able to accomplish that.

I heard Stew say, "Yeah, violence could happen. And yeah, the Mayor of Chicago did put out a shoot to kill order. But it wasn't against Yippies or mainstream MOBE demonstrators; it targeted Black people. Richard Daley is a stone cold racist. This was his racist response to the uprisings in Chicago's Black community that followed the assassination of Dr. Martin Luther King."

Then Stew, in what I recognized by its low cadence as his most authoritative voice, told the assembled hippies that he had learned from his friend Eldridge Cleaver never to give in to fear.

"But at the same time," Stew concluded, modifying Jim's warning with greater objectivity than I could ever muster, "I also agree with Jim. It would be wise to prepare the kids for a confrontation, even if it's a confrontation Yippie style."

I wondered if the hippies I saw squirming in their places felt uncomfortable with any type of confrontation. Not so, I thought, for me. My desire to avoid confrontation stemmed from my harsh and argumentative alcoholic family, not my opposition to unjust authority. I told myself I'd welcome the challenge to run from cops to protest a horrendous war and prove myself—at least abstractly, since I had not yet done it.

Jerry, an eternal optimist, appeared unmoved by Jim's statement; he believed sincerely that Mayor Daley would grant permits for a peaceful Festival of Life. Nancy looked dubious. Jim had jumped immediately to a worst-case scenario—that protesters would be attacked. I watched a bearded fellow rise effortlessly from the floor. He introduced himself as Wolfe, a tai chi master;

he volunteered to teach Yippies a nonviolent way to demonstrate used by students in Japan to prevent cops from breaking through their protest lines.

At that, Jerry interrupted: "Rise Up and Abandon the Creeping Meatball!"

The curiosity I've had my entire life won out. Even such an unremarkable act as speaking in a meeting for the first time can be an act of defiance.

In a voice as loud as my heartbeat, I stood and asked, "Jerry, what does 'abandon the creeping meatball' mean?"

"The way to eliminate fear is to do what you are most afraid of!" Jerry replied.

It came to me that if I chose to be a Yippie I could rise up and abandon all the creeping meatballs of insecurity I'd learned growing up that occupied my life. This process would be neither instantaneous nor easy, but to come into my own as Judy Gumbo, to act with that depth of courage all Yippies must, I'd have to do it.

* * *

EACH TIME I'D VISIT ANITA AND Abbie's apartment, I'd find a color television set blaring. I emphasize the word "color" since owning a color television in 1968 meant Anita and Abbie were ahead of the curve. Only two years previously had all three TV networks begun to broadcast evening shows in color.

Abbie'd prop himself against a door jamb, his energy too irrepressible to allow him to sit down. Stew'd squeeze in next to Paul and Anita on the brown couch. I, the newbie outsider, sat on an orange rug on the floor. But with Stew's legs as my back rest, I finally felt at ease enough to watch the news with Anita, Abbie, and Paul.

"Good evening. This is the CBS *Evening News* with Walter Cronkite."

Cronkite's deep voice exuded gravitas. He was authority personified.

He began, "The Pentagon announced today that 1,543 Americans died in Vietnam this April. Also last month, 9,409 Americans were wounded."

With that, Cronkite's face faded into images of Marines in full dress uniform saluting as coffin after coffin, each covered in a red, white, and blue flag, slide down a conveyor belt from inside the hold of a cargo plane. I could not draw myself away. Twenty-five years later, when American ownership of color televisions was long routine, President George H. W. Bush banned TV images of coffins coming home from the Gulf War. Coffins, especially those draped in patriotic colors, make explicit how war chews up its participants in an assembly line of blood.

In Canada, the Vietnam war seemed distant to me. I'd protested in front of the American consulate in Toronto but in a polite Canadian way. The sign I'd carried read: END CANADIAN COMPLICITY IN THE VIETNAM WAR. Now a U.S. resident, I rejected being "complicit"—being complicit was too indirect, too far removed from the action. By the time I spent time in Anita and Abbie's apartment, the war in Vietnam no longer felt so far away. TV and the anguish and anger of my Berkeley and now New York City friends had forced this war on me. To immerse myself in American culture—just like my involvement with the Panthers—I had to experience my adopted culture directly.

I watched on Anita and Abbie's newish color TV as white smoke billowed up from a pile of papers that smoldered in a parking lot. Two Catholic priests, the brothers Phillip and Daniel Berrigan, and seven other Catholic activists, had broken into a Selective Service office in Catonsville, Maryland, seized draft files, doused them with napalm, and set them on fire. Abbie grabbed Anita. The two danced a jig. Stew and Paul rose up as well, shouting their approval. My backrest vanished; I lost my balance then stood up and screamed, "Way to go! Stop this fucking war!"

That traditionally conservative Catholic clergy could be so audacious as to take napalm, a gel made from gasoline by Dow Chemical Company that decimated forests and burned the flesh of any human being on whom it landed, and turn that instrument of war back on the warmakers: this was for me an act of inspirational proportions. Even a kid in the kitchen poked their head into the hallway, as if to assure themself the planet still existed.

"And in other news," I waited as I saw Cronkite look straight at me through his horn-rimmed glasses, as if he was addressing only me. He paused, then continued.

"One hundred and seventeen student anti-war demonstrators have been arrested at Columbia University. Overseas, violent protests, hundreds of arrests of students, and a general strike of an estimated nine million workers continue to rock France, as they have every day this month."

"Yeah, Walter!" I yelled, as if Cronkite and I now shared a camaraderie of protest that put us on a first name basis. Walter went on to inform me that directors had withdrawn their films from the Cannes Film Festival. The Cannes jury had resigned. The festival itself shut down. All to support workers and student protesters in France.

It had to be—the revolution had arrived!

But Walter suddenly shed his civil tone. In a voice that sounded to me like a disapproving father, Walter announced, "In Chicago today, the office of Mayor Richard Daley reiterated the Mayor's determination not to grant permits for planned anti-war demonstrations this coming August at the Democratic National Convention."

At that, Abbie took a red Swiss Army knife out his pocket. He grabbed a bottle of cream soda and used the knife to flip the cap off with a fast snap of his wrist. Incensed, he yelled at the TV in what sounded to my Canadian ear like a foreign voice, but I soon learned was his working-class Worcester accent.

"Richard Daley! That sunnuva-bitch! He's got some hell of a fuckin' nerve! All we want are permits to sleep in the pahk. Have a goddam rock festival! Politics of Ecstasy, fah chrissake. Fuck him!" Abbie turned directly toward me and demanded, "You're coming to Chicago, right?"

I nodded yes, though I felt confused. In that moment, Abbie reminded me of my father: both men possessed the high-energy, deal-making machismo of entrepreneurs. But Abbie was a genuine performance artist, like the multicolored sparklers I used to light as a kid to celebrate Queen Elizabeth's birthday. And like any sparkler, over the time I'd know him, I watched Abbie's creative genius flare up, die down, flare up, and then burn out before its time.

"And that's the way it is," I heard Uncle Walter say. "Friday, May 17th, 1968."

CHAPTER 5:
THE PLAY'S THE THING

I WASN'T FAMOUS IN 1968. NEITHER was Stew, really. But Stew, along with Abbie and Jerry, possessed a celebrity machismo that turned me on. Perhaps it was their body language, upright and arrogant, projecting the power of their gender. Or the free flow of ideas that cascaded out of all three Yippie mouths. But unlike Jerry and Abbie who courted personal fame as a perk of making revolution for the hell of it, Stew was humble in a manly-man kind of way. He did not seek the spotlight for himself.

I was tempted to seek that spotlight, but I did not know how. When I'd open my mouth in Yippie circles I felt marginalized. Anita and Nancy did not speak up much at Yippie gatherings either, except to clarify what the boys said or if they were angry or upset. Apart from that, Yippie men talked; Yippie women listened. It wasn't that Yippie women were directly disrespected—it was more that what we said was passed over or ignored. I began my career in the Yippies by learning to watch, to listen, and to imitate, and finally to act with Yippie abandon. Like the Yippie men. I needed to be equal to these assertive but self-absorbed guys, but on my own terms.

One afternoon in late May, when Stew and I still lived on Bleecker Street, I heard Ellen Maslow's voice call down into our cellar's gloom. Nancy was on the upstairs land line. Her friend Robin Morgan was organizing a protest at the Miss America

Pageant in Atlantic City. Robin asked if Nancy, Anita, and I wanted to join her, to protest the horrendous way women are objectified as mindless sex objects—especially in the media.

I'd heard of Robin, a former child TV star and original Yippie. Robin had quit the Yippies before I ever showed up, incensed by the misogyny she encountered there. Nancy, Anita, and I declined Robin's invitation. We stood by our men. I wondered briefly whether the sexism that compelled Robin to quit the Yippies could one day become a creeping meatball in my own life, but I let it go. I was not yet ready to abandon my new lover and his exciting Yippie pals for what I considered at that time a "mere" women's demonstration. I convinced myself I was having too much fun with the Yippies.

Robin had scheduled the women's protest for the week following our Chicago protests. She and her cohort of women had borrowed a page from the Yippie handbook but transformed it. Instead of running a pig for president, Pageant protesters crowned a live sheep Miss America—a symbol based in the reality that Pageant contestants were treated and expected to act like conformist sheep. When I saw on TV that women protesters had stopped the show by unfurling a banner inside the Pageant Hall that read "Women's Liberation," I cheered—loud enough for Stew to hear. He did not comment. The women protesters also threw bras, corsets, and what they baptized instruments of female torture into a Freedom Trash Can. But they burned no bras. Miss America Pageant protesters had bested the Yippies at our own game: Out of an act that never happened, women created a myth much bigger than reality—the myth of bra-burning.

* * *

STEW AND I DEPARTED NEW YORK City for Chicago in early July 1968. Stew had completed his ritual dumping of the piss water, returning to our cellar with a bag of red New York State apples for the road—plus an adorable white kitten with a black patch over her left eye. The owner of a fruit stand next door had asked Stew to take the kitten to Chicago to protest in his place. The kitten was far worse off than I had ever been; she was a matted, homeless denizen of New York City streets while I was just a stranger in a strange land. I named my kitten Krupskaya, after the Russian revolutionary and Lenin's wife.

I took the wheel of a Plymouth Fury. On both sides of its front doors and clearly visible under a sparse topcoat of white paint, a shield prophetically proclaimed POLICE. It didn't occur to me this signage might be a prediction. In its retirement, this former cop car had been demoted to a drive-away, my generation's most inexpensive way to travel next to hitchhiking. The retired cop car came equipped with a full tank of gas plus papers I had signed that promised I would deliver the vehicle, undamaged, to strangers in Indiana who had bought it on the cheap—sight unseen.

I was happy to drive. To escape my family, I'd obtained my driver's license the moment I turned 16. Because of it, I had control—a major theme in my life. The plan was for the four of us—me, Stew, Jerry, and Krupskaya—to drive the Plymouth to its new owners, then hitchhike to Chicago. Nancy had stayed behind in New York City as Jerry's assistant to promote a manuscript he'd written. I tuned the cop car's radio to a rock and roll beat, to hear Janis Joplin urge me to take another little piece of her heart now, baby. I fancied Janis, Ritchie Havens, the Doors, the Who, Jimi Hendrix, and Jefferson Airplane as the upbeat soundtrack for our trip. But the more I drove, the more the radio began blaring far-right talk shows much more at home in a former cop car than I was.

Stew sat up front next to me in the passenger seat; Jerry and Krupskaya shared the Plymouth's spacious back. I had imprisoned Krupskaya inside an empty orange crate, in which I'd put a litter box. Since no metal suspect's grill separated the cop car's front from its back, I could see in the rear-view mirror each time

Krupskaya's paw thrust itself upward through wooden slats to meet a swat from Jerry.

As strips of white paint zoomed by on black asphalt, I continued to work on fitting in, to speak more like Stew, Anita, Abbie, Nancy, and Jerry. My Canadianisms had once served me well—people looked on me as polite and therefore compliant—as well as charming and cute. My passive way of speaking stoked male egos. But now I wanted to speak in that forthright way Americans do, more suited to the confident person I wished to become. The rhythm of the road helped me repeat in whispers the project I began in Liberty House—to let go of overt Canadianisms such as "Eh?" and "washroom" and not to apologize automatically if someone jostled me, as if it was my fault. I'd change "Aboot the hoohse" to "abowt" the "howse," turn "kohffee" into "cawwfee," and, most foreign of all, discard "zed" and change it into "zee."

"X-Y-ZEE." I muttered as if I was rehearsing a witchy incantation, "X-Y-ZEE. Zee. Zee, X-Y-ZEE."

Stew turned his head to stare at me as if I was going nuts.

Next instant, I heard a *crunnnnnch*. The cop car bucked then slowed to a crawl. Panicked, I pressed down on the gas pedal. No change of pace. It was as if the lines and spaces on the highway had themselves lost speed. Terrified, I babied the behemoth into a nearby Gulf Oil gas station I was relieved to see on my right and rolled the car to a stop. I watched Jerry frown. A young mechanic ran out to examine the car and then informed us that we needed a new water pump—which would take a full day to arrive. At that, Jerry opened his back door and jumped out, leaned his brown head of hair into Stew's open passenger window.

"This is terrible guys. Abbie's already in Chicago. Working the media. I can't wait around. I NEED TO BE THERE TOO!! Now! You understand right? It's OK, right? With both of you, right? You agree it's what I should do, right? I'll give you money for the car and for a place to stay, OK?"

Stew's job as Jerry's best friend was to give advice and counsel but not stand in Jerry's way. My job as Stew's partner was not to challenge. The attendant told Jerry where to find a Greyhound bus to Chicago, while Stew and I checked into a Motel 6 in a one-horse town I'd renamed Bumblefuck, Indiana. That evening, under an ink-black sky sprinkled with stars, I coaxed the cop car into a drive-in movie. I purchased two hot dogs, popcorn, and two cokes at a concession stand whose faded exterior bore witness to a changing American reality—that television, and especially color television, was forcing drive-in movies out of business. Stew and I snuggled with each other inside the comfort of our cop car while on a giant movie screen the embattled idealist, Dr. Zhivago, forged his heroic way across frozen Russian steppes. Stew whispered that he loved me. I deflected. I told Stew that, given my immersion in Soviet cinema as a child, for me the movie focused too much on the flaws of the Russian Revolution and not enough on its accomplishments.

That night, I could not sleep. I got out of bed, wrapped my naked body in a thin beige blanket, and stood at the motel's screen door to hear the *tzzt* of three brown moths with furry wings bump themselves against the surface of a yellow bug lamp. Chicago may have been the light toward which I, brave moth, was heading, but I did not take the moths' attempts at suicide as an omen. Just the opposite: for the first time since Hemblen's betrayal, I could admit to myself that the calmness in my body came from a source beyond physical release—I loved Stew.

I came to Chicago to re-fashion myself through action, to prove my courage and yet have fun—all this underlined by my moral imperative to help end the war in Vietnam. I was looking for adventure and to become my own person. Stew too had something to prove. He subsequently wrote that he went to Chicago to fight against the war, but also to prove his love for me, to impress me politically—and, like me, to fill the hole created by his failed marriage. Stew also said he needed to demonstrate his manliness not just to me but also to Jerry and Abbie, his nationally-famous friends, who would not waste their time with anyone they considered unworthy. My energy and happy ferocity had impressed him. I did, however, feel a tinge of guilt—about which I could do nothing—when I saw the faces of the elderly white couple, who were the drive-away's new owners, as two Yippies and a kitten pulled up to their mobile home in a former cop-car belching black fumes from its still-rattling engine.

Stew, Krupskaya, and I, romantic heroes of our own Dr. Zhivago movie, headed down I-80 toward Chicago. I was buoyed, not frightened; I'd realized that, underlying it all, I also came to Chicago to prove my love for Stew. He and I would face whatever helluva revolution awaited us—together.

* * *

IN CHICAGO, JERRY, STEW, AND I lived at 506 West Armitage Avenue, in the apartment of a man who had advertised free lodging for out-of-town Yippies on a bulletin board in the office of the *Chicago Seed*, Chicago's underground paper. I no longer recall our host's name, but he was rumored to be a former CIA informant. Abbie had warned us that the man had been recruited by the Russians to pass information to them about Francis Gary Powers, a CIA pilot whose U-2 plane had been shot down over Russia in 1960. Abbie told me later he and Anita had stayed in but then quit the man's apartment, convinced the man was still in thrall to government overlords. Abbie turned out to be right. Our host did serve government overlords—not the Russians but the FBI. I later discovered the following comment in my files:

> *This informant was utilized in a soviet espionage investigation in 1959 through 1960, but was discontinued in 1961.*

I wasn't surprised when Jerry had a viewpoint opposite to Abbie's.

"You don't have to worry about this guy," Jerry assured Stew and me. "He's definitely come over to our side."

I chose to believe Jerry, though to be safe I named our bald and lanky host "The Spy," but never said so to his face. My files claim our host reported to the Chicago Office of the FBI about his Yippie guests on a daily basis through 8/30/68. But The Spy failed at his job. He was, according to my files, **unable to furnish any information of substance regarding the Yippies since no planning or strategy sessions were held in his presence.**

I also wasn't surprised to read this. Given our Yippie chaos, to hold any form of Yippie planning/strategy session would be a miracle of its own. Stew, as was his way, opted for a middle ground.

"Accept reality. Once a turncoat, always a turncoat. Now we are aware of who he is, let's stay here anyway. We just have to be careful in everything we say."

Free lodging in Chicago was hard to come by. Jerry, Stew, and I moved in.

The Spy acted as if he had nothing to hide; even the windows in his apartment had no curtains. For his daily Yoga practice, I'd observe The Spy hoist himself up on both elbows, stark naked, head toward the floor, in front of a window that overlooked a narrow side street, his elongated old man's balls hanging in full view like hairy plums on a rope. Such was the image that welcomed me to Chicago. But in my head, I'd hear my father Leo make his standard prediction: "Ya ain't seen nuthin' yet."

* * *

MY RIGHT OF PASSAGE TO BECOME a Yippie began in Lincoln Park. Assuming we got permits, Lincoln Park would be the venue for our Festival of Life, and where we'd sleep during Convention Week.

Stew and I met up with Abbie in the park on Sunday, August 18, 1968, one week and a day before our Yippie Festival of Life was scheduled to begin. Abbie handed me a leaflet, an Abbie Hoffman manifesto that spelled out what to expect in a New Nation built on Abbie Hoffman expectations. In Yippiedom, the Vietnam War is over, Black Panther Minister of Defense Huey P. Newton is free, as is health care, education, art, love, contraception, abortion, money, and toilets. The planet is in ecological balance and human beings, having overthrown the shackles of capitalist consumerism, live as equals. For Abbie and for the rest of us, Yippies must go beyond organizing resistance to our Yippie version of revolution—direct action to create all that is good.

I returned to Lincoln Park the next day, Monday, August 19, 1968, to perform my woman's task—to paint pink and purple Yippie logos on protest signs. I was not asked, and with mild jealousy had convinced myself I did not care, to accompany the boys—Stew, Jerry, Abbie, Paul Krassner, and our friend Abe Peck, editor of the *Chicago Seed*—to a high-level meeting with Deputy Mayor David Stahl, a Chicago bureaucrat. The boys' job, together with the MOBE—that sober, mainstream organization led by Dave Dellinger, Tom Hayden, and Rennie Davis—was to negotiate permits. Like any well-meaning but still naive Canadian, I assumed Mayor Daley's administration would grant those permits to protest peacefully in Chicago's streets and to use Lincoln Park as an overnight camping ground.

My task of making posters soon began to try my patience. For excitement, I decided I'd just show up unannounced at the *Seed* office on Halsted Street, where the boys' meeting was taking place. I found Stew, Abbie, and Jerry standing together, heads of bushy hair held high, one blond, two dark, a boy band minus instruments. But by the time I arrived, their meeting had run its course. Stew kissed me on the forehead, interrupting what I'd come to recognize as a typical Abbie rant.

"We didn't come to Chicago to oppose the Democrats; we came to oppose the war. That's what I told him. That fuck!"

Abbie's Worcester accent inflated his usual intensity.

"Staaaahhhl. That's all he'll ever do. Staaahhhl."

Seed editor Abe Peck had turned out to be a naysayer. Abe, our local expert consultant, had concluded that if the Yippies did not receive permits, demonstrators should not come to Chicago. Abe, a long-time Chicagoan, insisted he knew from direct experience the vicious way Chicago cops behaved. Like Jim in New York City, Abe insisted that Abbie, Jerry, and Stew warn incoming protesters of the potential for police violence. I refused to admit Abe might be right. Jerry and Abbie glared at the pony-tailed editor—deflecting onto Abe the frustration each one of us felt about Mayor Daley's intransigence. I saw Abe frown behind his wire-rimmed glasses. Jerry retorted that such a warning would discourage protesters from turning out. I stayed silent as I often did. The thrill-seeker in me wanted our Yippie protest to take place, but to speak out I'd need a compelling argument—which at the time I lacked. To be a woman who puts together ideas so radical they convince a group of Yippie men takes time—at least it did for me.

For Stew not so much.

"For sure," he repeated what I'd heard him say in New York, "Chicago cops had quelled uprisings in Chicago's Black community with force and violence. It'd be prudent to prepare kids for a confrontation, but Eldridge and the Panthers taught me never to give in to fear."

This prompted Abbie to attack Abe's argument as fearmongering. The confrontation between the guys hid an ideological fault line that I've seen roil every social movement I've been part of—to what degree do you encourage risk if you believe your cause just?

That night, after Jerry and The Spy were asleep, Stew and I lay side by side on our mattress on the floor. I had only a torn white sheet to absorb my sweat. Still a newbie to America let alone Yippie politics, I asked Stew why he thought Mayor Daley was being so intransigent. Stew rubbed his fingers over my belly—arousing in me an expectation not of politics but of orgasm. Instead, his goatee scratched my cheek.

"Here's how I think it's gonna go, Gumby," Stew began speaking in a murmur that grew passionate the more he spoke. "President Lyndon Johnson is a Democrat. FBI Director J. Edgar Hoover is a Republican. It'd be in Hoover's interest to exaggerate what Abbie says about us Yippies fucking on the beaches and putting LSD in Chicago's drinking water. But Mayor Richard Daley is a Democrat. He doesn't want a confrontation."

"So, Stewie, what'll happen?" I asked, intrigued.

"Mayor Daley is known to be short-tempered. If J. Edgar Hoover can convince Daley we Yippies are an actual threat, Daley will call in the cops. Against," Stew emphasized, "the interests of his own Democratic Party. Then, if riots do erupt, the Democrats will get blamed, the Republicans will win, and Richard Nixon will get elected as a law-and-order president."

"So, ask yourself, Gumby," Stew finished up, "who benefits from a confrontation?"

That question—"Who benefits?"—is one every resister must ask themself. Who benefits from confrontation? Who benefits from acts of violence? Who benefits from encouraging risk if they believe a cause is just? I decided up front that Stew was right, a riot in Chicago would serve the interests of FBI Director Hoover and Republicans. So I asked myself—if violence arose out of our Yippie protests, would it make me, a protester, complicit if Richard Nixon won his election?

At the same time my inner voice insisted, "Gumbo, do you really want to be in Chicago if there's gonna be a confrontation?"

I've long agreed with the Chinese military strategist Sun Tzu, who famously claimed, "Know your enemy and know yourself, in a hundred battles you will never be defeated." I had not yet read Sun Tzu, but I could identify my enemies—war, misogyny, racial injustice, despoliation of the earth. I also know myself—I enjoy taking risks. I like to be where the action is: did then, do today. The majority of risks I take end up being worth it. I've reflected on this moment over decades, and my answer remains the same—confrontation with Chicago cops or no, in August 1968, I'd run a pig named Pigasus for President to help stop a horrific war.

In Yippiedom the play's the thing. The show must go on.

CHAPTER 6:
THE BIG PIG FIGHT

PIGASUS GAVE YIPPIES A PLATFORM TO laugh at adversity. Even a Yippie newcomer like me understood that to run a live pig for president of the United States would be media gold. But why a pig, and not some other animal?

Two years before the summer of 1968, the Black Panther Party newspaper published Emory Douglas's cartoon of pig as villain. Emory's pig was a brutal, abusive, racist cop with a pig head on a human-like body—a protruding, hairy beer belly, a bandaged head, one arm in a sling, with tears running out of one eye. Emory's pig stood upright on crutches, surrounded by buzzing flies. Under the headline "What is a Pig?" Eldridge wrote the definition of a pig as:

> A low natured beast that has no regard for law, justice or the rights of people, a creature that bites the hand that feeds it; a foul, depraved traducer usually found masquerading as the victim of an unprovoked attack.

A traducer is a liar. At least according to Eldridge. Which means that anyone who acts with dishonesty and deception deserves to be labeled pig.

In Berkeley, I'd read issue after issue of the weekly Black Panther Party newspaper and seen Emory's pig, surrounded by its signature buzzing flies, morph into new, creative guises—a scheming FBI agent pig; a Pentagon pig with dollar signs for eyes;

a fat, American, imperialist pig who suckled slobbering pink piglets from around the world. Giant rat/pigs named Richard Nixon and Attorney General John Mitchell handed an indictment of the Panthers to Chicago's Mayor Richard Daley. When astronauts landed on the moon in 1969, Emory's astronaut pig, again complete with flies, claimed the moon for white people only.

Over time, the word "pig" entered my vocabulary as a generalized descriptor for all oppressive forces—racist pigs, sexist and male chauvinist pigs, ruling class pigs, fascist pigs. Which is why, in August 1968, I was just fine with running a pig named Pigasus for President of the United States.

* * *

ON THURSDAY MORNING, AUGUST 22, I passed Jerry in The Spy's hallway, right after I woke up. Jerry, in his favorite yellow and black striped T-shirt was in furious bumblebee mode. The idea to run a pig named Pigasus for President was his and Stew's, not Abbie's! Abbie had one-upped him! Abbie had betrayed him! Abbie had gone out and already purchased a pig to be the Yippie candidate for president! Without consulting Jerry. Or getting Jerry's approval.

Differences of opinion are endemic to free speech. But divisiveness based in political difference can become destructive, especially in situations dominated by men so passionate about their cause that their egos run amok. We Yippies may have been experts on how to manipulate the media, but we lacked processes to resolve interpersonal conflict. Even over a pig.

Jerry had called a meeting at The Spy's apartment. Urgent. High level. Insiders (and spies) only! I knew this gathering could have only one outcome—trouble. Abbie arrived sans pig but trailed by Anita, Paul Krassner, and a friend of Abbie's I'd met in Lincoln Park. I seated myself in front of The Spy's bare windows as audience for my opening performance of the Yippie Theater of Masculinist Confrontation.

Jerry placed one fist on each hip, glared at Abbie and started in. "Your Pigasus is too small!"

Abbie volleyed back, "What the fuck does it maaahtta, the size of the pig?"

"Small means cute. Your Pigasus makes us look cute."

Unstoppable, Abbie continued.

"Size don't matter. It's politics of the absurd, in case you've forgotten, Jerry. Cops identify with pigs. And Nazis. And fascists. It makes 'em feel like real men. Your fat pig will give the cops somethin' to relate to."

I'd never been anywhere close to a pig, but I identified with Abbie's reasoning. I too wanted an explanation: Why did size matter? For me, it was the authenticity of having a live pig that counted.

The next day I heard a rumor that proved Abbie right. Someone had spotted a Chicago cop with a tiny, gold-plated pig pin on his uniform—his medium was his message.

I watched Abbie take that same red penknife I remembered from St. Mark's Place and weave it over and under his fingers. At the same time, his voice filled with as much fevered blaming as I'd ever heard, Jerry bellowed, "Throwing money from the balcony was your idea, Abbie. You turned Wall Street greed into a myth. Pigasus has gotta be more mythic than the Stock Exchange! He's gotta be the largest, smelliest, most repulsive hog that ever stunk up the earth! That is, if we want people to take us seriously."

"Take us seriously? Are you serious? We're not serious, we're Yippies! Yippies don't want serious!" Abbie yelled back.

Jerry countered with, "Abbie, you're a hippie. You think Yippie should be nothing more than peace, love, and good vibes."

For a nanosecond Jerry stopped speaking in an un-Jerry-like loss for words. Abbie pursued his advantage,

"Jerry, you want the clenched fist; I want the fist and the flower. We're putting on a Festival. A Festival of Life! A rock concert, for chrissake! You sound like a Ma-a-a-a-ahxist, Jerry. A boring, doctrinaire Maaahxist! Whaddaya thinking, May Day in Havana?"

At which Paul Krassner, Abbie's constant ally, invoked the champions of Hollywood comedy.

"Yippies aren't Marxists, Jerry—we're Groucho Marxists."

Growing up a communist Clavir meant that any conflict, but especially conflicts over Marxism, made me anxious. In my family, ideological disagreement between my father and my mother came accompanied by invective as my mother inhaled doubles of rye whiskey, which, in turn, led to a stream of hideousness that exacerbated the intensity of their conflict. To soften this Yippie conflict, I plucked up my courage and decided I'd make a joke, but one appropriate to a child of Jewish communists.

"If I had to choose my Marx," I said, "I'd ally myself with Karl not Groucho."

I've come to love the freedom of creating chaos, an act at which both Yippies and the Marx Brothers excelled. But at the time I heard Abbie criticize Jerry for his May Day in Havana comment, I felt more at home with Karl than Groucho. Brief laughter followed my remark. I told myself I'd won a minor victory.

But Jerry ignored me. He focused on his opponent, his eyes narrowed to slits; his words emerged at breakneck speed.

"Abbie, you call yourself a hippie organizer. But I know you, Abbie! You put your body on the line in the South. You support the NLF. You want to stop the war, free Huey, legalize pot. All the good stuff. You say you're a revolutionary, Abbie. But now I wonder?"

Ouch, I thought. Good guilt-trip, Jerry.

Jerry paused. With a smile of triumph so broad it crinkled the freckles on his cheeks, I heard Jerry say, "Abbie, ask yourself— what does it mean if you put together Karl Marx and Marshall McLuhan? It means the Yippies need to create a legend. A myth of revolution bigger than reality."

Jerry's hands made brush strokes in the air as if he was conjuring up an actual pig. He barreled on, "Pigasus has gotta be big, ugly, fat, and mean. Like LBJ. Like the entire American government. Small and cute ain't mythic, Abbie. It just ain't."

Then Jerry threatened to hand out a leaflet in Lincoln Park denouncing Abbie as a media-hungry ego tripper. Finally, purged, Jerry sat down.

The room devolved into an uncharacteristic silence. I saw Abbie press his lips together to stifle his rage; he looked as if he wanted to fly across the room and strangle Jerry. Smoke might as well have been pouring out of his ears and up through every one of his brown curls. I wasn't surprised to see Anita's green eyes glare at me. Rumor had it that behind Stew's back, Abbie's friends referred to him as Jerry's sidekick. Anita had assumed, rightly, that Stew and I would side with Jerry. Stew again held back. As a child, little Stewie, with his angelic blond curls, had shuttled between his mother Raizel and his father Harold on those frequent occasions when Raizel stopped speaking to Harold for up to a month based on some unidentified slight or misdemeanor. Acting as a mediator between his parents had forced young Stewie to be an adult, to prize loyalty and stability in personal relationships. This soothing quality of Stew's was one reason Jerry, Abbie, and I all loved him. I have no doubt that Stew used his skills and reputation as a mediator and facilitator to enhance his influence within the Yippies and the more mainstream anti-war movement. And influence is power.

I watched Stew tug on his goatee as if to extract from it expertise on how to broker a peace. He then took advantage of the quiet to begin.

"Uh . . . Well . . . Uh . . . You know . . . I was thinking. . ."

"Stew—you're just the white tail of the Black Panthers," Abbie snapped, an insult based on the reality of Stew's friendship with Eldridge.

"Abbie—you're just the TV antenna of CBS." Stew, once roused, was quick on the uptake. The laughter that followed Stew's remark failed to dissolve the tension. As grown men can if they don't get what they want, Abbie's voice rose to the pitch of a six-year-old's.

"Fine. If you want your own Pigasus, go get one!" Trailed by his coterie, Abbie stomped out of The Spy's apartment.

The confrontation I witnessed that morning has got to be the only faction fight in history to occur over the size of a pig.

Stew talked Jerry down and stopped him from creating an equivalent of a Twitter storm—to put out a leaflet in Lincoln Park attacking Abbie. Stew's intervention created a moment of reason in a summer of over-reaction. But for the rest of Convention Week, that last key week of August 1968, Abbie and Jerry did not speak to each other. This left the Yippies with divided leadership during the most significant of our protests.

If I ask myself today what triggered Abbie and Jerry's big pig fight, the answer is obvious—who, Abbie or Jerry, could claim to swing a bigger dick? I suspect Jerry gave himself away two years earlier when, paranoid he might not get subpoenaed to testify before the House Un-American Activities Committee, he named the phenomenon himself: Subpoenas Envy. My conclusion is elementary: If anyone can explain why Jerry Rubin insisted on a bigger pig than Abbie Hoffman's to be the 1968 Yippie candidate for president, that person, obviously, is Sigmund Freud.

* * *

THAT SAME AFTERNOON OF ABBIE AND Jerry's Big Pig Fight, Thursday, August 22, 1968, I was the only woman on an expedition to purchase the largest, most repulsive hog we could find. I sat in the back seat of a station wagon whose fake brown wood paneling peeled off its sides, a car that a surveilling FBI agent, with the usual fanatical attention to detail, identified as "a 1957 Willys Jeep."

Stew squeezed his body in on my right; next to Stew sat a Black flower child named Vince whose dreadlocks coiled down his back. Wolfe, the bearded Jewish/Buddhist tai chi master sat next to him. "Head Shop Jim," the station wagon's owner (a head shop being what today we call a marijuana dispensary), occupied the front seat. The famous folksinger Phil Ochs drove; Jerry, the instigator of this trip, was crammed in next to him. Not one of us was buckled in. Our station wagon had no seat belts. Only eight months earlier had federal law mandated seat belts be installed in cars.

This was the first occasion at which I met a celebrity musician. With his boyish face and brown hair swept to the back into a duck's tail, Phil gave off a mid-western shyness that I thought belied his fame. I'd later learn the folk-singer's humility hid a heart-felt discontent. Phil didn't find it easy being Phil, even though Joan Baez's version of his song, "There but for Fortune," had been nominated for a Grammy. Phil wanted to make it to the top. But Bob Dylan had cornered the market on protest songs five years earlier; that reality was for Phil a source of lifelong frustration. Phil Ochs was one among the very few performers to show up in Chicago that August to protest against the Democrats and their war in Vietnam.

Phil bounced the station wagon onto a gravel road. A faded red barn came into view. Inside a square of earth enclosed by wooden posts with wire fencing, I saw pigs: some solid pink, others mottled pink and gray. From that distance, the pigs did not appear ferocious enough to hold the highest office in our land.

I prefer to run toward the action, not away from it. The instant the car stopped, I opened the station wagon's door, inhaled a breath of musty straw and fresh manure, then took off toward the enclosure to see a real live pig close up. A first for this urban girl! Through a space in the wire fence, a pink snout pushed its way into my hand My fingers touched velvety softness. I found no trace of viciousness. But every single animal was huge. No question.

This was a time in parts of rural America when Black people like Vince or white activists like Stew and me who dressed in non-conforming tie-die garments could find ourselves confronting signs that read "Whites Only." Or "No hippies or dogs allowed." I was relieved to see a man in overalls and battered straw cowboy hat approaching, whose quizzical but friendly look defied my stereotype.

Ignoring me, the farmer asked, "What can I do for you boys?"

"We wanna buy a pig."

"What kinda pig?"

"A big, fat, ugly one."

"Take your pick," the farmer said. "They're all big, fat, 'n' ugly."

"Could you pick one out for us?" I piped up.

The man replied, "Naww, This ain't some fancy store, Missy. If you want a pig, you gotta get it fer yourself."

Everyone except Phil but including Jerry, who I'd seen act finicky on numerous occasions, jumped into the pigpen. I slipped and landed on my butt. At age 25 I was no expert in pre-planning, so had worn for this excursion my leather sandals from India that attached to my feet with a single toe strap. My sandal lodged itself in a pile of green muck. Or what I convinced myself was muck. A snout backed by twinkly black eyes headed toward its food. I grabbed my sandal and looked up to find Stew also on his butt, a hair weave of pig shit embedded in his curls. In a scene worthy of our Yippie mentors the Marx Brothers, Jerry, Stew, Wolfe, Vince, Head Shop Jim, and I managed to separate a huge pig from its friends. Head Shop Jim went for its tail. Once. Twice. Then he caught hold. The rest of us grabbed Jim around his waist in a pig vs. people tug of war and dragged our reluctant presidential candidate out of captivity.

Phil, not yet wholly socialized into our Yippie ways, remained outside the fence. He paid the farmer $20. It was the old joke come alive: Four Yippies, a Buddhist, a folksinger, and a Rastafarian walk into a farm and emerge proud owners of a 150-pound pink and black hog. Our presidential candidate squealed and oinked their way back to Chicago. Phil parked our station wagon at an undisclosed location at 1250 North Wells—a.k.a. Jim's Head Shop. We bedded Pigasus down for the night on a floral bed sheet, violating every possible statute prohibiting farm animals inside Chicago city limits.

"I'll stand guard," Wolfe volunteered.

At The Spy's apartment, green/gray water from my hair and body circulated down the shower's drain, cleansing me of pig shit and the odor of rotten eggs. If all Yippie protest felt as exhilarating as this, I'd fit right in.

* * *

YIPPIES MEASURE SUCCESS BY HOW MUCH press coverage we get and how frequently we get it. We understood that widespread press coverage spread an anti-war message to far-flung communities that we Yippies would otherwise not reach. By the time I emerged from the shower to join Stew and Jerry in The Spy's living room, Jerry had scheduled a press conference at the Picasso statue in Chicago's Civic Center. There, we would introduce our presidential candidate to the world.

But first we needed to figure out, together, what we'd say.

Jerry began with, "America controls the world, right? So everyone in the world should be allowed to vote for Pigasus! He must be treated as a legitimate candidate. Let's demand Secret Service protection for him!"

"Let's say Pigasus should get invited to the White House. Let's demand foreign policy briefings for him," Stew added.

"He" was the generic pronoun used in the 1960s and 1970s to apply to any gender. Jerry and Stew were not alone in assuming Pigasus must be male—no one that I knew considered the possibility of a female presidential candidate, to say nothing of one who was a pig. By August 1968, I'd heard the chorus of complaints from feminists such as Betty Friedan and Gloria Steinem—and especially

Robin Morgan—about male domination in politics. I decided on the spot I wanted our candidate to be female. Why not? Men had screwed up the world so badly I figured women could do better.

"What about we say Pigasus is female? If she gets elected, she can be the first woman president," I added, still in my questioning Canadian way.

It pissed me off that Stew and Jerry ignored what I considered to be a brilliant Yippie suggestion.

At 10 a.m. on Friday, August 23, 1968, Jerry, Stew, Vince, Head Shop Jim, Pigasus, and I arrived in what was then called Chicago's Civic Center—the largest public space we knew of in Chicago. It was jammed with cameras, photographers, local, national, and international media. As a result of their Big Pig Fight, Jerry had excluded Anita, Abbie, and Paul from his invitation to participate. Still, with Yippie expertise in mobilizing media, Jerry's half of Yippie Central did a terrific job telephoning newspapers and TV stations to publicize our candidate's inaugural event. Media far outnumbered Yippies. We'd found a perfect venue to give our candidate the attention she deserved.

More rational than human candidates and Yippies, Pigasus declined to meet the press. Jerry, Stew, and Wolfe had to drag her, stiff-legged and oinking, out of Jim's station wagon into Civic Center Plaza. Pigasus continued to be uninterested in her candidacy. Bystanders swarmed, trying for a closer look; reporters shouted questions as they pushed and shoved their way toward us; photographers took pictures of the most recent entrant into the 1968 presidential race. Pigasus ignored the crowd and the flashbulbs; she flopped on her belly, a sow sit-in for animal rights. She also declined to enter into a vigorous question and answer session or specify her gender to the press.

"We stand for a garbage platform," I heard Jerry shout.

Chicago cops appeared. They arrested Jerry, Stew, Wolfe, and four other human Yippies, including a woman named Gayle Albin and Vince Black. The cops also arrested Pigasus. Fearful I might get deported back to Canada, I stayed on the sidelines. But my job was crucial—I'd ask Dennis Cuningham, a well-regarded Chicago attorney to donate $300 to bail the Yippies out. I did, with so much verve and confidence that Dennis easily agreed. I am truly grateful to Dennis, to the Yippies, and especially to Pigasus. She gave me my first opportunity to raise funds for women's causes, a profession that evolved for me into a highly successful post-1960s career as a fundraiser for Planned Parenthood.

The FBI, never ones to credit Yippies with success, minimized our event, reporting that, **The only emotion displayed by the crowd during this time was mild laughter.**

Our Pigasus rally had lasted a grand total of five minutes, perhaps the shortest ever presidential rally on record. Among the eleven cops who surrounded and arrested Pigasus, photos reveal many wore tiny, gold-plated pig buttons pinned on their uniforms. All human Yippies were charged with disorderly conduct. Vince Black was the only arrestee to refuse on Yippie principle to plead guilty. Vince was later released with a $250 fine.

Stew told me afterward that, as he and Jerry sat inside an airless jail cell, a burly Chicago cop, his belly hanging over his belt like a real-life version of Emory Douglas's cartoon, had stared at them through the bars and declared with a straight face:

"Boys, I have bad news for you. The pig squealed."

I never saw Pigasus again.

I did hear a rumor that Pigasus was sacrificed and eaten at a Chicago cop's barbecue. But an article in the Chicago Tribune describing Pigasus's arrest has her happily ensconced in Chicago's Anti-Cruelty Society "until police decide what to do with him." If Chicago cops did barbeque Pigasus, it would have substantiated every nasty thing we Yippies assumed about them.

J. J. Shaffer of Chicago's anti-cruelty society held an opposing view.

"Not only is Pigasus on a farm, but he has been joined by his wife, Mrs. Pigasus,"

I'll never know Pigasus' final fate, but it's clear that Shaffer's is a misogynist interpretation. None of us, the Chicago media, Yippies, bystanders, or me, were eager to gather the necessary data to prove conclusively that Pigasus was female—in other words, to examine the back end of a live, ill-tempered, 150-pound pig close up. But I affirm categorically that Pigasus was indeed female. She had no prominent male tusks. All photos of Jerry's large—and Abbie's small, cute—pigs (the actual number of pigs in Chicago in 1968 remains a mystery but for sure more than two appeared) reveal at best an indeterminate gender.

I recently received greetings from Susy Barsotti who assured me that Pigasus was female. As a long-time member of the counter-cultural Hog Farm, Susy would know. Victoria Woodhull may have run for President of the United States one hundred years before Pigasus, but by 1968, women still could not legally marry women and only men had held the highest office in the land. For me, Pigasus was and still remains this country's first non-human black and white female presidential candidate. Still, Pigasus taught me that you may be huge and mean, small and cute, all of, none of, or a combination of the above—but you can always become a powerful, political woman.

CHAPTER 7:
THE WHOLE WORLD IS WATCHING

THAT SUMMER OF 1968, I WALKED—OR rather ran—with the love of my life, chased by Chicago cops down the aisle of the United Church of Tear Gas. Stew and I joined together in a savage wedding ceremony not of our own making. I'm guided even today by the lessons I learned that summer: Don't delay. Don't procrastinate. Don't over-think the consequences. Take your life—and your freedom—into your own hands. Or as Jerry said, "Do It."

On Tuesday, August 20, 1968, five days before our Yippie Festival of Life was to begin, mainstream media reported that Russian tanks had invaded Czechoslovakia to squelch demands of dissidents for political reform. As if channeling his literary idol, John Reed, who reported from the front lines of the 1917 Russian revolution, Stew's exclusive on the front page of the *Berkeley Barb* caught my mood:

> *Here in Chicago I know there will be a revolution; because it has begun, and I am in the red and black center of it.*

That same day, I marched with Stew and Jerry down North Wells Street in Chicago's Old Town, past narrow streets and alleys lined with classic Victorians of red brick. Perhaps twenty of us were in the streets. A teenager had been shot. Shot dead. The young person's name was Dean Johnson. He was seventeen. From Sioux City Iowa. Dean Johnson was an Indigenous American.

Jerry, his voice strident with rage, said the cops claimed Johnson had been shoplifting; that he'd taken a pistol out of his bag. Of course, Chicago cops claimed the kid had fired on them—twice. Jerry announced Dean Johnson was a Yippie. For Jerry, every young person that summer in Chicago was a Yippie.

I marched past a young Black man dressed in a faded Jimi Hendrix t-shirt who guarded a stain on the sidewalk. No woman could mistake that rusty red.

I heard him cry out, "Watch your step, sir, there's a dead man. Pardon me ma'am, you just stepped on a dead brother."

Then, as if to confirm Abe Peck's prediction of police violence, a row of cops in white helmets shoved aside all passers-by. Nightsticks smacked against gloved hands. Jerry, Stew, and I retreated two miles down Halsted Street to our free turf of Lincoln Park. The crowd around me multiplied—Jerry speed-rapping, Stew and I sitting silent, absorbed in Jerry's words. Despite their Big Pig Fight, I was surprised—and pleased—to see Abbie, Anita, and Paul Krassner come sit with us. Along with Abbie's friend Brad Fox, a young guy who called himself Peter Rabbit, a blond teenager named Super-Joel, and a tall, skinny man named Keith Lampe. Keith's wife, also named Judy, had designed the Yippie flag with its black background for anarchy and a red star for revolution, covered by a green marijuana leaf.

Wolfe Lowenthal, the bearded man who'd volunteered at Nancy and Jerry's apartment to teach tai chi in Lincoln Park, introduced his friend Jerome Washington. I recognized Jerome. He was the young Black man who'd guarded that bloodstained sidewalk. Jerome said he was a Yippie and a friend of Ellen Maslow's from Liberty House days. He and an army—buddy, a member of the Blackstone Rangers, a street gang out of Chicago's Southside—had made a Rangers/Yippies alliance. Rangers would bodyguard Yippies—just as they had done for Dr. Martin Luther King Jr. early in 1966, well before Dr. King's assassination. As my Toronto past floated out of reach, I was happily amazed that a Black Chicago street gang would help protect me.

By then, I no longer felt alone. Nor did I feel strange for having lived in a New York City cellar where I met only Stew's close friends. My horizons had expanded beyond exclusive personal relationships. I had arrived into the company of compatriots who looked and thought like me. I sat on the green grass of Lincoln Park and pledged my heartfelt allegiance to a new tribe of polit-ical hippies. Together we would end a war. And make America counter-cultural and whole again. This may be Yippie exaggera-tion, but I also recall thinking we would soon number in the hundreds of thousands—if not millions, planet wide. Within a year, thanks to Nancy Kurshan, we'd use her name for us—Woodstock Nation.

* * *

ONE LEGACY OF THE 1960s IS the term acid flashback, a form of recovered memory that emerges unbidden in your brain as a result of having ingested LSD. I've only taken LSD three times in my life but images of what occurred in Lincoln Park that summer remain embedded in my consciousness to recur without notice. I recall a man with short black hair, black beard, black pants, and T-shirt inserting himself on the grass between Jerry and Stew. The man wore aviator sunglasses and chain-smoked cigarettes; he looked like any biker dude. Jerry introduced him, telling us the man's name was Bob Lavon. Lavon had volunteered to be Jerry's bodyguard. For reasons I'm not clear on, Jerry had accepted. Bob's affect disturbed me but I couldn't say exactly why.

I'D STARTED TO GET BORED JUST sitting in a circle on the grass listening to Jerry needle Abbie as the two men jockeyed for position. I'd wonder if Jerry was jealous. Jerry was good at working in groups, very democratic as long as he got treated first among equals. Abbie, even more an individualist, possessed greater charisma. But Abbie's genius at getting people to do what he wanted was being tested by his recalcitrant rock band friends like Judy Collins and Jefferson Airplane who, he complained, were deserting the Yippie Festival of Life like passengers on the Titanic. Conflicts over who could entertain the crowd in Lincoln Park gave me an idea I felt confident the boys could not refuse. I interrupted.

"How about we ask Eldridge?"

I spoke too softly; no one paid attention. Frustration helped me raise my voice.

"Eldridge. Eldridge Cleaver. How about we ask Eldridge Cleaver to speak? He's a great speaker. He's well known. Everybody wants to hear what he has to say. And we haven't got anyone from the Black Panther Party."

Everyone in the Yippie leadership knew that in addition to Jerry, Eldridge was Stew's other best friend. Stew smiled and squeezed my arm. Jerry nodded, as did Anita and Abbie. My suggestion must have been Yippie enough, or imaginative enough, or off-the-cuff enough or outside the box enough to cause the male decision-makers to pay attention. Eagerly, Biker Bob offered to guide Stew and me to the nearest bar in Old Town to find a pay phone—pay phones being the only means available back in that day to make a public call. Despite my instinctive dislike of Bob, I took his volunteering as an affirmation of the worth of my idea.

The bar's wood walls were stained with cigarette smoke; a neon red, white, and blue Pabst Blue Ribbon Beer sign buzzed each time it flashed. In one corner, a dark-brown wooden phone booth waited for Clark Kent to change into Superman. Stew pulled the phone booth's glass doors open, picked up its black receiver and deposited a series of quarters into metal slots at the phone's top. I leaned inside the booth as best I could to listen. Biker Bob pushed in close behind me. Stew placed the call.

Eldridge turned Stew down. If he left California, he would violate the terms of his parole. But he told Stew that the Black

Panther Party had made a decision: They'd send Party Chairman Bobby Seale to speak in Chicago in Eldridge's place.

Decades later, I asked Bobby what he thought about the Party decision. He answered, "I went because we were for human rights and against this damn war. We, the Black people, shouldn't have to be fighting this war, dying in Vietnam if this country isn't recognizing our civil, democratic, human rights."

My suggestion to invite Eldridge had its butterfly effect—it rippled into a tsunami. Eight months later, on March 20, 1969, Bobby Seale, a Black man, along with seven white men including Abbie and Jerry, were indicted by the Nixon Administration's Justice Department for conspiracy to cross state lines to incite a riot. Their trial would achieve global fame—plus a legacy of movies, books, and Academy Award nominations, as in Aaron Sorkin's 2020 film *The Trial of the Chicago 7*.

* * *

I BEGAN THE DESIGNATED FIRST DAY of the Yippie Festival of Life, Sunday, August 25, 1968, grumpy and irritable. I fought a hangover from a tablespoon of honey infused with hash oil which we Yippies had ingested as a lark the day before—courtesy, or so I heard, of Paul Krassner. Thanks to Paul's medicinal intervention, I can recall only a visual image of Stew lying flat on his face on a sidewalk in front of The Spy's apartment.

That humid afternoon, Stew and I met up with Abbie in Lincoln Park. The crowd was much smaller than everyone had hoped. About 2000 Yippies lay on the grass smoking weed or wandering around aimlessly, waiting for our Festival to begin. The muggy air in Lincoln Park caused rivulets of moisture to run down my back, reminding me of Waterfront Park in Toronto—until I observed wave-like motions under a green blanket. This, a truly un-Canadian sight, told me the woman in a tie-dye t-shirt and man in jeans had taken Abbie's call to fuck on the beaches as a holy commandment. I saw silver-haired women avert their eyes as they pulled minuscule dogs with bejeweled collars away from such a sight, while older men, both of color and white, hid their faces in racing forms—and peeked surreptitiously at the couple. I had no question that reactions would be the same in both my countries.

Two Chicago cops wearing white shirts and blue pants strolled through the Park distributing leaflets that politely read: PLEASE COOPERATE.

In response, Wolfe Lowenthal, his duties corralling Pigasus complete, had organized Yippies into a line to break through lines of cops, should cops attack. One behind another, arms akimbo, legs at every angle, Yippies laughed and shouted, *WA-SHOI! WA-SHOI!* As he had offered in New York, Wolfe was teaching snake-dancing, that form of self-defense used by students in Japan. Snake-dancing looked to me like fun, a well-intentioned game. But to count on good intentions, plus a sunny, peaceful heat-filled afternoon, turned out to be magical thinking.

Always an agitator, Abbie had prepared his own leaflet to counter the cops. It read, LOCAL COPS ARE ARMED AND CONSIDERED DANGEROUS!!!!—a Yippie hyperbole that asserted a truth.

I opted not to take either leaflet seriously. After all, Abbie had minimized Abe Peck's warning, as well as claiming the previous week that Yippies did not tolerate serious. Nor was I ready to cooperate with Chicago cops, even if their leaflet said please. I crunched Abbie's leaflet together with the cops' flyer into the back pocket of my jeans, along with a tiny bottle of kid's tempera paint I had brought with me to make protest signs.

"You know who ain't here? Everybody!"

I stepped back as I heard Abbie escalate his attack.

"Cowaads. Stinking rotten cowaaaads. Phil, Ed Sanders, and Tuli Kupferberg—they're the ones with balls! Them and the MC5! Didja hear about Country Joe? He got attacked. By the pigs. In the lobby of his hotel. He's hopped a plane back to Berkeley."

Abbie ranted on—against Mayor Daley, the traitorous media, and even against mild-mannered Abe Peck, who had done his best to warn us Yippies about police violence. I wondered if Abbie now agreed with Abe but, in a typical Yippie move, had appropriated Abe's warning as his own and conveniently overlooked its origin.

Angry Abbie did not let up. His next target was the blond teenager Super-Joel. By 5 p.m. that Sunday, Super-Joel, the driver of a flatbed truck that carried the stage for the Festival of Life, had gone missing.

"Ya think the cops stopped him?"

Stew replied slowly, as if his measured tone could cool Abbie out. "Naaaah. You know Super-Joel. He's so stoned he's always late."

I did know Super-Joel. Everyone in Yippie Central knew Super-Joel. No Yippie, including Stew or I, questioned Joel's assertion that he was the hippie in a turtleneck sweater who had placed a chrysanthemum in the barrel of a rifle of a military policeman at the 1967 Levitation of the Pentagon. A photo of this courageous act had been published in the *Washington Evening Star*—and nominated for a Pulitzer Prize. Joel also told everyone that his grandfather was a Mafia boss, the legendary Sam Giancana. We believed Joel. Yippies took pride in Super-Joel's pedigree; it affirmed our inclusiveness. Super-Joel's favorite story was that, as a result of this photo and his Yippie affiliation, his Mafia grandmother had kicked him out of the Family. And welcomed him back after he became a dealer of hard drugs.

Super-Joel's Mafia origins—and his entire story—turned out to be Yippie exaggeration. Krassner, always an investigative journalist and also good friend of Super-Joel's, discovered that Joel was just an ordinary middle-class boy, son of a Sicilian doctor and a Norwegian-Irish carpenter from Franklin Park, a suburb of Chicago. It shocked me to hear this. Joel seemed so genuine.

Protest movements can be vehicles for activists to re-invent themselves. I know; I did. To create a myth about yourself that is bigger than reality was standard practice in 1968—and remains so today. To me the issue is not the act of reinvention itself, but a moral one—do not lie to your compatriots about who you are to advance your personal ends.

I spotted what I thought looked like Super-Joel's truck near a temporary fence. I turned my head to tell Abbie, then turned back to Stew—to see blood running through his golden curls, across his domed forehead, and down into his eyes. I'd never been afraid of blood, but I froze. I stood immobile as I watched Stew fold himself in slow motion, knees first onto the grass.

"You're bleeding," I sputtered—as if Stew didn't know that.

Unprepared for such an emergency, I reverted back into the help-less woman I wanted so desperately to reject—a state of being which only magnified my fear for Stew. A white VW van with a giant Red Cross adorning its side began its journey into the crowd at the same time as two people in green army jackets ran toward us. I learned later that Abbie had used a walkie-talkie to summon the Medical Committee for Human Rights, volunteers who patrolled the Park and Chicago's streets treating protesters injured or tear gassed.

The van and volunteers arrived. Blood still dripping down his forehead, Stew stumbled toward the van, a medic under each arm, to be wedged between a journalist and a stack of blue and white boxes of bandages. I attempted to climb in, but someone shut the ambulance door in my face. My lover, van, and medical volunteers vanished into the crowd.

Like every human, I have control issues; for an activist like me to be forced to wait without taking action when a loved one is in danger is torture. I could not rise up against the creeping meat-ball of fear that had paralyzed my psyche.

I wandered Lincoln Park alone, my world out of balance. I barely heard the Detroit band MC5 beat out its soundtrack of hard rock in contrapuntal rhythm to the *Whomp! Whomp!* from blades of a green army helicopter that hovered overhead. I thought naively that barbarous events like Stew being attacked did not occur in the Canada where I grew up. But even my bucolic Canada is not exempt from barbarity. Now, in 2021, I read reports of more than 1,000 indigenous children who were killed and buried at state-run residential schools in my home country.

The MC5 thumped on, their music discordant to my ears. I saw, as if through a kaleidoscope, fuzzy images of cops surround a man who may or may not have been Abbie climbing onto what may or may not have been Super-Joel's flatbed truck. Assigning blame to others helps me avoid the need to face myself. I blamed Krassner—not my fear—as responsible for my altered state, since Paul may or may not have distributed that honey laced with hash oil that I had ingested the day before.

Out of nowhere Anita Hoffman showed up. To my surprise she hugged me. Jerry appeared and did the same. Nancy also hugged me, saying, "Judy, I just got in from New York. What happened?"

Forgiveness did not come fast or easy for me or for the Yippie inner core. Anita ignored Jerry, gave Nancy the tiniest of smiles, then walked away. What remained of Jerry and Abbie's Big Pig Fight had transferred to us Yippie women. Until I caught a glimpse of Stew, blond curls hidden under a turban of white bandages, being escorted toward me through the crowd, I existed only in that state of deep disbelief that can dominate any medical emergency, even if you are surrounded by friends.

After I let Stew go, he puffed out his chest underneath his bloody shirt.

He crowed, "Six stitches. Isn't that far-out? It doesn't hurt too bad either. The doctors said the wound was made by a blackjack."

"Undercover cop," Jerry opined.

Since Stew wasn't dead, I gave myself permission to take my painfully bitten fingernails out of my mouth. I realized that Stew's being hit over the head by an undercover cop would confer on Stew a red badge of courage in which I and every other Yippie shared. The spilling of first blood defines a protest. To my knowledge, Stew's was the first blood shed in Chicago's parks that summer of 1968. It would not be our last.

* * *

ON SUNDAY, AUGUST 25, 11 P.M. was curfew hour, or so claimed placards put up by Park employees. The Daley administration's edict was final: No permits would be issued; no individual was allowed to sleep in Lincoln Park. I stood side by side with Warrior Stew under streetlights that illuminated park paths with yellow circles. Wet heat drifting off Lake Michigan made time pass so slowly I felt as if I was walking through molasses. Jerry chomped on his fingernails; I was grateful for the companionship of a fellow nail-biter. On occasion I'd see an orange spark shoot high in the air as protesters set fires in trash cans. The thickly built men in plaid golf shirts I'd seen earlier in the day appeared to have increased in number. As dusk fell, I watched a familiar apparition dart from one illuminated circle to another.

"Is that Abbie? I asked Stew.

"Looks like."

"What's he doin'?"

"No idea. Maybe telling people it'll be safer to stick together in affinity groups."

An affinity group is a pre-selected group of your compatriots who have agreed to march with, watch out for, and defend each other from attack. In the distance I heard a drum beat out a rhythmic, war-like chant: *"Nah-na-na-na-nah! Nah-na-na-na-nah! Off the Pig!"*

I joined in as the chant died down. I'd enlarged the Panther slogan in my subconscious: I'd defy the atrocities of war, the curfew, Chicago cops, and anything or anyone who dared hurt Stew, or put limits on my freedom. A line of protesters snaked past me, legs bent, kicks coordinated, not clumsy like earlier that day. I heard a shout. I turned. Behind me, on a hill, a grey-white cloud billowed a few feet off the ground while in front of the cloud an army advanced. They looked to me like robots marching in lockstep, illuminated by globules of white light like landing lights on an alien spacecraft. I did not feel afraid. Just the opposite, I reveled at the thrill of being in a live action anti-war documentary. A sense of power surged through me, to deliver to me that moral courage I needed to do my part. My hatred of injustice had triumphed over fear.

Stew, Jerry, Nancy, and I scrambled to our feet. The spectral line advanced. Screams punctuated the gloom. I opened my mouth to breathe, only to inhale gas so toxic I might as well have snorted Drano. Tears burned a channel down my face; my eyes shut of their own accord. By the time I was able to open them, Nancy and Jerry had vanished. My courage did not. I grabbed Stew's hand and ran down a slope and toward a tree now outlined in flashes of rotating red and blue light. Under it, famous poet Allen Ginsberg sat prophet-like in lotus position, chanting *Oh-m-m-m-m-m* as if to remind the planet that even in the midst of chaos all life is interconnected. In high school, I had been so taken with Ginsberg's epic poem *Howl* that I'd smear black make-up over and under my eyes then walk to my high school pretending to be a Beatnik but looking like a raccoon. Passing cars honked at me in derision. Stew and I fled in Ginsberg's direction seconds before the gas. I arrived to find the renowned poet now on his feet leading a procession of his acolytes out of the park, still chanting *Oh-o-m-m-m-m-m-m*. So much for mantras, peace, and loving spiritual practice. Even Buddhist serenity must surrender to amber waves of gas.

So ended Day One of the Yippie Festival of Life.

* * *

By Monday, August 26, Day Two of what had become an Un-Festival of Life, I had survived what I believed to be the worst the Chicago cops had to offer and emerged determined to fight another day.

Stew, Nancy, Jerry, and I arrived in Lincoln Park that afternoon, our noses running, eyes still red and puffy. Stew began to report on the previous night's victory: A driver of a public transit bus had pumped his fist in the air in a Black power salute, its passengers held up two-fingers in a V sign of peace. Despite the foul smell still embedded in my clothing, I did not feel demoralized. Nor did my companions. If anything, we buzzed like a swarm of manic bees ready to defend our hive from the arrival of the bears.

A stranger joined our Yippie circle. I identified him by his clothing—he was a young Vietnam veteran dressed to bring the war home. He had sewn a U.S. Army tag on his olive-colored vest, next to a white peace sign; on his head he wore a sun hat made of camouflage with a decal of red, white, and blue stars and stripes. A "Fuck the Army" button with the logo of a fist hung like an earring from one ear. I told myself this man had likely been drafted into the army at age eighteen, against his will. He began to cough loud enough for me to hear.

When he stopped, he said, "That gas last night? The gas they used on us? It must have been CS. I recognize it, I used CS in 'Nam. Until army brass outlawed it, that is. I'll never forget that one V.C. He came up out of a tunnel. He was coughing so hard, crying, he kept scratching at his face 'cause it was all burnt up. I watched him die. Just like that."

I nodded my head in sympathy. I looked up, and he was gone.

The anti-war vet was right. The robots and the spacecraft in Lincoln Park were not hallucinations. The lights that looked like spacecraft came from a squadron of City of Chicago garbage trucks equipped with rotating searchlights and protected by barbed wire. They spewed at protesters that same CS gas first used by U.S. troops on civilians and guerrilla fighters in Vietnam, then outlawed. I still ask myself how my newly adopted homeland could outlaw use of poison gas against a country the USA had invaded, but then bring that same gas home for use against its own children.

* * *

MONDAY AFTERNOON, AUGUST 26, I HEARD brakes squeal. A black and white Chicago police car had penetrated Lincoln Park. Stew and I joined jeering protesters to push the cop car down toward the ground to a chorus of "Hell No," then release it upward to "We Won't Go." I spotted a phalanx of Chicago cops rush toward us to rescue their cop comrades. I did not retreat.

"Commie faggot," I heard one cop yell at Stew, using the idiom popular in my day to insult gay men, lefties, and varieties of anyone police considered "un-manly."

"Fuck you, pig!" I screamed back, happy to defend my lover's honor with an arrogant, upward thrust of my middle finger. In Stew's case, I knew the cop got the commie part right.

My fingers curled around my tiny glass jar of tempera paint that rested inside the pocket of my jeans, covered up by Abbie's leaflet warning that, as I now easily admitted, "Cops Are Armed and Dangerous." My jar was perhaps three inches high, like those samples from a paint store you get to test colors on your wall. A genie must have dwelled inside that bottle, urging me to set it free, to rage against the Vietnam War, Eldridge's forthcoming imprisonment, Stew's bloodied head, the evil gas, Mayor Daley's intransigence, everything I hated, all the way down to Hemblen's adultery and the vicious ministrations of my mother.

I tightened my fingers around my jar, pulled my arm back, and let my non-toxic missile fly. I hoped to see it shatter and decorate the roof of that police car in Yippie purple. My jar hit the cop car's roof. I heard it ping. It bounced off unbroken. I didn't care. No girlie throw for me, I had hit what I had aimed for! To throw and hit my cop car target immersed me in a new sensation—freedom as an act of joyful protest.

I couldn't believe I was having so much fun.

Stew and I plus crowds of anti-war demonstrators streamed out of Lincoln Park into Chicago's streets, pursued by cops and clouds of CS gas. After we grew tired of the battle, Stew and I made our way behind police lines to The Spy's apartment. We made love as if it were our last time. Tomorrow we might be in jail or even dead. Then, spent, we watched on TV as bloodied demonstrators fled rampaging cops.

The Chicago cops and Walter Cronkite's deep baritone voice did as Jerry had predicted; they turned our Yippie protest into legend.

* * *

BLACK PANTHER PARTY CHAIRMAN BOBBY SEALE arrived in Lincoln Park on Tuesday, August 27, amidst a lingering, rancid but unmistakable odor of CS gas. Decked out in his Panther uniform of black leather jacket and blue shirt, Bobby brought with him Fred Hampton, the 20-year-old leader of the Chicago Panthers. Hampton acted as Bobby's bodyguard. I could not make my way through Bobby Seale's adoring crowd to greet the Panther leaders. Again, I didn't care. I had done my part. Thanks to my inspired suggestion, the Chairman of the Black Panther Party had come to Chicago to speak in Lincoln Park.

Bobby began:

"We must understand that as we go forth to try and move the scurvy reprobative pigs: the lynching Lyndon Baines Johnsons, the fat pig Humphreys, the jive double-lip-talkin' Nixons, the slick talkin' McCarthys—those murdering and brutalizing people all over the world—when we go forth to deal with them—that they're gonna always send out their racist scurvy rotten pigs to occupy the people, to occupy the community, just the way they have this here park occupied."

He ended with, "Black people, we seem to be lost in a world of white, racist, decadent America. I'm saying we have the right to defend ourselves as human beings."

I am not Black, my experience with injustice was not nor could ever be Bobby's. Still, I'd choked on gas and seen my lover's head split open. Lincoln Park was under occupation by an army of pigs. I knew the Panther leader wasn't riffing about Pigasus's untimely end. In an escalating trajectory that breaks out when peaceful protest is put down by brutal police violence, if I translate my reaction to Bobby's words into 1960s Panther Speak, this white mother country radical could dig where Bobby was coming from.

* * *

ON WEDNESDAY, AUGUST 28, THAT FINAL, fateful day of the 1968 Non-Democratic Un-Convention, Nancy, Jerry, Stew, and I gathered in Grant Park near the white half-dome of Chicago's Bandshell. Short of breath, nauseous, and dizzy from inhaling toxic gas, I had not slept well the night before. Nor had Stew. We woke up late to watch gleefully on The Spy's TV as a woman and her compatriots climbed Grant Park's Logan statue. She carried with her a red, blue, and yellow NLF flag, demonstrating their and our support for the NLF—America's "enemy" in Vietnam. Chicago cops pulled all of them down, shattering arms. Like Stew, the Grant Park protesters came away bloodied but unbowed.

But unlike Abbie, a natural performer, Jerry's first few words from the Bandshell stage came out strained.

"Welcome to the most important convention that's going on in this city."

Jerry quickly hit his stride.

"Everybody in the world should have the right to vote in an American election because America controls the world. People think it's a free country. But not if you try to change it! We came here to express our point of view and what do we get? The only way they can nominate a pig for President is by bringing out all the pigs to protect the pig they nominated!"

His voice hoarsened by fatigue and tear gas, Jerry exhorted us, his mostly young, mostly white audience, to take to the streets. To put ourselves at that same risk as Black people, even if it meant risking our own deaths. I had by then enlisted fully in the Yippie army; I would have leaped inside Death's carriage had it unkindly stopped for me.

I noticed Abbie's tall, thin friend Keith Lampe sprint past me, a gray gunnysack in his arms. A squirming gunnysack with a snout. Keith ran toward Jerry and the Bandshell stage. Our heroic giant Pigasus, now languishing in porcine prison, had been replaced by Abbie's small cute pig! Glimpsing Abbie's pig was the closest I came to Anita or Abbie that day. And, as best I can recall, Stew and I, and perhaps Nancy and Jerry, did not talk to Anita and Abbie for the rest of that week. Possibly for almost a year. Even after Anita's embrace of me in Grant Park, I realized the residue of the Big Pig Fight between the boys would make it painful for me, an avoider of inter-personal conflict, to spend much time in Anita's and Abbie's presence.

On stage, Jerry ignored the porcine arrival. He pumped his right fist in the air, goading protestors not just to issue policy statements, but to take action, to Do It.

"We say to the Democrats—we can run this country better than you can!"

Perhaps. I do occasionally wish Jerry and the Yippies had got our chance to run the U.S.A. Our tenure would have been very brief, fun, and ultra-chaotic.

"See you in the streets!" Jerry finished up.

Shortly after Jerry's speech, an unknown resister followed his advice. He lowered a U.S. flag flying near the Bandshell to replace it with a white T-shirt spattered in blood. In response, yet another phalanx of helmeted cops rampaged through Grant Park, turning neatly arranged white chairs into a field of chaos. I was astounded to see a short-haired man in a gray business suit run past me, cops close behind him screaming,

"Get that *Newsweek* bastard."

If police were targeting mainstream reporters, they'd show no mercy for grungy counter-cultural Yippies like Stew and me.

We'd crossed into Grant Park that morning over a small bridge with a concrete railing, one of many that connected the Park to mainland Chicago. I've always had a stellar sense of direction; Stew not so much. As Chicago cops advanced, I decided I'd be a hero—I'd lead our personal charge to safety. Stew and I ran to that familiar first bridge to find our escape blocked by a green National Guard jeep with a five-foot square of barbed wire mounted on its front. Foiled, I ran toward a second bridge, Stew trailing behind me; this time we faced what looked to me like a cannon on wheels pointing straight at us. A scene from *Battleship Potemkin*, the film by the Soviet director Eisenstein that my father had screened for me in my grandmother's living room, arose unbidden in my mind. To escape Tsarist rifles, a young mother, alone, helpless, and bleeding after being shot, had leaned against her baby carriage to send it down what I recall as an endless flight of marble steps so that, even in dying, her infant would live. I tamped down a similar terror in me.

Stew hunkered into a wrestling move he must have learned in high school. He thrust his big head forward, a red-faced bull with blond curls. Concerned that Stew had chosen to stay and fight without consulting me, I stopped; I pulled him toward me; together we ran off to find another bridge. And another. Finally, Stew, the crowd, and I came to an unguarded, open bridge. I don't recall catching a glimpse of Tom Hayden, but he must have been there since he describes crossing that same bridge as a parting of the Red Sea. Tom was right. Relief washed over me in biblical proportions.

"Fuck yeah, Gumbo," I told myself, "You did it. You made it. Through the cops and the clubs and the gas and the guards' blockade." With that, despite all its contradictions, my world of Yippiedom gave birth to a new me.

* * *

LATE THAT WEDNESDAY NIGHT, AUGUST 28, Nancy, Jerry, Stew, Phil Ochs, and I gathered in the gloom on the Grant Park side of Michigan Avenue. I felt no fatigue. Just the opposite. Bright lights from TV cameras had again turned the scene into a live action anti-war documentary filmed in noir-ish black and white— interrupted only by a splash of color as a woman in a red or bright green evening gown entered the Hilton lobby. I joked with Stew that delegates who'd paid extra for a top floor front room at the Hilton should demand a refund since their lake view now came complete with protesters, cops, and tear gas. On the Grant Park side of Michigan Avenue, Stew and I faced a line of National Guard soldiers in army fatigues and helmets pointing their rifles directly at us.

"Join us! Join us!" Stew, the crowd, and I chanted, hoping a soldier might risk imprisonment and lay their rifle down. The troops stood rigid in formation.

Like Yippies, the National Guard were my contemporaries— young, mostly white men and, I assumed, potential weed-smoking counter-culturalists. The Guard were not the older, better trained, armed Chicago cops with their history of vicious racism. I figured these young men had never experienced direct combat. I empathized—neither had I. I noticed folksinger Phil Ochs slowly walk the line of troops. I abandoned Stew to join him, figuring Phil would remember me from our Pigasus excursion. Phil had pinned an American flag pin on the lapel of his sports jacket—that same pin politicians wear to advertise their patriotism. To me the flag pin was—and still is—an emblem of conservatism, so I asked, "Phil, why are you wearing that pin?"

Phil turned his lapel over. Underneath he'd pinned our pink and purple Yippie button.

"Jerry once asked me to switch the buttons around," Phil said, "I told him no."

To me our Yippie button represented an alternative America, not the Amerikkka I spelled with three K's, to represent the initials of the Ku Klux Klan. I wore it proudly. Was Phil, a celebrity, entitled to a more traditionalist standard? I told Phil I thought it was incongruous of him to wear both buttons and not take sides.

Phil answered, "I was born in El Paso, Texas. I grew up in rural Ohio. I love America. It's my duty as an American to do whatever I can to change things when I know my country is wrong."

I had my personal litany of America's wrongs—napalm that burned Vietnamese babies and defoliated forests; white supremacists who lynched and murdered Black people; to say nothing of the evils done by Amerikkka to every woman, Indigenous peoples, student protesters, and young men drafted against their will to die in foreign wars. Growing up communist plus my friendship with Black Panthers made me view the world as binary—you're either part of the solution or part of the problem. Plus, I had not grown up in the USA; I found it hard to give myself the complexity to love and hate America at the same time, as Phil did.

I walked with Phil down the line of the National Guard as guardsmen's fingers tightened around their rifle stocks. They pointed bayonets attached underneath straight at us. To me those metal blades appeared twelve inches long. Unintimidated by such a show of force, Phil smiled, then introduced himself.

"I'm Phil Ochs. I'm a folksinger. You ever heard my song, 'I Ain't Marching Anymore?'"

A guardsman in front of me fidgeted in the heat, then piped up: "I once spent $10 for two tickets to one of your concerts. That's an awful lot of money."

"You're right," Phil responded, then I heard him sing these words softly to himself, "Too many martyrs. Too many dead."

I remembered this Phil song. It linked the death of civil rights worker Medgar Evers to deaths of American soldiers in Vietnam. The young man and the older man stared at each other; I imagined the distance between them diminishing as pre-conceptions melted. Mine included. The guardsman lowered his bayonet and grinned at us. I decided he must be jubilant that a singer he admired could empathize with him.

At that same moment, a distorted voice, loud and male, came through a megaphone:

"Delegates, if you're with us, flash your lights."

The four front towers of Chicago's Hilton lit up like a Christmas tree; the presents underneath were Yippies, mainstream protesters, tanks, and National Guardsmen posing like GI Joe action figures. I grabbed Stew and Phil in a three-person hug. Through my tears provoked by joy, not gas, I heard myself cheer.

My experiences that August summer in Chicago stay with me as imprinted memory, even decades after the fact. Late into that night of August 26, 1968, or perhaps it was early morning of the following day, I stood with Phil, Stew, Nancy, and Jerry, five among 5,000 demonstrators. A line of Chicago cops attacked with truncheons and CS gas. In addition to Stew, the list of injured friends and compatriots that day included Yippies Abbie Hoffman and Wolfe Lowenthal; MOBE elder Dave Dellinger; Michael Drobinaire, a young MOBE sound tech; and MOBE stalwart Rennie Davis, whose blood dripped down his face. Both Dave and Rennie were knocked unconscious. Cops shoved Tom Hayden through the Hilton's plate glass window. Convention delegates inhaled CS gas. Hundreds of demonstrators and passers-by had their heads bloodied, or were gassed and thrown into paddy wagons; those clubbed and/or arrested included mainstream reporters such as CBS's Dan Rather, photographers, TV camera operators, local Chicago residents, participants in Dr. Martin Luther King Jr.'s Poor People's Campaign, and even a woman member of the British Parliament.

Inside the Convention Center, Walter Cronkite, close to tears, stared over his horn-rimmed glasses at his TV audience of millions.

"They're beating our children," he declared

Outside I joined the chant.

"The whole world is watching! The whole world is watching!"

As the world was. Our new medium of color television turned "the whole world is watching" into a reality that exposed the brutality of established authority.

Inside the Convention Center, Chicago Mayor Richard M. Daley gave himself away by castigating an outraged Senator Abraham Ribicoff using an anti-Semitic diatribe captured on tape and later translated by a professional lip-reader for the deaf.

"You motherfucking Jew bastard, get your ass out of Chicago."

In early December 1968, a commission headed by Daniel Walker, chief attorney for former retail giant Montgomery Ward and then-president of the Chicago Crime Commission, concluded that even though a majority of police had behaved responsibly, police actions in Chicago constituted a "police riot." According to the *Walker Report*, Chicago police had, however, been provoked to violence by demonstrators using obscene language.

To which I say, "Fuck you, motherfuckers," and plead guilty.

CHAPTER 8:
"STUPID REVOLUTIONS"

THERE ARE RISKS YOU TAKE, ESPECIALLY when you're young, that you can't believe you took when you look back; but when I was in my 20s and wound up in my passions, to take a risk for revolution felt both natural and easy. At times this led to behaviors that were so utopian—and stupid—Kathleen and Eldridge called them "stupid revolutions."

After Chicago, Stew and I hitched a ride back to Berkeley with a Bay Area anarchist couple. Their rickety green Ford truck broke down in Denver. A stranger in a plaid shirt and hunter's vest took us in.

"It's disgraceful what they did to you. Un-American," the stranger said.

Un-American? No. In those four months preceding our protest, Martin Luther King Jr., Robert Kennedy, and Lil' Bobby Hutton lay dead; during Chicago, 17-year-old Indigenous American Dean Johnson had been murdered. Five thousand of us were gassed and beaten at the Democratic Convention. I hated to think my mother had been right in disparaging the United States, but by then I fully bought into H. Rap Brown's assertion that violence is as American as cherry pie.

Before Chicago, I had become briefly infatuated with gun culture. I purchased a cheap Japanese bolt-action rifle at a Bay Area gun show—not for retributive violence but to defend myself. Mine was no high-powered assault rifle. It was a .22 bolt-action rifle with a nicely polished barrel. I bought it for its looks. It was a Gumbo kind of gun—cute, petite, and made of brown wood that matched my hair. After I brought it home, I realized the big-bellied gun dealer with flag tattoos on both arms had profited from my naivete. The bullets he sold me were an odd, un-American size, next to impossible to obtain. Nonetheless, I looked on that rifle with that same romantic pride as does a teenage boy who keeps a condom in his wallet.

One morning after Stew's and my return to Berkeley, I sat at Keith Street's dining table inhaling morning coffee as if it were weed. I heard a knock. Two men in dark blue suits had planted themselves side by side on Keith Street's porch. Based on their short hair and wing-tipped shoes, I decided the men must be FBI agents. I slammed the door in their faces.

"Stew, it's the pigs!"

Stew headed down the stairs barefoot, in jeans, fumbling with the buttons on his paisley shirt. As he passed me, Stew whispered, "Get the gun! Cover me."

I possessed at that time a sense of divine invulnerability typical of younger generations. I was so fully immersed in my romantic fantasy of self-defense that I gave no thought that I might actually harm a human being. I failed to see my housemate Miche, newborn baby in her arms, staring at me with eyes wide open. Instead, I sat like a gun-toting Christopher Robin halfway down Keith Street's stairs, out of sight—or so I hoped—of the FBI agents. I could see Stew's back as he stood between Keith Street's double wooden doors. Stew waved his hands at the two agents who shimmered in my rifle sights. It did not occur to me as I pointed the rifle's barrel toward the front doors, through the opening in the stairwell wall where the hookah lived, that, had I actually pulled the trigger, my bullet would have mowed Stew down first.

My arms began to shake. My neck muscles cramped. But Stew ranted on.

"Stew," I muttered, "shut up already!"

It may have only been a few minutes, but time typically stretches out in stressful situations. Soon I relented. I laid the rifle gently down in my lap. My heart beat hard but steady. I crept back up the stairs to Stew's and my bedroom and shoved the rifle into its hiding place inside my closet. Which is exactly when I noticed that my rifle had no bullets. In the interest of safety, I had stored the bullets separately from the rifle. In crisis time, I forgot to load it.

I was so relieved I barreled down the stairs and inserted myself into the conversation. My FBI files claim:

> *During interview of STEWART ALBERT Subject interjected without invitation and endeavored to hinder the interview. She demanded to know why the Agents required such information and urged ALBERT not to answer questions. She was sarcastic and vitriolic in her remarks and attitude.*

Shortly afterward, I watched the FBI agents make their way politely down our front path and disappear.

This memo is the first evidence I have that contains comments by FBI agents on my personality. In the interests of full disclosure, the report contains a truth. My bitchiness was real. The instant the agents departed, I began to berate Stew like an Elizabethan fishwife.

"Who do you think you are, talking to the FBI? Why the fuck did you ask me to cover you? What did you expect me to do, shoot them?"

Stew, crestfallen but still defiant, deflected my question.

"I was testing my intelligence against theirs. I didn't tell them anything they didn't know already."

"What fucking stupidity!" I announced bitterly, hands on hips.

Stew then proclaimed that the FBI wanted to take him out for breakfast to talk a second time. His offhand remark made me want to nuke any human or animal within a three-mile radius of Keith Street. In their birdcage next to the double doors, Miche's yellow finches, perhaps sensitive to the new toxicity of their environment, fell silent. I refused to let it go. I raged on.

"You don't know what they know! You have no idea what they'll do with what you already said! You're an idiot! An arrogant, asshole idiot! I hate you!"

I burst into tears. Stew's mouth drooped.

"I'm sorry. I didn't mean to upset you. Stop crying, please. I can't stand it."

Stew always did what I wanted if I cried.

Stew wrapped his arms around my rigid body; I wiped my nose on his shirt.

To me, Stew's was a primal sin. If I had learned one rule at my communist parents' knee, it was *never under any circumstances talk to the FBI.* Julius Rosenberg's brother-in-law, David Greenglass—known around my parents' house as "the Traitor Greenglass"—had, and with what result? The Rosenbergs were executed.

This event marked the first real fight of Stew's and my nine-month relationship. Ours was a battle over core values—both sides needed victory. And I won. Never again did Stew make any move to talk to the FBI. But I did begin to question whether, by pointing that unloaded bolt-action rifle at two FBI agents, I had so identified myself with Panther World, where arming to defend oneself was a matter of survival, that I had taken a leap I could not justify—a leap far beyond Yippie theatrics. I idealized heroes from the Black Power movements, but I did not live in Black America's world of death by cop.

* * *

IN ADDITION TO CHAMPIONING AN END to police brutality, stopping the murder of Black people, and implementing Serve the People programs, the Black Panther Party condemned Black violence against hippies. On September 28, 1968, I read a severe and anonymous, "warning to so-called 'Paper Panthers'" (Panthers in Name Only) in the national Party paper:

> *Black brothers, stop vamping on the hippies. They are not your enemy. Your enemy, right now, is the white racist pigs who support this corrupt system. Your enemy is the Tom who reports to this white slavemaster every day. Your enemy is the fat capitalist who exploits your people daily. Your enemy is the politician who uses pretty words to deceive you. Your enemy is the racist pigs who use Nazi-type tactics and force to intimidate black expressionism. Your enemy is not the hippies.*

> *Your blind reactionary acts endanger BLACK PANTHER PARTY members. WE HAVE NO QUARREL WITH THE HIPPIES. LEAVE THEM ALONE. Or—the BLACK PANTHER PARTY will deal with you!*

In late September 1968, Jerry had arrived at Keith Street from the east coast. Jerry was nervous, seeking Stew's advice about what to do with the rest of his life now that Chicago was done. Eldridge also showed up. The four of us sat around Keith Street's communal dining table, a wooden spool six feet in circumference formerly used to store PG&E's electric cables. At this table and at Eldridge's request, *Barb* photographer Al Copeland took a photo of Eldridge, his expression stern as he ate a slice of watermelon, a photo soon to show up in the underground press. At first, I looked on Al's photo as a Yippie send-up of a noxious stereotype, until Eldridge later told me he regretted it.

"This shit," Eldridge had decided, "is not funny."

At that same table, Eldridge, Jerry, Stew, and I went on to write an intersectional manifesto to oppose the forthcoming election of Richard Nixon. I typed our words on a black non-electric Underwood typewriter. At the same time as I despised my woman-as-typist role, I rationalized it: I was a faster and more accurate typist than any man present.

"Come into the streets on Election Day. Take your clothes off. Release hundreds of greased pigs in pig uniforms downtown," Jerry dictated to me; a great example of where the word "dictator" comes from.

"Rise Up and Abandon the Creeping Meatball!" I jumped in, insisting we include my newest favorite slogan.

"The American election represents death," Stew proclaimed, "and we are alive."

Eldridge's contribution broadcast his anger—at the pigs, at the indignities suffered by people of color forced to live in racist America:

"America is a house on fire," Eldridge wrote, "Freedom now or let it burn, let it burn."

On October 4, 1968, a two-inch tall headline in capital letters "YIPPIE/PANTHER PACT" dominated the entire front page of the *Berkeley Barb*. This headline was the culmination of Stew's lifelong dream—to use the media to promote a strategic alliance between Black and white revolutionaries. "Pipe Dream #2: Opening Salvos from a Black/White Gun" rallied our respective communities to rebel.

My name did not appear on the signer's list. I took this omission as a personal affront to me—but not to Eldridge, Stew, Jerry, and Abbie, whose names appeared. I complained bitterly to Stew about being sidelined. I had won my Yippie stripes in Chicago. As a contributor to their thinking as well as their typist, I believed I should be treated as an equal. Abbie's name appeared and he wasn't even present when we wrote it! I had been marginalized. I was once again powerless to make a change—since the paper was already in print. Nor, I knew, would the *Barb's* male-dominated editorial staff see fit to apologize. Frustrated and angry, I excused the omission as just the way things always happened.

The "Yippie/Panther Pact" was utopian—and split—in its political vision. In the part that Eldridge wrote, he visualized an

armed Black revolutionary alliance with the "disenchanted, alienated white youth, the hippies, the Yippies, and all the unnamed
dropouts from the white man's burden—these are our allies in
this human cause." Meanwhile Stew, Jerry, and I wrote of non-
violent, guerilla theater—of bringing our Yippie revolution to
Washington armed with thousands of kazoos.

* * *

SHORTLY AFTER *OPENING SALVOS* WAS PUBLISHED, Eldridge
ran for President of the United States as a candidate of the Peace
and Freedom Party. Jerry became Eldridge's vice-presidential
running mate—Eldridge's second choice after SDS honcho Carl
Oglesby had declined. The slogan on Eldridge's campaign poster
read, "POWER TO THE PEOPLE, BLACK POWER TO BLACK
PEOPLE." I loved that slogan! But Eldridge lost. On November 5,
1968, a white man given to paranoia named Richard Milhous
Nixon defeated Hubert Humphrey for that office.

By then, Panther World was speeding past me like a bullet train to
hell. Legal maneuvering over Eldridge's arrest at the Bobby Hutton
shootout had ended. Eldridge Cleaver, best-selling author, charismatic
speaker, Minister of Information of the Black Panther Party, misogynist, and my friend, was headed back to prison. As Panther women
did after Panther men were killed or carted off to jail, Kathleen threw
herself into managing the crisis. She raised bail, worked with attorneys, organized community support, and worried about her and
Eldridge's future. I saw her rarely. Eldridge, too, traveled on his own
trajectory. His visits to the hippie palace became less frequent.

Three weeks after Nixon's election, Eldridge paid Stew and me
his first post-election call. The naked alabaster lady and boy in
turquoise pants surveilled us from Keith Street's mantelpiece.

"I'm not goin' back," Eldridge announced. Unlike the kidding
chatter Eldridge, Stew, and I had enjoyed when the three of us
hung out together with the hookah, Eldridge's voice now came
out hard—and severe.

Eldridge had a plan. He'd barricade himself inside an Oakland school. With shotguns, rifles and pistols. Like a siege. Oakland's Black community would rise up to support him, just as the Algerian people did in that famous movie *Battle of Algiers*. Eldridge stared directly into Stew's blue eyes.

"I'll need ya there, Stew. Inside. With me. To get the word out to white mother country radicals."

And I heard Stew reply, "Right on, I'm with ya, man."

At that, I pushed the finger of my right hand into my mouth. On it, I wore a ring that resembled a silver snail with a blue moonstone for its head. I'd bought my ring in London to remind me to never again fall victim to a betrayal such as Hemblen's. Now I bit my ring nail so deep I tasted blood. If Hemblen's was a 10 on the betrayal scale, for Stew to agree on the spot, without consulting me, was a solid 9. Abbie was right! Stew was the white tail of the Black Panthers! I stood up, turned my back, marched into Stew's and my bedroom, and slammed the door. The cherubs on my fireplace jiggled in rebuke.

In less stressful times, Kathleen, Eldridge, and even the Central Committee of the Black Panther Party might have labeled such a dangerous and impractical plan a "stupid revolution." No more. The pattern of all our lives had escalated beyond anything we'd previously experienced. Kathleen wrote later that during this painful time she became mentally and physically exhausted, convinced she would die. Eldridge never shared his plans with her; he referred to them merely as a showdown.

For Stew and me, this became the first make-or-break moment in our relationship.

The instant Stew climbed up the ladder into our bed, five feet off the ground, I began to scream at him. I pounded my fist on Stew's chest so hard I flattened the blond hair between his breasts. Had I known Stew had an arrhythmic heartbeat I might have stopped, but I did not. I did hear an echo of my mother's voice as I yelled at Stew, "God damn you to hell! I don't want you dead!"

The person I was most furious at was me. For buying that stupid rifle in the first place. For complying with Stew's absurd demand. For not speaking up. By way of response, Stew became as intransigent as I was. Our relationship devolved into a hell of yelling: me at Stew, him at me. Punctuated by silence. And no sex.

Four days before Stew's 29th birthday, the last Sunday in November 1968, Eldridge arrived once again at Keith Street. Resentful but still reluctant to be excluded, I joined Stew and Eldridge on Keith Street's balcony, our special place to conduct conversations we wanted only the wind to hear. Fingers of grey fog blocked out our view of the Golden Gate Bridge. Eldridge told us he'd consulted Don Duncan, a companion journalist at the lefty *Ramparts* magazine. Eldridge respected Don, a stocky, white, muscular, crew-cut-wearing former U.S. Marine Special Forces operative who, like Eldridge, wrote for *Ramparts.* Don had warned Eldridge—if he went through with his plan, authorities would simply cut off the water, then fire in tear gas and make the school uninhabitable.

Don told Eldridge, "You'll come out with your hands up, just like when Lil' Bobby Hutton died."

To my huge relief, Eldridge announced he'd given up on his "barricade myself in Merritt College" plan. It took long minutes before I could allow my affection for Eldridge to re-emerge, but, especially after I lit the hookah, it did. Our conversation meandered: Eldridge asserted that the United States had become death row for the majority of its inhabitants. I agreed. Eldridge said he had re-named the United States "Babylon" because of this country's decadence and corruption. In his mind, the pigs would never stop vamping on the people and especially on the Panthers. Again, I agreed. Eldridge then informed Stew and me he'd soon leave the United States for an undisclosed location. Leaving the country, Eldridge said, was his only option to avoid jail. If he didn't disappear, he might be murdered in prison or killed in the streets. He allowed that Kathleen plus hundreds of friends and co-workers agreed. But, like many an important leader who does what they can to preserve their legacy, Eldridge did not want, by leaving, for Panthers or white mother country radicals to think him any less a revolutionary.

Cold fog blew in. Perhaps it was a release of pent-up tension that blended with my gratitude that Eldridge had made the right decision, plus my ideological conviction that action for a righteous cause can conquer all—I volunteered to help Eldridge escape.

"Eldridge, can I give you a lift somewhere?" I inquired.

Next day I headed south down I-80 in my brown VW bug, Stew in his usual place beside me in the passenger seat, Eldridge in back. Stew and I had dressed in our Yippie power leathers to mark such a historic occasion. Stew wore his brown leather jacket; I dressed in my brown faux-leather miniskirt with matching jacket. I caught a glimpse of Eldridge in the rearview mirror. He'd put on a short-sleeved white dress shirt, Nation of Islam-style but without the bow tie. Over it, he wore a bomber jacket, navy blue. He looked like a security guard. I noticed Eldridge's eyes dart side to side as if Oakland cops intent on his demise inhabited every passing vehicle.

He said, "Gumbo, I need you and Stew to do this one thing for me, ya dig?"

By then, whether Eldridge would ask me to risk my life or stop my car so he could take a leak seemed of little consequence. I was determined to do the right thing—to help the Black liberation struggle as best I could. Through the space between my VW's front seats, Eldridge handed Stew an iconic piece of his identity— his black leather jacket.

"Give this to Kathleen," he requested.

Our journey ended at a single-story pink stucco house in West Oakland. All three of us got out. We hugged. Eldridge smiled with what I recognized as tenderness and appreciation. I watched his broad back as he climbed up four concrete steps and knocked on the door. He did not look back.

* * *

ANY SOCIAL MOVEMENT THAT MIGHT HAVE emerged from the intersectional Yippie/Panther Pact was wrecked by government pressure—particularly on Black Panther leaders. Eldridge was driven from the USA shortly after we wrote the Pact; Bobby would be forced to focus on the legal problems he faced at the upcoming Conspiracy Trial, and a false indictment in New Haven. Panther Minister of Defense Huey P. Newton, now released from prison, had no personal knowledge of or personal interest in white mother country radicals or Yippies. At the time, "Opening Salvos" had no more impact on actual events than what it was: an overstated pipe dream.

The FBI reported:

> *Leroy Eldridge Cleaver is presently a fugitive from justice in the State of California, owing to his failure to comply with conditions of his 1966 parole from a California state penitentiary. Kathleen Cleaver is publicly known as the National Captain of Women, BPP. (BLACKED OUT) has previously advised that Albert and Hemblen consider themselves to be good friends of Eldridge Cleaver and his wife Kathleen.*

"Police Issue All-Points Bulletin for Cleaver," headlines blared the next day when Stew and I arrived with Eldridge's jacket at Kathleen and Eldridge's Pine Street House in San Francisco . The windows of their Victorian were wrapped in knotty plywood.

"Why's your place boarded up?" I needed an explanation to satisfy my curiosity.

"Misdirection; bulletproof the house. Make anyone watching think Eldridge was prepared to shoot it out," Kathleen replied.

Kathleen had good reason to barricade the house. But, like the Yippies, she and Eldridge also possessed expertise in creating political theater. They had created a visible false flag operation. Kathleen told us a *New York Times* reporter had taken the bait. The reporter told Kathleen she had information that Eldridge and a woman had hijacked a plane to Cuba—such hijackings being an actual but infrequent occurrence in 1968.

Kathleen said, "I decided to fuck with her mind. I asked her— Goddammit, what is my husband doing with another woman?"

Joking was foundational to Kathleen's and my relationship; but guilt, like plaster, has a way of sticking with you. Kathleen's reference to Eldridge being with another woman indicated to me Kathleen knew enough about Eldridge and his white women "friends" to make fun of whatever she'd decided went on between them. With that, Kathleen partially assuaged the guilt I had for concealing from her what I knew concerning Eldridge's infidelity.

"At least the pigs don't have the slightest idea where Eldridge is," Kathleen went on, "So, I guess that means I'm in a good mood."

I never discovered if Stew and I had aided and abetted Eldridge's actual escape or if we were mere decoys, a ruse, an act of Panther/ Yippie theater designed to throw Eldridge's pursuers off the track. I do know that Eldridge devoted part of his last months over ground to tying the Panthers to the hippie/yippie cultural revolution—white mother country radicals. For me, driving Eldridge on one leg of his journey to an undisclosed location was a farewell gift to a prominent Black revolutionary I admired, from the partner of his best white friend. Eldridge Cleaver gave me my real name. From it, I would create a new identity. The least I could do was help transport Eldridge out of his.

CHAPTER 9:
MEET THE PARENTS

By Christmas 1968, Stew and I had been living together for close to a year. It was time for my new boyfriend to meet the parents. Eldridge had arrived in Cuba that same week, looking for a revolutionary's welcome he did not find.

I cleaned Stew up. I washed his jeans and paisley shirt. I trimmed his blond curls so poorly he looked like a lion who'd developed mange. I needed to win my parents' approval—but on my own terms. I dressed to provoke battle—black fishnet stockings underneath my knee-high Frye boots and faux leather miniskirt. And I counted on Stew's temper. He could be provoked.

My father Leo picked us up at Toronto's airport. He looked the same—same black hair, slicked back 1950s style—and I got that same happy hug of welcome I remembered.

But almost immediately, my father waded in.

"Stew, I hear from my daughter you know a little something about politics?"

Stew responded mano-a-mano.

"Well Leo, I hear from my girlfriend you know a little something about the Soviet Union."

My father rose to the challenge.

"So then Stew, what's your opinion about the Hitler-Stalin Pact?"

My father was a true believer, a lifelong and faithful member of the Communist Party of Canada. This stayed true until he died. It was appropriate to him that he pass judgment on the worth of a potential son-in-law based on an event thirty years in the past—before Stew or I were born. If, in Leo's view, Stew gave an incorrect answer about the moral meaning of the Hitler-Stalin Pact, Stew would not be worthy to marry his eldest daughter. I see this now as an old-fashioned conflict between men that comes disguised as ideological difference. My father was testing Stew, just as Abbie and Jerry had tested each other over the size of Pigasus. The issue was the same: which man—Jerry or Abbie, my father or my lover—got to be the top dog, and who the underdog?

Unintimidated by being in what was for me a "normal" family setting, I jumped in, pleased that I could call up what I considered a boring detail from my boring undergraduate class on World History Since 1914. I went on the offensive.

"So, Leo, what's so important about the Hitler-Stalin Pact? It lasted only two-years! Why should I care that a Nazi and a dictator divided Poland between them twenty-nine years ago?"

Leo replied, "I'm your father. Don't I have a right to know what your boyfriend thinks?"

This fight between my lover and my father stays with me, while the specifics of the Hitler-Stalin Pact have long since entered my personal version of Trotsky's dustbin of history. Only in my Communist Party family did your position on the 1939 Hitler-Stalin Pact determine your potential as a future son-in-law.

I have no recollection of what the correct position on this issue was.

Stew and Leo came to enjoy their political debates, which took place in my mother's living room. They'd sit one across from the other under one of her treasures—an oil painting of a bucolic Canadian lake by Frederick Varley, a famous Canadian artist. Varley had once accompanied my father on one of his trips to Russia, but the peace of Varley's portrait of a pine tree backgrounded by a deep blue lake did not transmit inside my family home.

Stew, a seasoned tactician, began by quoting a famous meme from *The Communist Manifesto*.

"Yes, Leo, you are right, the working class has nothing to lose but their chains." But Stew went further. "Sure—we work in factories. But we, the young people, are the driving force of history. We go to universities. We support the Black Panthers. We die in Vietnam. We smoke pot and listen to the Rolling Stones. And we're not straight-laced either . . ."

My father interrupted with what was for him an all-important Marxist question:

"Yeah, and what's your relationship to the means of production?"

"It don't matter," Stew replied. I was pleased that Stew didn't explode but kept his temper. He finished up with,

"For us Yippies, all young people are the working class. We take action, even if we're not well organized or top down like you communists. And we will make the revolution!"

As Jerry had advised, Stew "killed" my parents. He bested Leo at his own game—Stew killed Leo's ideology with his words. My father, a flexible man by any communist standard, conceded. Satisfied that Stew had proved his Marxist credentials, Leo covered his capitulation by modifying a famous communist maxim.

"Yippies of the world unite! You have nothing to lose but your pot pipes!"

My mother, naturally, was less flexible. In 1956, with the Party's sudden change in political line, over which Harriet had no control, my mother felt no need to repress her rage at what arbitrary Soviet authority demanded of her. Bitter, my mother turned the rigidity of her former true-believer communism into its opposite—she stayed authoritarian but accumulated material goods. I don't blame her—by then my entrepreneurial father had made a tidy fortune producing bingo games for local Toronto television stations, which—he rationalized—gave the working-class opportunities to win big bucks and helped to share the wealth.

Freed from an ideology that disparaged class privilege, but dependent on a husband who now made money, Harriet indulged herself. For work she managed Leo's business. For pleasure she went shopping. And drastically increased her alcohol consumption.

When Leo, Stew, and I arrived at 378 Cortleigh Blvd. in late December 1968, I found my mother standing coatless in the cold, between the two thin white columns that marked her home's front door. I put my arms around my mother as a dutiful daughter must, inhaling her aroma of cigarettes long dead. Harriet looked past me; her blue eyes narrowed, trained on Stew. The two shook hands quickly, as if each was desperate to wash contagion off. I had by then entered that state of exaggerated mental vigilance which, like LSD, may give my memory a greater luminosity than it deserves, but I recall feeling more foreign as I entered my mother's bourgeois home than I had ever felt as an immigrant in America.

Upstairs in our living room, Harriet directed Stew to sit. Stew leaned back into my mother's couch, a striking portrait of blond curls set in the couch's gold brocade, behind a coffee table of dark mahogany. Stew crossed his legs. He shifted the position of his scuffed Frye boots. My mother froze.

"No! No feet on the table!" she commanded in that same harsh tone I'd heard her use on Davey, our loyal West Highland White Terrier. In hindsight, I should have felt grateful. My mother was treating Stew like a member of the family.

The days that followed became a merry-go-round of booze and boredom. Photos from our visit show Stew with a hangdog look; I appear—and likely am—drunk. The day before Stew and I were scheduled to depart, my mother summoned me into her kitchen. She and I sat on white chairs with orange cushions on opposite sides of her white Saarinen table with its picture-window view of tree-lined Cortleigh Boulevard. My mother held what I hoped was her first whiskey of the day in her hand. A circle of cigarette fumes wafted toward the ceiling, creating that familiar barrier between us.

"I feel obligated as your mother," Harriet began, "to give you my considered opinion about Stew."

Reduced in an instant to a child with attitude, I glared back.

My mother continued, "And I don't mean to be critical."

I recognized that sentence. It translated to, "My sharp and painful critique of you is about to begin." Years later, when I'd see Harriet and Leo once or twice a year on holidays, I'd do as therapists advised and put on, metaphorically, a child's protective yellow slicker—hoping that her vitriol would fall off me like drops of rain. But at age twenty-five my mother's words still wounded.

"Stew is a very smart man."

I knew that any compliment from my mother must inevitably be followed by critique. I waited as Harriet took a sip of rye, ground her cigarette stub into her ashtray, and extracted a fresh cigarette from her red packet of Du Mauriers. *Uh oh, here it comes*, I thought. I watched my mother light her cigarette, pull smoke deep into her lungs and exhale.

"Have you considered Stew might be a hoe-moe-sexs-syu-al?"I heard her ask in all seriousness

I had to pull my cheeks inside my mouth to stop myself from giggling. My mother's question was hilarious. And outrageous. When I managed to speak, I replied in sternest possible tone I could muster.

"What in God's name makes you think that?"

"He looks like a girl. His hair *is* extremely long, you know."

With that, my mother conflated two noxious stereotypes— for a man to have long hair meant that man was queer and being queer was bad. I, however, had landed on a new perch of objectivity. This incident took place before gay pride and well before gay marriage; still I knew my response would make or break this battle. I stood up, smiled politely, put my hands on the back of my chair and, in my best cowgirl style and in the strongest voice I had ever heard myself use to address my mother, I spoke deliberately and with that identical cadence and phrasing I'd learned—and knew my mother would recognize—from those anti-communist hearings conducted by the evil U.S. Senator Joe McCarthy.

"Stew is not now, nor has he ever been, a homosexual."

Which I followed immediately with, "And so what if he was? What the fuck's wrong with being homosexual?"

"Well dearie," my mother responded, her voice tight, "Be it on your own head."

Harriet used this trope whenever I acted in ways of which she disapproved. She meant I must take responsibility for whatever calamity ensued as a result of my own actions. With that, my mother both insulted me and acknowledged my independence. For my entire life, my mother held inconsistent standards of right and wrong that she'd inflict on everyone but herself. But in the long run of history, as my father used to say, my alcoholic mother did me a favor. She taught me to despise hypocrisy, which, to put it in Marxist terms, is a necessary but not sufficient condition to become a Yippie.

* * *

ON DECEMBER 31, SO FILLED WITH relief I could almost taste it, I departed Toronto with Stew and flew to New York City. At my insistence, Stew had put in each pocket of his brown leather jacket a codeine/caffeine/aspirin combination called 222's, available over the counter in Canada. I had purchased two bottles of this Vicodin-like product for headache relief and preservation of my sanity. A U.S. customs agent spotted bulges in each of Stew's pockets.

"What have you got there?" He demanded.

"Two-twenty-twos." Stew replied truthfully.

The agent mistook Stew's answer to mean he carried a lethal product with him—not Vicodin but two .22 caliber pistols. The agent tensed, blanched, then ordered, "Step away from the counter! Put your hands on your head! Now!"

To my relief, Stew complied.

I watched the agent reach gingerly into Stew's pocket, first one, then another, and extract from each not a .22 caliber pistol or a revolver but a brown glass bottle, two inches tall, with the numbers 222 printed in bright red on its label.

Stew, never one to be intimidated by cops or anyone in uniform, said, "See! That's what I told you! Two-twenty-two's."

In 1968, Stew could joke about carrying two pistols while crossing the U.S. border and not immediately be arrested as a terrorist. A relieved customs agent returned our pills. On the plane, a flight attendant handed us a copy of *The Toronto Globe and Mail*. Its headline summarized that day's true atrocities: "14,500 U.S. Soldiers Killed in Vietnam in 1968."

Back in New York City, Stew and I walked to the by now familiar former tenement at 5 St. Marks Place where Nancy and Jerry lived. Old Year 1968 was on its way out; Baby 1969 beckoned. The Yippies as a brand name would be one year old this night; rock stars Janis Joplin and Jimi Hendrix would be dead within two. As Stew and I huffed our way upstairs through the narrow tenement hallway that led to #16, a sweet, familiar odor of marijuana brought me home.

I found Jerry in prophet of doom mode, unusual for him. He'd heard a rumor that federal indictments would be issued for the previous summer's demonstrations in Chicago. What Jerry called the United States Department of Injustice had acknowledged to Jerry's lawyers they had put his apartment under electronic surveillance.

"1969 will be the Year of the Bum Trip," Jerry, rattled, opined.

Next day, New Year's Day, January 1, 1969, Stew and I strolled east down St. Marks Place toward Anita and Abbie's apartment at #30. Even Abbie the Eternal Optimist predicted a grim future. He hoped Eldridge would establish a community of exiles so Yippies could flee to Cuba. I refused to join their gloom parade. I had escaped the grim Toronto of my childhood; I was ecstatic to be back in my world.

CHAPTER 10:
WHY THE WOMEN ARE REVOLTING

THE FRONT PAGE OF MY LOCAL underground newspaper the *Berkeley Barb* welcomed January 1969 with a photograph of Nazis rallying under a swastika banner next to a photo of the Fuehrer shaking hands with a member of the Hitler Youth. Next to Hitler, a photo of President Nixon in front of a gigantic American flag,predicted a grim future. "HEIL 1984," the *Barb* headline read.

"There are rumors of concentration camps," Stew wrote, referring to our New Year's conversations with Jerry and Abbie.

It's easier to agree with a generalization than take a position on specifics. I was skeptical about the camps, but like many of the *Barb's* 250,000 readers, I too considered President Nixon a genocidal Hitler. And I believed George Orwell accurately portrayed Nixonian doublespeak. Still, no matter how repressive an America I thought I lived in, somehow the *Berkeley Barb* continued to publish.

* * *

THE *BERKELEY BARB* WAS AN AGGREGATOR, a *Huffington Post* with sex ads. I started work there in early 1968, shortly after I hooked up with Stew. I coordinated classified sex ads in the *Barb*. My ads upheld the lowest end of the *Barb's* revenue stream; the paper's economic engine was powered by full page display ads for records, concerts, and most often for sex worker services: "Beaver Like You Can Never Imagine;" "BIG BUSTED BROADS OVER 21 looking for easy work with groovy hours & good pay. For Men Only," and the Normandy Massage Parlor, a regular, who promoted "the best beaver, shaved and bushy, ever shown." By standards of modern feminism, I ought to have been shocked, horrified, appalled, and dismayed at this blatant exploitation of women's bodies for profit, but at the beginning I was not. I was glad to have my job.

Office gossip had it the *Barb* generated a profit of $300,000 a year. This figure may have been accurate. It may also have been pot-inspired exaggeration, or deliberate obfuscation from the *Berkeley Barb*'s publisher and editor Max Scherr. Max paid full time staff 65 cents an hour. The Clavir family mantra that money equaled love had no relevance for Max—he paid me $3 a week. The FBI, with their usual exaggeration, claimed in Stew's file both that Moscow funded our resistance, and that Max was paying staff a magnificent **rate of $1 per column inch for published work.**

No. Max's reporters earned a Dickensian 25 cents a column inch, a wage so low that articles in the *Barb* wandered down a path of dense verbal irrelevances so reporters could add inches to their columns and earn more money. As I recall, Stew earned about $25 a week. But for certain, Stew's and my income did not sustain what FBI agents called our spartan—and I considered opulent—hippie lifestyle.

Still, FBI agents were correct to suspect that Stew and I were funded by foreign sources—just not Russians. I had received a grant from the Canada Council to write my Ph.D. thesis and I counted on my father Leo's largess, which no longer "came from Moscow" but from producing bingo shows for Canadian television.

FBI agents also got the *Barb* right:

> **In addition to sexual matters, the Barb opposes present leadership and authority in virtually every area of American life including government, business, labor, education, and religion.**

Max filled the *Barb*'s pages with diatribes based in what we called "participatory journalism." Stew, I, and many others reported on the marginalized by taking part in protest, reporting facts as we experienced them, then agitating readers to join the action. As a result, a wild west of intersectional characters populated the *Barb*'s pages: draft resisters and active soldiers, Black Panthers, Latinx and Asian folks, hipsters, the homeless, LGBTQ+, runaways, marijuana growers, women's liberationists, and environmentalists, anarchists, communists, and John Birchers (*Don't Call Us the Radical Right!*), plus advocates of sexual freedom, hippies, Yippies, students, physicians, fortune tellers, factory workers, poets, journalists and writers both published and wannabes, scions of the ruling class, folks of low and no income plus every protest group known by their initials—SDS—or by the number of activists persecuted—like the Oakland 7. As a writer for the *Barb,* I could be as political as I chose.

Two times out of three a photo or a cartoon of a naked woman appeared on the *Barb*'s front cover, a photo that confirmed that, for Max, profit was in command.

"Tits above the fold. It's how ya sell papers," was Max's motto.

The deadline for *Barb* classified ads was Monday at 8 p.m. I had dressed for success at work in my favorite brown fake leather miniskirt and knee-high Frye boots. One Monday afternoon, just as I congratulated myself on how in-charge I looked, I heard the sound of chains clanking their way down the street. I saw my favorite repeat customer George come through the front door of 2042 University Avenue and knew immediately that his outfit had my neo-Panther attire beat to hell. Two silver chains coiled around George's neck, secured by a 3-inch padlock. Four rows of shiny steel looped down his butt, connected to three smaller chains over each wrist. A black leather vest with silver studs covered his chest, from which protruded curls dyed red; his black leather pants stretched so tight across his groin I could not miss the outline of his balls and penis.

"Hey, George, nice to see you again. How're you?"

"Jus' fine," George replied.

Laconic as usual, George handed me his ad, pre-printed on a form adorned with a cartoon of two naked women next to two obese cops patting down a hippie:

"WANT TO MEET YOUNG MASC. GUY INTERESTED IN WILD LEATHER AND WESTERN GAMES. If 33, 6'1", 165 well-endowed turns you on call George. Photo please." Decades later, a gay male friend told me that "western games" meant you got tied up with your butt in the air, and, if you were hard core, this included branding.

George offered me $5, waved away my $1 change, smiled a gentle smile, then clanked his way out the door. That same evening, Stew stepped behind my counter and drew me close, as if to button me up inside his gray and green plaid jacket. I told him about George. Stew's answer challenged what remained of my Canadian prudery without hurting my feelings.

He said, "You're doing good."

"How so?"

"You're helping people satisfy their sexual needs. No matter how unorthodox you think they are. It's making you a more tolerant person."

Only once did I receive an ad from a woman hoping to meet a woman. It arrived in the mail.

* * *

MAX'S TROPE ABOUT TITS ABOVE THE fold turned out to be a call to action.

By the spring of 1969, a comic book heroine named Lenore Goldberg had become my role model. R. Crumb, known for being a misogynist, was Lenore's creator. I ignored Crumb's misogyny but I identified with his portrayal of Lenore's muscular thighs, dark wavy hair, black leather stomping boots, and Jewish name—and fantasized that I, like Lenore, would someday lead a group of Girl

Commandos who karate chopped a fat hairy cop while shouting "JOIN THE WORLD-FAMILY REVOLUTION OR DIE!!! POW!"

Lenore was fictional; reality was different. I carry with me an image of Jane Scherr, bent over an ancient white kitchen stove, her brown hair stringy from steam that belched up from pots of boiling water. Everyone thought of Jane as Max's wife although they never married. Jane was the mother of Dove and Polly, Max's two youngest children. Max had abandoned his oldest child Raquel and wife Estella to move in with Jane.

On Wednesday nights, one staff person would drive the *Barb*, laid out and pasted by hand onto sheets of blue-lined paper, to a printing plant in San Francisco's Mission district. The rest of us descended on Jane and Max's two-story house at 2421 Oregon Street in Berkeley where, on the front porch, a blue vinyl back seat of a car extruding stuffing reminded me of a rural dwelling gone to seed. But living in my Greenwich Village cellar had modified my rigidity; I could empathize with making do.

Jane's kitchen looked as if a truck had dumped its load there: unruly stacks of mail, yellowed newspapers, paper bags, photographs, and an army of bottles—beer, molasses, vinegar, soy, and hot sauce—marched along a black vinyl counter, along with a thrift store of cups and plates to hide the stains that peppered the oak table.

One Wednesday I asked, "Don't you mind? Doing all this cooking I mean?"

Jane brushed beads of sweat from her forehead. She spoke so softly I could barely hear her.

"No. Not really. It makes me feel useful."

Jane had no income of her own. Rumor had it Max did not give Jane money to buy food while insisting Jane cook a weekly meal for the *Barb* staff. Decades later Jane revealed to me that, to comply with Max's demand, she'd skim nickels, dimes, and quarters from the cash receivables Max had her deposit into the *Barb's* bank account.

"It was never a good idea to ask Max for money," she confided to me, "Because he would say no. Then call me stupid. Or a cunt."

* * *

By spring 1969, much of my life, that of my contemporaries, and my world of resistance politics had moved into a world at war. Stew and I now lived on the second floor of a mustard yellow, stucco Craftsman house we called the Ashby House. The FBI had recruited two elderly women neighbors who lived across Ashby Avenue as sources for the following:

> Subject is now residing as a paramour of
> STEWART ALBERT at 2917 Ashby Avenue
> Berkeley, California, where other young
> radicals live, including THOMAS HAYDEN who
> is currently awaiting trial re offenses
> occurring during the 1968 Democratic
> National Convention in Chicago. This house
> is frequented by members of the Black
> Panther Party (BPP) and white radicals.

Ashby was a collective typical of the inclusive demographic of my generation. Stew and I consummated our paramourishness in our second-floor bedroom on Ashby's sun porch. A draft resister lived with us under a fake name, Gentle Waters, as did sundry *Barb* staffers, including the pregnant daughter of famed historian William Appleman Williams. Tom Hayden paid Ashby's rent but actually spent his nights on Parker Street with his own "paramour," my friend Anne Weills.

Anne was a tall, blond, native Californian. I was a short, dark haired, east coast Jew. Anne considered herself a serious revolutionary; I was a Yippie. In high school, Anne had fought back alongside her good friends, the six tough Irish sons of Vivian Hallinan and her husband, Vincent, an attorney whose run-ins with Senator Joe McCarthy had made him famous. I identified as a beatnik in my Toronto high school, had an Afro-Canadian boyfriend, and fought back against my parents. Anne and I shared an affinity for miniskirts, knee-high leather boots, and a commitment to confront injustice. Neither of us intimidate easily.

I sat with Anne one afternoon in the sunlight that lit Ashby's living room, engaged in what today we call teambuilding. We cut out images from fashion magazines of women with bouffant hairdos who posed in front of kitchen sinks or modeled bikinis as a come-on for men to buy cars. Such symbols of subservience demanded action! We would challenge women's traditional roles! And revolutionize our lives!

We glued our cut-outs onto red construction paper. No bridal shower for us; ours were invitations to a women's liberation meeting. But Anne surprised me. She turned to me and remarked with what I heard as my mother's severity, "Judy, there's something I need to say to you."

I flinched. Anne continued.

"Judy, you're a strong woman. And you're intelligent. Please don't be offended but every time I see you, it's bring Stew this, bring Stew that. Drive him here. Drive him there. You act like you're Stew's servant."

"You're wrong," I barked back, unwilling to absorb what Anne was saying. "I'm my own person. I do what Stew wants because *I* want to."

"I'm just wondering is all. I didn't mean to hurt your feelings."

Later, Stew and I made love as an orange California sunset shone through curtains I'd sewn out of my mother's gift of Buddhist monks' robes. Reassured by sex yet insecure and needing affirmation, I snitched Anne out.

"It's not true what Anne says, Stewey, is it? I don't only do what you want, do I?"

"Of course not. You drive because you like to drive. I never learned. I can't cook. You can. You want me to learn to cook? I'll do it. I'll do whatever you want me to. I love you, Judy. You know I do."

"I love you too," I sniffed, mollified, and nestled my butt into his.

By way of preventive atonement, Stew published an apologia in the *Barb*. He denounced hippies who believed it was cosmic karma for women to clean up. Stew declared that if he could not cook, he was not entitled to eat. *Barb* readers saw Stew vow—in print—that he would learn to make his favorite meat sauce. I chose to believe Stew. Max also bought into Stew's apology. As if equating all men with racist Southerners, known as crackers, Max titled Stew's article *I Am a Male Cracker*. He printed my name in smaller type as Stew's technical consultant.

I took that citation as recognition, even if of secondary status, that I had won this battle, unaware that it would evolve, as gender conflicts do, into perpetual war. Even the San Francisco office of the FBI, an institution not known for sensitivity to gender issues, reported to Director Hoover that Stew had written an article about male chauvinism.

* * *

I CAME OF AGE IN A macho, hetero-sexist end of late-1960s protest. Radical feminists labeled women like me "male-identified," implying, unfairly I thought at the time, that I took my primary identity from observing male leaders. I call this period one in which I "learned and grew"—a phrase Stew coined that is patronizing but accurate.

Stew, Tom Hayden, Jerry, Abbie, Bobby Seale, Eldridge Cleaver, and even Max Scherr were Movement influencers. We called them "heavies"—home-grown, overwhelming male, mostly white leaders and celebrities. "Heavies" were both admired for their leadership and resented because we were not them. A "heavy" could come off as intimidating—especially if, like me, you were a woman and/ or foreign born. But I learned from Kathleen Cleaver—a true "heavy"—that it is the moral quality of an individual, not only fame, that gives a person influence and power.

In April 1969, fifteen women trooped into my second floor living room. I had banished my "heavy" from the Ashby House. Stew departed without protest. Many of us were *Barb* staff and/or in relationships with a male protest movement "heavy." Our jeans, boots, and hair down to our shoulders made us look as if we occupied a boarding school for hippie women. Relieved Max's partner Jane had shown up, I sat her next to me on my red-brown couch with its uncomfortable upholstery.

Anne started in, "Those images in the media that turn us into sex objects and infantilize us—like what we put on our invitation. I hate them. They're degrading."

Revolutions come in stages. By then I had gone so far as to stop wearing a bra—I have small breasts; bras inhibit my personal freedom. I had yet to internalize the rallying cry that "the personal is political," with which Carol Hanisch had revolutionized the east coast women's movement that same spring of 1969. Part of me still envied those tall, slim women in the car ads even though my body's architecture was as far from theirs as Mars. I deflected Anne's remark with what I thought of as a Yippie joke. Like any joke, mine contained a grain of truth. Remembering my jealousy of Lenore's big—albeit cartoon—breasts, I said, "Yeah, but I wish I had big breasts like they do."

No one laughed.

Jane whispered to me, her voice so low I could barely hear her, "Oh Judy, how do you dare talk like that out loud?"

"I hate the word chick," Alta, a poet who published under her own imprint, Shameless Hussy Press, interrupted, a quaver in her voice as if any word that denigrated women offended her poetic sensibilities. She went on.

"A chick is a baby chicken. And a bitch is just a dog. I won't let Simon call me an old lady either."

To my surprise, Jane picked up the narrative. She said, her voice again subdued, her eyes downcast, "It's a revelation to me how everyone's experience seems to replicate mine."

I told myself that my relationship with Stew did not compare to what I'd seen of Jane's to Max. Still, Anne's "you act like you're Stew's servant" comment had burrowed into my subconscious like that underground worm in *Dune*. I also bought into Eldridge's binary division of the world—I would *not* be part of the problem; I *was* part of the solution.

"Who's women's enemy?" I demanded. "The Panthers rightly hate the pigs; the North Vietnamese hate U.S. imperialists—who are ours?"

"Society," came a chorus.

"Men," said a lone voice I did not recognize.

Provoked, I shot back, "Stew's NOT my enemy. Didn't you read the *SCUM Manifesto*? By Valerie Solanas? She shot Andy Warhol! With a .32 Beretta pistol! Almost killed him. Is that what we want?"

I was by then swimming in a sea of liberation struggles—for a peaceful, independent Vietnam, for the liberation of Black people and all people of color, for the National Liberation Front (Viet Cong) of South Vietnam, for the Chicago Conspiracy defendants, even for sexual freedom (led by a man who soon began to call himself Jefferson "Fuck" Poland). But I had yet to identify "The Patriarchy" as my enemy. The phrase "The Patriarchy" felt too amorphous and unstructured for me. I preferred to jump directly into opposing a concrete—and evil—target.

Which is why, by meeting's end, my ambivalence had melted into elation. My singular "I" had merged into a collective "we." No wussy women's group for us macho broads; no sitting around in circles venting feelings. We'd organize a women's march! We'd lead ourselves! Beginning at Sproul Plaza on the male-dominated UC Berkeley campus! We'd demand the

impossible—freedom and equality for women. We set a date—
May 15, 1969.

I do not presume to speak for Everywoman, but I believe that,
to become a free person, you must put your metaphoric tits above
the fold, face down those who oppress you and by so doing find
the courage to be yourself. Over time, Jane and every member of
our women's group found that courage. For me it would take six
more months.

* * *

IN APRIL 1969, BLACK PANTHER CHAIRPERSON Bobby Seale,
Tom Hayden, Jerry, Abbie, John Froines, and Dave Dellinger—
six of eight about-to-be defendants in what became known as the
Trial of the Chicago 8—arrived at the Ashby house to discuss
resistance tactics. I waited impatiently on the first floor. The
meeting ended. Bobby came downstairs and looked into my fish
tank, which I had filled with half a dozen neon tetras who swam
alongside a Siamese fighting fish, a fish who, for unknown
reasons, I'd named Mergatroyd. Mergatroyd's tail of cobalt blue
blissed me out when I was stoned.

"What's that?" Bobby asked, pointing to the fish.

"It's a Siamese fighting fish. Her name is Mergatroyd."

"A fighting fish! Why do you put Mergatroyd in jail? Free
Mergatroyd!"

Bobby raised his fist in a Black Panther salute and declared,
"Free all fighting fish! Power to the People!"

Then Bobby looked down at me from his six-foot height and said,
"You know, Gumbo, the Party is holding a Free Huey rally. On
Mayday. In front of the Federal Building in San Francisco. You're
right on about women's liberation. Do you wanna give a speech?"

What white mother country radical woman could ask for more?

Today, Black Panthers are depicted in right-wing media as
street thugs; on occasion parts of the left claim Panthers were
Black nationalists. In my experience, neither was true. As I'd

learned at Panther School a year before, the Black Panther Party welcomed white allies—as long as we recognized that Black Panthers were in command. Now Bobby had welcomed me—a white woman—to speak at a Panther rally to free Huey. I see now that by asking me to give a speech in support of women's liberation, Bobby was agreeing with Eldridge about the importance of our Yippie/Panther alliance. I remember well Bobby's intersectional message. It went like this:

"Power to the people—Black people, white people, brown people, yellow people, blue, red, green, and polka-dot people. Panther Power to the vanguard!"

For Bobby, the revolution was one revolution. Period.

Overjoyed, flabbergasted, and determined to do my best, I rehearsed in front of Mergatroyd with the discipline of a professional athlete. I expected hundreds of people to attend. When Thursday, May 1 arrived, I stood in front of 3,000 people under a cloudless San Francisco sky. I'd dressed in my neo-Panther leathers, a proud but nervous expert in women's liberation. Stew waited twenty feet behind me, pretending to be my bodyguard. He was accompanied by Big Man, a Black Panther whose large, square face and oversize torso prompted his name. Just as I opened my mouth, I heard Stew's voice together with Big Man's shout, "Gumbo! Gumbo!"

Against my better judgment, I turned my back to my audience and shrieked, "What the fuck do you want?"

"Are you OK? Do you know what you're gonna say?"

The patronizing concern in Stew's and Big Man's tones affirmed the righteousness of my cause. I yelled back, "Shut up, you idiots! Shut up and listen."

I put the microphone up to my lips as I had watched male speakers do, kissed it like a penis to make myself heard and began.

"As women we are getting our shit together and overcoming the alienation that the system foists on us; as revolutionaries we are learning and teaching those skills necessary for our survival. We don't hate men. We dig 'em . . . We are part of the solution and we will ally with anyone who wants to overthrow this rotten system."

To a chorus of, "Right on! Right on, Sister!" I pumped my right fist in the air, and ended my speech by quoting from a conversation I'd had with Eldridge.

"When you are fighting for your own liberation, you must fight to the death on all fronts."

My rhetoric was extreme; I had no direct experience with the reality of death, let alone what it meant to die for women's liberation. But I stand by my statement—to fight for freedom as a political progressive gives you life; anything less is a death. I strutted back to Stew and Big Man to see Stew's blue eyes shine with pride. "Right on!" Big Man said and patted me on my back. Judy Gumbo, independent woman, had arrived—or so I thought. The *Berkeley Barb* cited both Stew and me as speakers. Their reporter quoted directly what Stew had to say about People's Park. That same *Barb* reporter ignored my speech about women's liberation.

CHAPTER 11:
PARK HERE ANY TIME

ON JUNE 29, 1969, FOUR DAYS after my 26th birthday, I was home alone in the Ashby house listening to KPFA, Berkeley's politically progressive radio station. I listened to an announcer, their voice hoarse with excitement, explain that at that very instant the New York City tactical squad was attacking a gay bar in New York City's Greenwich Village. I heard folks singing as they overturned police cars and realized the confrontation was taking place a block-and-a-half from my old Bleecker Street cellar.

Ashby's doorbell rang. Two strangers had made their way onto our yellow stucco porch. They both had dirty blond hair, long sideburns, and wore identical jean jackets. The older man asked if I was Gumbo. I said I was. He introduced himself as Konstantin Berlandt.

"I liked what you said at the Free Huey rally. My friend and I would like to talk with you, ok?"

I've always been a sucker for a compliment. LSD guru Tim Leary had by then infused 1960s counter-culture with a cosmic interconnectedness which carried with it a sense of instant trust. I invited the pair upstairs past the aquarium to my inner sanctum living room. Konstantin sat; I watched him press his fingers into the blue jeans worn by his companion. Such an overt gesture of affection between two men in front of a female stranger could only be one thing: a test of my tolerance. I waited. As did Konstantin, who asked, "Am I the first person you ever met to tell you out front he was a homosexual?"

Remembering George, I felt unsure whether to nod or shake my head. In a voice as rapid-fire as Jerry's, Konstantin's friend jumped in.

"I once had a job interview to be an investigator. For the government. They asked me, 'What if you had to reveal someone was homosexual?' I don't remember what I said. All the time I was answering I wondered what would happen if they found out I was one."

"You must know Leo Lawrence," Konstantin added. "He writes for the *Barb*. Did you know he was fired from ABC when he came out?"

In fact, I did. Leo Lawrence, a dark-haired *Barb* reporter as short as I am, was a *Barb* pal.

"What made you come to me instead of Leo?" I asked.

"We have. He's with us. But what you said at the rally inspired me. About fighting to the death for your liberation. I want to go public. As a homosexual. In the *Barb*. Can you help too?"

"I'll do my best. I'll speak to Max. But I can't promise," I replied, all too familiar with Max's penchant for ignoring me.

Max titled Konstantin's piece *Been Down So Long It Looks Like Up to Me*. I never saw Konstantin again, but his public coming out gave me a private gift—I could motivate people to action with my words.

* * *

IN 1969, THE PASSION I INVESTED into events could both speed up and slow down time. It may be a cliché, but the intense activity of each moment made me feel as if an hour had passed; hours felt like days, days became weeks. In early 1968, the University of California had torn down a bohemian neighborhood of old brown-shingled Berkeley homes allegedly to construct dorms and an athletic field on a plot of land between

Dwight Way and Haste Street. By May 1969, the land remained an empty, muddy parking lot.

> *"HEAR YE, HEAR YE . . . At one o'clock our rural reclamation project for Telegraph Avenue commences in the expectation of beauty. We want the Park to be a cultural, political, freak out, and rap center for the Western world."*

Using a pseudonym—People's Park Commissioner—Stew wrote this call to action which Max published in the April 18 edition of the *Berkeley Barb*.

I've been called a co-founder of the Park, but so were hundreds of my closest radical friends. Two days later we began work. Stew and I broke hard, clay-like earth into brown clumps to plant tomato starts. Students in bell-bottom jeans dug the land alongside us, as did musicians in jester's hats and bells that tinkled. Older women who I, an advocate of youth culture, once disparaged as little old ladies in tennis shoes, watched in awe as young men with shaved heads danced and chanted: *"Hari Krishna, Hari Krishna, Hari Rama, Hari Hari."* Younger women danced, their naked backs and barely concealed breasts clear evidence of lack of bras, which I too longer wore. But if men could go around bare-chested, why not me? My former Keith Street roommate David Minkus, now People's Chef, served up brown rice and beans he cooked inside a steel garbage can that, knowing David, I knew would be clean. Musician and anti-war vet Country Joe McDonald sang, "One, two, three, what are we fighting for, don't ask me I don't give a damn, next stop is Vietnam"—the ballad he had not had a chance to sing after being attacked by cops nine months earlier in Chicago. We, the residents of Berkeley, were building a Park for the People—liberated territory in which free speech, music, and gardening took hold. Women ensured the Park would be a safe space to work, to hang out, and for children to play—so different from the sexual violence that had defiled the Summer of Love two years before.

Abbie visited. Black Panther Party chair Bobby Seale also arrived to say, "This Park is really socialistic! We got to get some Panthers down here working on it!"

Bobby's statement was, like what he'd said about polka dot people, another example of the Panther leader's imaginative, intersectional point of view. Such overt Black Panther support for People's Park delighted Stew, me, and thousands more mostly white *Barb* readers and Berkeley residents.

Stew's label for People's Park was "soulful socialism." It recognized and validated our emerging eco-consciousness. Within a year, Stew would comment: "People's Park was the beginning of the Revolutionary Ecology Movement. We founded it a full year before the first Earth Day. And it was an early model of the struggle we are going to have to wage if life is going to survive at all on this planet . . ."

Like the Yippies, People's Park had no elected or official leaders, just strong personalities, although, as so often was the case in 1969, after Wednesday, May 14th, more white men ended up "leaders" than the rest of us. Nobody supervised; I'd hear Stew say the trip belonged to those who dreamed. Some but not all decisions—such as they were—came about by mutual agreement or what we called consensus. To underscore our message that usurper land must be seized for a free people, a poster that looked like a no-parking traffic sign proclaimed, *"Park Here Any Time."*

* * *

TUESDAY, MAY 13, TWO WEEKS AFTER my triumph at the Free Huey rally, I handed Max a call to feminist action. I wrote that every woman who worked in People's Park or took part in anti-war demonstrations adopt as their own this fundamental principle: women deserve equality and liberation. Max printed it under my "Gumbo" byline and headlined my piece: "Why the Women Are Revolting." I'd adapt this headline but use it on my own terms: Women must continue revolting to achieve our freedom.

To paraphrase that infamous Brit monarch Queen Victoria, I was not amused. *Berkeley Barb* in hand, I stomped like Lenore Goldberg toward Max's designated space at the rear of the *Barb* office. But I lacked Lenore's superpowers so I could not hit Max with a karate chop. I did hurl the most aggressive Lenore Goldberg words I could come up with at him.

"Max Scherr, you are a two-faced sexist pig."

"Too busy. Don't bother me," Max replied, his bald head bent over a sheet of layout paper. He dismissed me with a wave of his hand.

I left, incensed. And conflicted. Max had insulted me with his demeaning double entendre, but at the same time he considered my piece important enough to stand on its own. Even if I strip away what reads to me now like a turducken of rhetoric stuffed with cliche and basted with expletives, I still stand by my message:

If it takes a revolution for men to accept that women are as good—in fact better—than men are, so be it. We will have our freedom. We will not be ignored.

On Wednesday, May 14, my women's group met in my Ashby Avenue living room. We planned a march for women's liberation for the next day. We'd meet at Sproul Plaza on the Cal campus. Anne Weills would speak on our behalf; she'd urge every woman present to march with us.

Thursday, May 15, I awoke to discover our beloved People's Park surrounded by a chain link fence. California Highway cops frolicked on slides and swing sets intended for toddlers. Ronald Reagan, Republican Governor of California and subsequent President of the United States, had ordered up the California Highway Patrol and Berkeley City cops to pacify the City of Berkeley.

Without benefit of social media, three thousand angry protesters assembled in Sproul Plaza.

"Take the Park!" U.C. student body President Dan Siegel exhorted the crowd.

Anne's speech, and any hope I had to march for women's liberation, evaporated into chaos. External events had overwhelmed my primary agenda—freedom for my gender and for me. I convinced myself I didn't care. I had to accept that People's Park had a greater moral compass since it inspired resisters of every gender. But, like so many protests women attempt, our Berkeley March for Women's Liberation became forgotten history. Until now.

I raced down Telegraph Avenue alongside Stew, my disappointment transformed into a second honeymoon of protest. When I reached the Park, I pushed so hard against its chain-link fence I left red diamonds imprints in my palms. Shortly thereafter, President Reagan's Chief of Staff called in the Alameda County Sheriffs, who had a reputation both for carrying shotguns and being vicious. They marched first on People's Park, then through Berkeley's tree-lined streets. Familiar, rancid tear gas assaulted the entire city then wafted upward on ocean breezes to wealthy homes on Grizzly Peak. I heard the *thud, thud, thud* of shotgun fire.

PIGS SHOOT TO KILL—
BYSTANDERS GUNNED DOWN

This three-inch tall headline in black capital letters dominated the front cover of the May 16–22 *Barb*. Right below the headline, as if to mourn the loss of what once had been, a charming photo of Max's younger daughter Polly appeared, looking upward. An even more gigantic headline **PEOPLE'S WAR ON** spread across the top of pages two and three. My piece, "Why the Women Are Revolting," appeared under my Gumbo byline. Max had ignored me, but he did not ignore my piece. He—or perhaps a rebellious layout person—had placed it front and center on page five.

The following week, *Barb* headlines screamed:

In Cold Blood! Gentle Waters hit by .38 caliber bullet!
Artist Alan Blanchard blinded!

***Bystander James Rector succumbs to shock, hemorrhage,
and multiple gunshot wounds at Herrick Hospital!***

The *Black Panther* newspaper printed its own analysis about the
meaning of police and government brutality in the Park:

> *No one should think that all of this repression was brought about
> because of someone trespassing on a piece of land. As this article
> was being written, news came that one of the persons shot by the
> pigs died of shotgun wounds. The pig power structures of
> California are trying to make examples out of the people who
> want the People's Park. Power never takes a back step to anything
> but power. There are more people than there are pigs, and all
> power belongs to the people. Period!*

The government of California placed Berkeley under martial
law. They called in the California National Guard. The Berkeley
City Council resisted, voting 8–1 against military occupation. They
lost. Public meetings of more than three people were forbidden. In
response, about-to-be Conspiracy 8 defendant Tom Hayden called a
group of twenty of his closest friends together, including Stew and
me. We met at an art-deco hotel on the Oakland border. Tom's goal
reflected his militant idealism—we'd write, collectively, a vision of
resistance for the City of Berkeley—and the world. Inspired by the
Black Panther Party's 10 Point platform and program, we titled our
creation *The Berkeley Liberation Program*. Our program began:

> *The People of Berkeley Passionately Desire Human Solidarity,
> Cultural Freedom, and Peace*

and ended with,

> *Power to the Imagination, All Power to the People!*

I and every woman present met separately in an equally art-
deco women's restroom to proclaim, in print, our anger at male
domination, combined with our unwillingness to give men up.
Ours was Point #5. We began with abstract rhetoric:

We will struggle for the full liberation of women as a necessary part of the revolutionary process . . .

and ended with a call to action:

We will end all forms of male supremacy BY ANY MEANS NECESSARY!

To supplement our education in revolution, Tom screened his friend Robert Kramer's movie *Ice* in Anne Weills's living room. *Ice* was a black and white movie shot in cinema verité style about white American guerillas who resisted a dictatorial U.S. government. Although I don't recall if Tom did this himself, I do know many of us went to the nearby Chabot Gun Club to practice self-defense. Tom Hayden was the main mover and shaker of the Berkeley Liberation Program; he also founded in the Ashby House what he called our International Liberation School. The militancy of 1969 was a militancy Tom Hayden shared.

But our idealism did not match our practice—I still possess a favorite photo that clearly documents Tom bloviating while I sit next to him doing women's work—typing his immortal words.

* * *

THE FENCE STAYED UP. A WASTELAND of thorny weeds choked out our tomatoes. The sod Stew and I had planted dried into a carpet of brown. National Guard helicopters dropped gas. On May 30, Stew and I plus thirty-thousand Bay Area residents marched in peaceful protest to save People's Park—to no avail.

Stew, the *Barb* staff, and I deflected our anger at the Park's demise onto Max Scherr.

The satisfaction I once had at being paid $3 for two days work dissipated. I felt as if I wore around my own neck the chains I'd seen on my favorite *Barb* customer George—but lacking his sexual perks. We, Max's wage slaves, demanded higher wages. Max refused. The *Barb* staff went on strike. Max decided to sell.

Two weeks prior to July 20, 1969, when astronaut Neil Armstrong would make his historic landing on the moon, Max's pal Timothy Leary, High Priest of the Aquarian Age and my generation's historic explorer of inner space, had arrived at the Ashby house. Leary came accompanied by Billy Hitchcock, a short, balding multimillionaire scion of the Mellon banking family. Leary wanted to buy not just the *Barb* but the services of its entire staff as a vehicle to help him run for Governor of California the following year.

Perhaps it was Leary's master of the universe stride, perhaps it was his silver hair slicked back into a Brahman-like ponytail or his chin that jutted movie-star-like over a necklace strung with tiny bells that tinkled as he walked, but I did not detect a scintilla of sincerity in Leary's being. Common wisdom dictates that first impressions stick. To me Tim Leary appeared to be the P.T. Barnum of Con.

Radiating goodwill, Leary and Hitchcock made their way to my couch, now covered with a yellow Indian cotton bedspread. Stew, the *Barb* staff, and I sat on my wood floor, acolytes at the feet of the master. By way of greeting, a *Barb* staffer repeated Leary's mantra, "Turn on, tune in, drop out."

"My purpose is to turn on the world," Leary replied.

I admit it; I began with a bias. I wanted to tune in but in fact I had turned off. I figured Stew would be more tolerant; he'd met Leary once with Jerry and considered Tim a likable rogue. Still, despite my initial dislike, I felt obligated to listen—given that Leary was the supreme sales rep for a colorless, odorless pill that dissolved the boundaries of human awareness and revealed to its user their connection to the universe. My Stalinist upbringing receded; I'd grant this man his grand visions.

By then I had experimented with LSD. Once. Before I met Stew, I'd shared a single tab of LSD with an erstwhile suitor who had torn it off from what looked to me like a white blotter. I'd driven through Tilden Park on the back of the man's motorcycle, greedily sucking in blue, white, and yellow stars as if I was ingesting celestial gummies. As the saying goes, I was what I ate. Now in my living room I saw Gentle Waters, *Barb* staffer and resident of the Ashby house, wince as he massaged his shattered right arm. He'd been among those shot on bloody Thursday.

G. W. asked Leary why he was running for Governor of California.

As evasive as any mainstream politician, Leary smiled with teeth as white as a dental ad and dodged G.W.'s question. He claimed his "Luv for Guv" campaign existed beyond structure. He'd hold love-ins! For young people! With major rock artists! Leary impressed me only when he said his campaign enjoyed the support of wealthy "heads" like John and Yoko, and I saw Billy Hitchcock, who was one, nod.

Leary asserted, "If I'm elected, People's Park will be green with grass, and police helicopters will drop flowers on the free campus. I'll meet the reasonable demands of the John Birch Society and the righteous demands of the Blacks."

This felt like a bizarre beginning to a tough labor negotiation. To unite revolutionary Black Panthers with alt-right white John Birchers or drop flowers on a campus now consumed in tear-gas was way too contradictory to inspire confidence—even for this fantasy-loving Yippie.

"Let's hear him out," I heard Stew's quiet voice in my ear.

Leary assured his audience he'd give away tabs of orange sunshine—pure LSD! In the tens of thousands! For free! And, Leary proclaimed, "If a beautiful person handed troops and police something to eat, be warned, it will save their souls."

Charlatans claim they're saving souls. Abbie Hoffman never did. When he boasted in 1968 that we'd put LSD into Chicago's drinking water, he used typical Yippie exaggeration to scare Mayor Daley. For all his theatrics, I decided Leary might actually pull off what I considered a harmful act—dosing unsuspecting folks with LSD. For me, any rationality I thought Leary possessed dissolved like a tab of bad acid.

Leary went on to assure his audience of *Barb* staffers that LSD would be his campaign's antidote to getting sprayed with mace. For me, Leary's LSD as cure-all was problematic; I could tell by Stew's pursed lips that such a tactic contradicted even his Yippie tolerance—and Stew's patience for the absurd was far greater than mine.

"You can't transform a pig like Max by re-programming him with LSD against his will," I heard Stew mutter.

Amid the rustle of bodies shifting position on my floor, Leary went on to make this promise:

"I won't try to control the *Barb*'s politics. I'll open the *Barb*'s books. You won't have to do anything you don't want to."

Timothy Leary, politician, gazed around my living room; it appeared to me that Leary's eyes focused only on the men, as if men alone would care about such matters. Again, I, a woman, felt invisible. Then, with the facility of a quick-change artist, Leary also changed the subject.

"What's your position on guns?"

In my mind, I congratulated Leary for finally asking what I considered to be an informed question. I didn't have a good answer; I knew only that, after the violence in Chicago, a minority of activists of every color, Stew and I included, had purchased rifles or even shotguns, but not semi-automatic assault weapons. Perhaps ours was just a fantasy—no white person I knew had picked up a gun and actually shot a cop—but I and a majority of the *Barb*'s 90,000 readers believed owning a firearm meant we could, if called on, defend ourselves against police attack.

I discovered a hole half an inch around with jagged edges in the lower right-hand corner of the Ashby house's first floor window. The hole came from a bullet. The window had not shattered. Nor did I, or anyone else, repair it. That hole symbolized our defiance. After People's Park, photos and cartoons of rifles or pistols appeared in the *Barb*, not as frequently as women's tits above the fold but certainly with regularity. Now I watched in amazement as Stew reached underneath a pile of Indian pillows I kept on the floor, under which we concealed our new but second hand .22 caliber rifle.

I observed my lover slowly raise the rifle above his head and heard him say, "Here's our position on guns. We've got 'em and we'll use 'em."

I had in front of me two Houdinis competing over which illusion—armed self-defense or cosmic interconnectedness—would control the *Barb*. In my mind, I flashed back to Jerry and Abbie's battle over what size Pigasus had to be. Stew triumphed in this theater of toxic male absurdity. Trailed by Hitchcock, Leary stood up and walked out, his trademark Cheshire cat grin frozen on his face.

Stew carefully replaced our rifle under its bed of embroidered mirrored cushions then leaned back and announced to the assembled *Barb* staff, "I wasn't serious. I was just being a Yippie."

At first, I was proud of Stew for being arrogant enough to confront the arrogance I found in Leary. I took it as a lesson that a theatrical show of arms can get the powerful to cave. But late that night, as my lover snored beside me in our bed, surrounded by my orange curtains of Buddhist peace, Leary's—and Stew's—exaggerations kept my own sleep at bay.

I refused to accept that Leary and his followers would "save people's souls" by dosing them with LSD without their knowledge. But I did believe my lover when he said that lifting that rifle above his head was just a joke. For a Yippie, a joke creates a rebel stance. It can also cover up an inconvenient truth. I had once accepted Stokeley Carmichael's infamous rationale that he was "just kidding" when he made (and later took back) his statement that the best place for women in the Movement was prone. Stew claimed he was making a standard Yippie statement and Stokely may have liked to fuck. But—is a joke that insults, hurts, degrades, or frightens still a joke?

* * *

THE *BARB* SALE DID NOT HAPPEN. The staff, including Stew and me, struck for higher wages.

Max fired us. He went on to publish by himself a four-page *Barb* sans news or cartoons but stuffed with sex ads and what I took to be a truthful headline, *"MAX IS A PIG."* We, the now former *Barb* staff, put out the *Berkeley Tribe* as a competing publication. It's no accident we wrote the Berkeley Liberation Program in the middle of People's Park. The Park brought to fruition the ideals of socialist community we'd articulated in the Program—and helped us define the *Berkeley Tribe* as a communal, people's project.

In addition to updates on the Panthers and the Park, in the *Tribe's* first issue reporters covered a cop killing of a young Black man, a tear gassing of Berkeley's free medical clinic, and a communiqué from Eldridge in exile, followed by seven personal classified ads for male models including one from a self-described "hairy chested butch, six feet of well-hung Southerner," and a lone display ad from the Normandy Massage Parlor. Sex ads were quickly banished, replaced by ads for concerts and records. With such a loss of revenue, the *Tribe* survived four years.

A photograph that took up the entire front cover of the inaugural issue of the *Berkeley Tribe* in anarchist red and black showed all forty-eight former *Barb* staffers, butt naked. A close examination reveals I hold a tiny—and as I recall, borrowed—pistol in my hand.

CHAPTER 12:
THE BATTLES OF ALGIERS

ONE SUNNY BERKELEY DAY, A THIN blue envelope imprinted with the words *PAR AVION* arrived at the Ashby House. Above a drawing of an airplane flying out of clouds, images of bright blue magic carpets patterned with intertwined indecipherable script adorned the letter's stamps. Inside the envelope I found a piece of lightweight stationary typed and dated September 6, 1969. The return address read:

Alger
Algeria
Africa
At Large
Off the Pigs

Underneath the address I found this salutation:

Stew and Gumbo
Gumbo Stew
Jerry and Crew
Power to the Wrecking Crew!

I knew Jerry had asked Eldridge to write an introduction to *Do It!*—a book for young people about our Yippie counter-cultural revolution, a book now in the process of being published. Eldridge had told Jerry he would be honored to write an introduction.

Eldridge was about to leave Algeria to tour North Korea with a group of mostly white American activists, but, he wrote, "When I get back to Algeria, I can write the thing. So, Gumbo, plan like that and come on over heah. Let's get our shit across!"

The letter had three signatures, Eldridge, Kathleen and, in print two inches high with the "C" facing backwards, their three-month old baby, Maceo.

> *(BLANK) had occasion to be in the residence occupied by ALBERT, HEMBLEN and HAYDEN in Berkeley. At approximately 12:30 A.M. a telephone call was received at the residence which originated from Algiers, Algeria. The caller was reported to be KATHLEEN CLEAVER. Both ALBERT and HEMBLEN talked to KATHLEEN CLEAVER. (BLACKED OUT) gave the impression that ALBERT and HEMBLEN intended to travel to Algiers and were going to bring ELDRIDGE CLEAVER back to the United States via a secret route.*

That telephone call was real. An FBI informant claims to have overheard Stew and me confirm with Kathleen that yes, we'd travel to Algiers to meet with Eldridge. But our so-called "plot" to bring Eldridge back to the United States by a secret route was totally fake news—concocted by BLANK, an unidentified individual, either in the Ashby house or listening in on our landline. Either way, I give that unidentified FBI informant credit—their tale was as exaggerated and as imaginative a story as any Yippie could invent.

* * *

I DID NOT KNOW WHAT TO expect when Stew and I arrived in Algeria in October 1969, but Algeria was not what I expected. Eldridge and Kathleen now lived in Pointe Pescade, a seacoast town outside the city of Algiers proper. The apartment's balcony offered me a phantasmagorical view of cobblestone streets and narrow alleys lined with whitewashed plaster buildings, most with sloped, red tile roofs. Out of an occasional spire that resembled a golden tulip bulb I'd hear muezzins chant their calls to prayer. I felt at first as if I'd jumped into a childhood fairy tale; I was so excited by this new adventure that I, a perpetual optimist, expected only happy endings.

"Why here? Why Algeria?" I asked Eldridge after Stew and I had settled into the Cleavers's apartment. We were seated in Eldridge's office; it was furnished with a ramshackle desk, a green metal file cabinet, stacks of Panther papers, an old TV set that was never on, and a telephone that rarely rang.

"We're in Africa, Gumbo," Eldridge explained; then, as was his way, he went on: "I relate to African struggles against colonialism. Besides, there's all kind of embassies here. Vietnam, Korea. I'm gonna set up an international branch of the Black Panther Party, right here, in Algiers. To establish diplomatic relations, Panthers and the Algerian government—ya dig? As soon as that mutha-fuckin' bureaucrat quits stalling and gets his act together."

I recall Kathleen standing in a tiny yellow kitchen, coating slices of fresh eggplant with egg, flour, cornmeal, paprika, and salt, then gently sautéing them. I named these yummy morsels "Eggplant Kathleen Cleaver style." On occasion, Kathleen and I ventured out on errands into the streets of Point Pescade, and left their son Maceo, born in Algeria and by then three months old, with Stew and Eldridge. On more than one such occasion, bare-foot Algerian boys in baggy pants, their chests too young for hair, followed us, taunting us with incomprehensible yells. We'd hurry to a bus stop. Small stones clattered at our feet.

"Kathleen, what the fuck?"

Kathleen chuckled without warmth.

"It happens when I go out. Maybe because I'm a woman. Maybe it's my hair. I don't want to cover it," Kathleen said, unconsciously patting down her bronze Afro that glistened in the sun. "This is a poor community. Isolated. Berbers. They're Algeria's original people, you know? Maybe they're suspicious of strangers. Or of Black people. I just don't know."

"It's very Frantz Fanon," Judy the Sociology Ph.D. replied, relying on abstract rhetoric to mask her own discomfort. "The oppressed colonial subject taking their anger out on another oppressed group."

Kathleen looked down the road as if by force of will she could summon a bus.

"Maybe things will get better when the Panthers get diplomatic recognition from the Algerian government," Kathleen remarked, but at that moment I didn't pick up much optimism in her voice.

* * *

ELDRIDGE STALLED ON WRITING JERRY'S INTRODUCTION.

Two months before Eldridge invited us to Algiers, he'd achieved a resounding success—or so he said. He and Panther comrades had attracted thousands of visitors to their Panther Party booth at the 1969 Pan-African Cultural Festival in Algiers— in which photos of Huey in his rattan chair, Emory Douglas's art, and full-size Eldridge portraits dominated. But by the time Stew and I arrived in Algiers, it seemed to me that exile wasn't doing Eldridge much good. He was not the jocular, joking Eldridge of Berkeley days. He seemed distracted, moody, and dependent on the goodwill of an Algerian government he needed but was not familiar with. He'd abandon Stew and me inside the apartment for what he said were private meetings—made necessary, I believe, by his request that the Algerian government give full diplomatic recognition to an International Section of the Black Panther Party. I didn't expect Eldridge to explain his frequent absences to us, but, lacking any explanation, I got annoyed. My predominant memory is of being bored—Stew and I didn't venture much outside the confines of the apartment to explore cobblestone streets and narrow alleys on our own. I'd nap on a mattress or stare at the single window high up on our bedroom's ceiling. Stew and I were not in jail, but we did not feel exactly at liberty either.

Ultimately, Eldridge's quest for Party recognition from the Algerian government succeeded—until it did not.

One morning Eldridge announced, "We're gonna split this crib. Go to the Kasbah. I've arranged a private screening of *The Battle of Algiers*. I want you to meet someone. Her name's Elaine Klein."

Kasbah is an Arabic word for market. Most Middle Eastern towns and cities have one, but the Algiers Kasbah looked so archetypical and mythic any uneasiness I previously had dissipated. Eldridge, Stew, and I walked into an alley where apartments with latticework fronts shaped like star fruit circled a stone fountain—without water. In an adjoining alley, white-robed vendors squatted in cubbyholes which gave off a smell of tempting, broiling meat. An array of random stacks of stuff surrounded each vendor—rose, red, and blue carpets of varying sizes topped by intricately woven baskets were next to brown ceramic pots; knives with two-edged blades sat next to brass teapots inlaid with copper spouts, from which hung silver necklaces and earrings that tinkled when I picked them up.

I listened as an atonal *hmmmmmm* repeated itself, emerging from a reed flute held by a bearded man who sat cross-legged on a carpet. I found his offerings unique: stacks of what looked to me like transparent surgical masks made of muslin in delicate shades of white, light green, blue, pink, and yellow. Adorned with intricate borders made of lace, they were worn, I learned, by Muslim women who eschewed full dress burkas. I bought a stack of face masks as gifts for my women's group to personify what I considered the oppression of Muslim women. I was part right; I'd also discover that face veils could symbolize women's resistance—Algeria's colonial French occupiers tormented Muslim women by forcing them to be photographed with faces bare.

Stew bought three knives at an adjoining stall. Each had a handle of polished bone and, I'd discover, an almost invisible metal button which, when I pressed it, shot out a vicious two-edged pointed silver blade. One knife was for me, one for him; the third we'd give to Tom Hayden. On our way home, Stew hid the knives in his luggage. They disappeared. It didn't matter. Tom, fundamentally a pragmatist and by then on trial as one of the Chicago 8, would have refused our gift anyway.

A woman who had to be Elaine Klein descended stone steps in front of me. She was followed by a foursome of young, giggling Algerian women in skirts and blouses, faces uncovered. This was not unusual; Western dress was deemed by many as acceptable for women students in Algeria fifty years ago. Elaine guided Eldridge, Stew, and me up a curved black metal staircase. Elaine was a handsome, dark haired, white American woman, the respected Panther liaison to the Algerian government and, as Eldridge had confided to Stew, lover of the late, great psychoanalyst, my hero Frantz Fanon.

"Ah yes, Elaine Klein," Stew would stroke his beard and say when he and I occasionally reminisced about Algeria. "Elaine Klein was Frantz Fanon's mistress."

Had I known this when I met her, Elaine would have been a superhero in my eyes. But I never learned if this was true or just another Eldridge Cleaver tale.

In an ancient screening room, Elaine signaled an invisible projectionist and the epic *Battle of Algiers* began. At the movie's end, after enduring torture at the hands of French Colonel Mathieu, I, Judy Gumbo, now a selfless freedom fighter against French colonialism, emerged from the screening room heroic and unbowed. I snuck quickly through the curved doorway of a battered white building, took two red sticks of dynamite out of my bag, and planted my bomb for freedom inside the building's battered walls. I heard a loud, sharp *bang*. Startled, I faded out of cinematic dreamscape to see, directly in front of me, that same, actual curved doorway and white building that I had just viewed onscreen.

I chose my heroes from the freedom movements I admired, but I understood by then that I was no Black Panther. Nor was I a dark-eyed woman fighter from *The Battle of Algiers*, determined to adopt the violence Fanon made clear was imperative to overthrow the violence perpetrated by Algeria's French colonizers. The Algerian revolution was theirs to fight, not mine. For all my attraction to extremism, for all my passion to oppose evildoers by any means necessary, our satirical, humorous, and hopefully peaceful Yippie Revolution for the Hell of It had to be a revolution of our own.

* * *

IT TOOK THREE WEEKS BEFORE ELDRIDGE lit a joint the size of a Cuban cigar and sat down at his black Underwood office typewriter to write his introduction to *Do It!* He finished in two nights. I read it after Stew and I boarded a four engine Air Algérie plane that ferried us on to Paris. Eldridge wrote:

> *I can unite with Jerry Rubin around a marijuana cigarette, around some good music, around being cool, around a profound contempt for pigs, and around the need for moving to change the world in which we live. I can unite with Jerry around hatred of pig judges, around hatred of capitalism, around the total desire to smash what is now the social order in the United States of Amerika. Around the dream of building something new and free upon the ruins.*

I found what Eldridge wrote a better, more sophisticated, and nuanced version of our Yippie/Panther pact. I'm not a patient person; I insist on choosing for myself and not having my choices dictated by others. By the time Stew and I left Algiers, the boredom I'd experienced there had tried my patience. Stew was an easy target of opportunity. I poked him hard in his bicep, and said,

"Eldridge says he wants to smash the social order and build something new and free upon the ruins, right? If we're so new and free like Eldridge says, why couldn't we get out of there quicker?"

Stew appeared amazed at my ingratitude. As travelers will to keep their memories fresh, Stew reeled off a list of our accomplishments: we'd hung out with Eldridge and Kathleen, we'd visited the Kasbah, we got to know Elaine Klein, we'd seen *Battle of Algiers.*

"We spent time in Algeria, for chrissake!"

I heard in the tone of his voice that a Stewie temper tantrum was starting up.

"How can you be critical of such a stellar international adventure? Eldridge Cleaver does what he wants when he wants. You know that, Gumbo."

"Stew—you're too passive when it comes to your friends. You care about Eldridge and Jerry more than me."

"Quit complaining. We're outta there now. Leave me alone."

"Fuck you too," I muttered.

Our plane from Algiers arrived late at Paris's Orly Airport. We were close to missing our flight to the States. As I ran past a kiosk piled with newspapers, Stew jogging heavily behind me, I glimpsed a headline: *Panthère Enchaine.* I stopped so abruptly Stew almost ran me down. I recognized the Black man gagged and chained in the sketch above the paper's fold. It was Bobby.

CHAPTER 13:
THE GREAT CHICAGO 8 CONSPIRACY TRIAL

Repressive, authoritarian regimes put resisters on trial in order to control dissent. The Chicago Conspiracy Trial of 1969–70, also known as The Trial of the Chicago 8, or the Chicago 7, achieved a level of notoriety in 1969 to match that of two of my favorite anarchists Sacco and Vanzetti in the 1920s, or my parents' communist heroes Ethel and Julius Rosenberg in the 1950s. In Chicago, Black Panther Chairperson Bobby Seale plus Jerry Rubin, Abbie Hoffman, Dave Dellinger, Rennie Davis, Tom Hayden, John Froines, and Lee Weiner each faced ten years in prison for conspiracy to incite a riot the previous summer in Chicago, and for crossing state lines to incite that riot.

I thought the charges were ridiculous. Chicago cops had been the ones to riot during the summer of 1968, not us.

Here's my brief, highly personal summary of what I missed in that month before Stew and I arrived at the Trial of the Chicago 8. It was an American moment that filmmakers, authors, and journalists would turn into legend.

Jerry and Abbie nicknamed the Trial judge "Mr. Magoo"—a Yippie send up of the short, grumpy old-man cartoon character Judge Hoffman physically resembled. Only his bald head, shaped like an egg, poked over his judge's podium. But this Hoffman—unlike his namesake Abbie—was no Yippie; he possessed an affect and a temperament more intolerant and racist than I'd ever seen in 1960s cartoons.

Charles Garry, Bobby's attorney and longtime friend of Bobby, Stew, and me, was in a San Francisco hospital for gall bladder surgery. He could not attend the Trial. Hearing that, Bobby demanded he be allowed to represent himself. As was his right. The judge cruelly denied the Panther leader's request. Led by Bobby and backed by defendants and lawyers, a shouting war erupted in the courtroom until an irritated judge glared down at the defendant's table, and, directing his wrath at the leader of the Black Panther Party, intoned; "The Court has a right to gag you."

To which Bobby had retorted, "Gagged? I am being railroaded already!"

Next day, Bobby pointed to portraits of America's Founding Fathers that hung on a dark wood wall behind the judge's chair.

He declared, "What can happen to me more than what Benjamin Franklin and George Washington did to Black people in slavery? What can happen to me more than that?'

Marshal after uniformed marshal formed a phalanx around Bobby. Black and white, each the size of a construction worker, marshals handcuffed Bobby to a metal chair.

"I demand my constitutional right to represent myself," Bobby yelled as Franklin and Washington scowled down at such unseemly chaos, until the Judge announced, "Take that defendant into the room in there and deal with him as he should be dealt with."

When Bobby emerged, he was chained to his chair, unable to move his hands. Marshals had tightened pressure bandages around Bobby's head and forced gauze covered by a cloth gag into Bobby's mouth. Rennie Davis told me later he saw blood running down one side of Bobby's cheek. Other defendants heard only a muffled "*mmh, mmmh, mmmm.*"

"Bobby is being tortured," Rennie shouted at the same time that Tom Hayden screamed, "The marshals are going to beat Bobby."

"This is not a courtroom," Abbie yelled, comparing Bobby being tortured to a Chicago-style Nazi gas chamber. In a phrase that became a classic to describe the trial, Abbie yelled, "It's a neon oven."

Stomping, screaming spectators rose to their feet. William Kunstler, the defendant's lead attorney, demanded a mistrial. The judge refused, then severed Bobby's case. Bobby was gone. With that, the Show Trial of my generation became both famous and known by its more racist name—The Trial of the Chicago 7.

* * *

STEW AND I LANDED IN NEW York City at the end of the first week in November 1969. I carried in my purse Eldridge's new introduction to Jerry's book *Do It!* One week later, Stew and I showed up in Chicago at Nancy and Jerry's apartment. As the FBI reported, it was November 15, 1969.

I handed Eldridge's introduction to Jerry. The speed with which he flipped through the pages then discarded them on top of a pile of newspapers astonished me. Why, I asked myself, had I languished for three weeks in Algeria for such little appreciation? Not yet familiar with the stress Jerry and the defendants suffered daily in Judge Hoffman's courtroom, I offered Jerry what I thought of as support. I commented without forethought:

"Having hair that short sure must be hard on you."

At age 26, I had trouble expressing empathy—a trait for which I blamed my alcoholic mother, rather than taking responsibility for myself. Before the trial began, Bobby and Jerry had been incarcerated in California correctional facilities to ensure they showed up. Guards had shorn Jerry's hair when he was imprisoned; Jerry now looked to me like a diminutive Samson post-Delilah. His long curly hair that once attracted mainstream media attention was now shaved into a buzz cut, U.S. army style. Very, I thought, un-Jerry-like. To have short hair in 1969 was a sore point for any male counter-culturalist—and I had drawn attention to that hair. With some justification, Jerry took my words as disapproval from a woman who, at least in Jerry's mind, had intruded on his relationship with Stew, his best male buddy. Jerry spoke only to Stew.

"Stew—remember that biker? My bodyguard? His real name's Bob Pierson. BOB PIERSON! He's a pig. He testified against me. In the courtroom! All clean-shaven and everything, with a suit and tie. How could I have been such an idiot?"

I remembered Pierson for his aviator sunglasses, black T-shirt, and black hunter's vest. Pierson made me queasy. He'd shadowed Stew and me in Lincoln Park, he'd accompanied us to that Superman-style phone booth in Chicago's Old Town after I suggested we invite Eldridge to speak in Lincoln Park, and Bobby Seale had shown up instead. I decided I'd been an idiot as well—I'd had suspicions about Pierson at the time but deferred to Stew and Jerry; I'd assumed, without cause, that guys were better at identifying a police agent than I was.

"But Pierson did say you gave Jerry and me the cans of paint, and it was Jerry, not you, who threw the paint at the police car," Nancy interjected.

I was dumbfounded. Then outraged. That was *my* tiny bottle of paint, *my* throw that pinged the cop car, I was the one who'd aimed true and hit my enemy with a tiny jar of tempera paint as my only weapon! Jerry's ignoring me when I arrived felt like a minor insult compared to Pierson giving away my moment of glory! Worse than that, Pierson claimed Jerry's missile had *missed* the cop car, but in real life I had hit it! Why, I asked myself, is the good stuff always given to the guys and women's achievements diminished? Worst of all, that evil pig Robert Pierson had appropriated my successful act of resistance and turned it into a failure! By now, in my life, I've forgiven many people, but never will I absolve that lying undercover asshole, that pig Robert Pierson.

When Stew and I made love that night on yet another lumpy mattress in yet another Nancy and Jerry apartment, I could not come. I repressed my orgasm to suppress my envy. I whined to Stew that Robert Pierson, greasy black-haired pig informant that he was, had deprived me of my triumph. I also confessed to Stew that I felt guilty about Bobby getting indicted. I asked Stew if my great idea to invite Eldridge to speak in Lincoln Park had created a ripple in the cosmos that, after seven months, had offered President Nixon's Justice Department an opportunity to indict Bobby.

Stew sighed, removing his hand from my crotch.

"So, you threw some paint at the cop car? So what? Don't take it personally, Judy. Conspiracy means attributing acts to the defendants that other people did. That's why Pierson gave your throw to Jerry. No other reason. And Bobby? Bobby didn't come to Chicago because of you. He came to show solidarity with Fred Hampton and striking Black bus drivers. And the Chicago Panthers. Don't get grandiose, Gumbo. Who do you think you are anyway? You're not that important."

"Quit yelling at me." I yelled back. "You're no hot shit either."

Unable to extract myself from such an avalanche of rejection, I scrunched myself into a fetal position and, defeated, fell asleep.

* * *

By Monday, November 17, 1969, I felt more like the confident Judy Gumbo I knew I was. Nancy, Jerry, Stew, and I walked into Chicago's gleaming steel and glass Federal Courthouse. By then, Stew had become a pale and coughing macho man. He'd been diagnosed with walking pneumonia by a movement doctor, but as men can do when it comes to seeking medical attention, refused to stay at home even though his blond curls stuck to his feverish forehead. I did not feel especially sympathetic. I resented being expected to be Stew's nurse—especially if it took me out of the action. But guilt prevailed and I complied.

An elevator whisked the four of us to the building's twenty-third floor. Inside a wood-paneled courtroom, a high-backed chair of black leather rose behind a judge's podium. I saw marshals, all males, all Black men, lining the room in pairs. Portraits of slave-owners Thomas Jefferson, George Washington, and Benjamin Franklin stared at me from the appropriately dark walls of Judge Julius Hoffman's courtroom.

As if a hippie bride was marrying a Republican groom, marshals escorted spectators to opposite sides of the courtroom. Stew, Nancy, and I were ushered to our right, while Jerry shoved his way to a nearby table buried in random stacks of newspapers, books, and legal briefs. I was surprised to find myself seated front and center in a second row of wooden benches immediately behind a row of reporters and sketch artists.

In the game of who got to scale the highest peak of Yippiedom, Jerry had already claimed he'd won the Academy Award of Protest. As an unindicted co-conspirator, one of fifteen men and two women, Stew had made the "B" list. As Stew's girlfriend, I hadn't even placed. Still, my status as the partner of an unindicted co-conspirator did come with perks—especially my privileged perch from which I'd view the Trial of the Chicago 8.

The way you dress can signal identification with a cause. At first glance, the Trial defendants and their lawyers looked like movie actors costumed to showcase their ideals and reassure the jury of their peaceful intent. The defendants' lead lawyer was Bill Kunstler, Stew's and my friend from Liberty House days, who the media often referred to as "brilliant and fiery." Bill's light-gray worsted suit made him appear mainstream, but with sideburns long enough to make Elvis Presley proud. A younger, more methodical but equally brilliant (and hot in the eyes of many) attorney Leonard Weinglass, second in command, wore multi-colored paisley ties, as if to show Len's approval, but in moderation, of the counter-culture. In the front row immediately behind the lawyers sat a Black woman named Micki Leaner, an impeccably dressed law student who was Bill and Lenny's legal assistant—not Chicago Panther leader Fred Hampton as portrayed in Aaron Sorkin's 2020 movie Chicago 7. When I told Micki about this, she said, "What an honor having Chairman Fred as a stand-in for me at the defense table." Micki also said that Fred Hampton, as the head of the Chicago Panther chapter, would have been the one to OK her role at Bobby's side at the trial.

At the defendants' table, the houndstooth jacket worn by peace activist Dave Dellinger, the oldest of the defendants, evoked the image of a serious professor, while Tom Hayden's blue denim shirt turned him into a Southern civil rights worker. Jerry had dressed for court in his bee-like yellow long-sleeved T-shirt. He'd covered his cropped hair with a black wig, held in place by a head-band of red, white, and yellow beads. Abbie exuded masculine Yippie-ism in his brown velvet shirt with long sleeves and zipper open to reveal sexy chest hair. Rennie Davis smiled his 1000-watt smile while the two lesser-known defendants, John Froines and Lee Weiner, appeared distracted and concerned. Women with multicolored knit scarves and long-haired men in green Army surplus jackets who'd lined up since dawn outside the Federal Building cuddled next to each other in the three last rows on the right side of the courtroom—like young puppies seeking warmth.

Supporters of the prosecution were seated to my left, men in suits and women wearing pastel sweaters or red wool dresses and high heels: they sat closest to an elevated jury box. On a sturdy wooden table in front of them, law books neatly stacked and papers I assumed were legal briefs occupied the attention of two men, one gray haired, the other younger, both dressed in bespoke suits. In front of them a grey-haired female court reporter bent over what looked to me like a small black cash register. In the back row on the prosecution's side, old men in white shirts and wrinkled black suits too large for their skeletal frames nodded off to sleep. Nancy whispered Abbie's name for them: courtroom buzzards.

* * *

AFTER COURT STEW AND I, PLUS a passel of defendants, lawyers, legal assistants, reporters, celebrities, and hangers-on tromped through swirling snow a block and a half down Jackson Street to the Conspiracy Trial office. Two days before Thanksgiving, 1969, and without informing me beforehand, Bill Kunstler announced to anyone who cared that he'd given me a new title: Conspiracy Trial Office Manager.

I was initially delighted at my new title, but my job coordinating classified sex ads at the *Berkeley Barb* had not prepared me for a chaotic legal office at a Trial that would become world-famous. Rotary phones continually rang, celebrity onlookers lolled between gray metal desks, and a red and black poster of Cuban rebel hero Che Guevara gazed down as if he alone could impose order on such chaos. Unfortunately for me, I found everyone I'd been tasked to manage to be genetically unmanageable. The defendants, their lawyers, and their friends ignored me; no one did what I politely requested but did not demand. After a few short weeks, a strait-laced, unpretentious white man named Bob Lamb took over my position. I was relegated to traditional women's work; I answered phones and handed out mail.

Both annoyed and relieved, I volunteered to take on a task with which I was familiar. At the end of court each day, Bill and Lenny received one copy of that day's trial transcript. In a time before Copy Central or computers, I'd type every word from that day's Trial transcript onto a waxy, green sheet called a stencil, then attach the stencil onto a round black drum of a primitive but useful printing device known as a mimeograph machine. The mimeo forced ink through the letters on the stencil I'd just typed and onto sheets of paper to emerge as printed transcript. If I banged too hard on the typewriter keys while I typed, the mimeo printed out black blobs in place especially of the letters "O" and "R," as if I'd squished tiny bugs onto the paper. I'd collate my pages which gave off a rancid smell of duplicating fluid, then use my ink-stained hands to staple the pages into packets. I'd snail-mail my efforts to every underground and mainstream media outlet I could locate across America and in Europe.

Karl Marx famously said that philosophers have only interpreted the world—the point, however, is to change it. I did office work most often relegated to women. But I provided global media with daily transcripts from the Trial of the Chicago 8, and our Yippie defense strategy to turn the Trial into a vivid countercultural spectacle kept the Trial in national and international news. The Trial's injustices could not be ignored. In addition to those mainstream reporters and sketch artists who sat in front of me in the courtroom's first row, my word-for-word transcriptions of the daily drama of the Trial kept global media enthralled. She who disseminates history can rule worlds.

* * *

ON DECEMBER 1, 1969, *LIFE MAGAZINE* published a front-page full color expose showing bodies of Vietnamese civilians and children lying in a ditch, massacred at My Lai by U.S. Army soldiers under the command of Lt. William Calley. Three days later, on Stew's 30th birthday, Nancy and Jerry's telephone rang. Seconds after that Jerry, white faced and breathless, barged into Stew's and my bedroom, bellowing that we had to get up.

"Fred Hampton's dead! Mark Clark too! Chicago cops shot them!"

I remembered Fred Hampton. I'd watched him, the 21-year-old leader of the Chicago Black Panthers, act as Bobby's bodyguard the previous summer for his speech in Chicago's Lincoln Park. A vigilant FBI agent had recorded Bobby's speech and given it to Bobby's prosecutors at the Trial. What follows is a portion of that recording:

The lynching Lyndon Baines Johnsons, the fat pig Humphreys,
the jive double-lip-talkin' Nixons send out their racist, scurvy,
rotten pigs to occupy the people, to occupy the community, just
the way they have this here park occupied. Black people, we seem
to be lost in a world of white, racist, decadent America.

Bobby had spoken as I knew he would: that any oppressed person—especially but not limited to people of color—had a right and a duty to defend themselves against police attack. Sixteen months later, Chicago cops did not give Fred Hampton, or Hampton's deputy, Mark Clark—that chance. Both men were murdered by Chicago cops as they slept in their beds.

Nancy, Jerry, Stew, and I departed for Hampton's memorial. Reluctant Nurse Judy, freaked out and punitive, admonished Stew, still coughing and wheezing, to stay in bed. Stew refused.

"I'll die with my boots on," he insisted.

We arrived at a red brick church to find ourselves on the edge of a colossal, primarily Black crowd. Stew shivered in his too-thin jacket. A single loudspeaker distorted speakers' words. Between gaps in an electronic buzz, I heard Bobby Rush, Deputy Minister of Defense of the Chicago Black Panther Party and later Congressman from Illinois declare,

"Black people will be free or we will level the earth in our attempts to be free. We want liberty or death. There is no other way out."

Two days after Hampton's funeral, white Hells Angels stomped an eighteen-year-old Black man to death at a Rolling Stones concert in Altamont, California.

I have friends who say that, for them, these two racially charged and contiguous murders of Black men signaled the end of the 1960s. For me, Stew's birthday, December 4, 1969 personified our resistance. It marked the moment I grasped the real meaning of "white privilege": White Yippies are tear-gassed, clubbed, and put on trial; Black Panthers are chained, gagged, and assassinated.

It took thirty years for the City of Chicago to settle with the Hampton family, which they eventually did for several million dollars, based on information that FBI Director Hoover and Chicago Mayor Richard Daley had done their part to bring about those murders.

* * *

AT THE CONSPIRACY TRIAL, A CULTURE war erupted over defense strategy. I was excluded from attorney meetings, but Stew was not. Sidelined, I'd learn the outcome secondhand. Abbie, Jerry, and to a lesser extent Lee Weiner argued for a counter-cultural defense: that the Conspirators ought to put on a courtroom spectacle that ridiculed the American system of "in-justice." Bill Kuntsler tended to agree. Tom, John Froines, and Len Weinglass argued for a traditional, more legalistic defense. At first each side viewed the other as the problem and their side as the solution—until pacifist Dave, peace activist Rennie and, I'm proud to say, mediator Stew brokered truces. By then, Abbie had abandoned his fight with Jerry over Pigasus to engage in a more consequential, personal battle with Tom—the theatrical vs. the serious. This dialectic played itself out in terms of which wit-nesses the defendants called to testify. In the end, both sides won.

From my privileged seat, I ran an emotional gamut—despair to joy, anger to exhilaration—as Bill and Lenny called 100 wit-nesses to the stand: cops, psychologists, and peace activists, poets and politicians, investigators and journalists. I watched promi-nent writers William Styron and Norman Mailer testify, as well as Black comedian Dick Gregory, now serious. I felt proud to be a (dis)loyal subject of her Majesty when the Member of Parliament, who I'd seen on TV get thrown down, maced, and then arrested, testified on the defendants' behalf in her impeccable British accent. I studied former U.S. Attorney General Ramsey Clark as he attempted to tell the judge that he had refused to indict those on trial because, in his legal opinion, the charges were unwarranted. The judge denied a defense request to hear from Ramsey Clark. And I certainly paid attention to Reverend Jessie Jackson when he eviscerated American racism.

When Judy Collins sang, "Where have all the flowers gone?" her voice as sweet as dark cane syrup, I almost cried. But when Tim Leary, still smiley, still creepy, took the stand, I could tell he was that same self-centered sexist I'd encountered in my living room. He had not changed.

I also witnessed first-hand how right-wing prosecutors try to intimidate someone who opposes them, no matter how renowned. The world-famous gay poet Allen Ginsberg relaxed me as he came close to chanting in that same melodic out-breath I'd overheard in Lincoln Park. "Ten people humming *Ommmmm* can calm one hundred. One hundred people humming *Ommmmm* can regulate the metabolism of a thousand. A thousand bodies vibrating can immobilize an entire downtown Chicago street full of scared humans, uniformed or naked," Ginsberg claimed. After he spoke, lead prosecutor Thomas Foran insisted that Ginsberg explain just how "intimate" a friend he was with Abbie and Jerry. To prove his point, Foran demanded that Ginsberg read to the jury his poem "The Night Apple," which focuses on the smells and functions of a sexually explicit wet dream.

I was both sad and angry when I watched original Yippie Paul Krassner melt down on the witness stand, having ingested 300 micrograms of LSD before he testified. Paul barely got his words out; his brain had devolved into a science experiment. Bill had to cut his testimony short. Paul stumbled off the stand. Paul's testimony was no Yippie joke—it ignored the fact that defendants and attorneys all faced years of jail time. It took Abbie close to a year to forgive him.

At midnight on Tuesday, December 23, 1969, young people began to line up outside the cold glass and concrete of Chicago's

Federal Building as if waiting for a rock star. Abbie was scheduled to testify this day. By 5 a.m., young Yippies in the courtroom line had been arrested for violating Chicago's curfew law.

Under portraits of former American patriots who, thanks to Bobby being chained and gagged, were no longer venerated at least by progressives, radicals, and Yippies, Len Weinglass began to question Abbie—a true American patriot of my generation.

"Will you please identify yourself for the record?"

"My name is Abbie. I am an orphan of America."

"And where do you reside?"

"I live in Woodstock Nation."

"Will you tell the Court and jury where it is?"

"It is a nation of alienated young people. We carry it around with us as a state of mind in the same way the Sioux Indians carried the Sioux Nation around with them."

Abbie went on with, essentially, his platform for a New Yippie Nation which was, he said, "dedicated to cooperation versus competition, to the idea that people should have better means of exchange than property or money, that there should be some other basis for human interaction. It is a nation dedicated to . . ."

I could tell by the frown on Judge Hoffman's face that he was about to interrupt. I was not surprised; I had watched the Judge bully defense witness after defense witness but be polite and deferential to any witness called by the prosecution. In his squeaky Mr. Magoo voice, Judge Hoffman asked Abbie where Woodstock Nation was located.

"Just where it is. That is all."

"It is in my mind," Abbie responded. "In the mind of myself and my brothers and sisters. It does not consist of property or material but, rather, of ideas and certain values. We believe in a society . . ."

"No," the Judge, an obstinate literalist, interrupted yet again. "We want the place of residence, if you have one, a place of doing business if you have a business. Nothing about philosophy or

India, sir. Just where you live, if you have a place to live. Now you said Woodstock. In what state is Woodstock?"

"It is in the state of mind, in the mind of myself and my brothers and sisters," Abbie answered on my behalf and on behalf of every Yippie.

Perhaps it was the glare of courtroom lights, or the tension that I felt bouncing off the paneled walls, but as I sat next to Stew and listened to one powerful Hoffman interrogate another on equal terms, I recognized what was occurring: any crime that the Conspirators, I, and everyone I knew may have committed was not to sleep in Lincoln Park without a permit or march in the streets to end a hateful war. Their crime—and mine—was to oppose a conservative, narrow-minded but dominant American paradigm.

The Trial office emptied after court and on weekends. Defendants and lawyers hit the road to speak at campus rallies, cheered on by tens of thousands of students. I'd see Jerry and Abbie on TV, saturating the airwaves with permission to rebel. The defendants became American idols, singing the song of angry men. When the defendants returned to the office, their pockets bulged with bills that disappeared into collective legal and living expenses. Including Stew's and mine. The late 1960s were a prosperous time for counter-culturalists: food was abundant, lodging shared. It was easy for me and hangers-on to attend the Trial and live with little income.

One such hanger-on was a longhaired, long-bodied transient named Jurgen who arrived at the Trial office from Norway and never left. Alice Hogue, a local luminary and society wife of the editor of the *Chicago Sun Times,* would pal around. Movie stars made their pilgrimage—including Dustin Hoffman, Jon Voight, and Nicholas Ray, director of the classic 1950s film *Rebel Without a Cause.* I also heard consistent rumors that groupies offered sex: that Abbie and Bill, to use the vernacular of the time, "took advantage" of women. A frown rarely left Anita's face. She did not speak to me. I encountered Nancy rarely.

* * *

After a brief recess for Christmas, Abbie resumed his testimony.

Richard Schultz, the younger prosecutor, asked, "Now, the first person you saw bleeding in Chicago during the Convention was Stew Albert, isn't that right?"

"That's right."

"By the way, Albert is one of Jerry Rubin's closest friends, is he not, to your knowledge?"

"Yes. He's right in the courtroom here too. Still has the scars."

I glowed as Abbie directed his big-toothed smile at Stew. Indicted or not, secondary status or no, I felt proud Abbie gave Stew his due.

Then Prosecutor Schultz asked, "You and Albert, Mr. Hoffman, were united in Chicago in your determination to smash the system by using any means at your disposal, isn't that right?"

"Did I write that?"

"No, did you have that thought?"

"That thought? Is a thought like a dream? If I dreamed to smash the system, that's a thought. Yes, I had that thought."

Abbie's answer to Prosecutor Schultz's question clarified everything: an Orwellian U.S. government, under the direction of President Richard Nixon, had launched the Conspiracy Trial to target Yippies and the anti-war movement based not just on what we wrote or said or even what we did—but on what we thought.

High school graduation, Harbord Collegiate Institute, Toronto, late 1950s.

Above: Stew Albert and the author, initial romance in the Berkeley Barb *office, Spring 1969. Right: The Kathleen Cleaver I met in 1968.*

*Top: Stew Albert,
Abbie Hoffman,
and Jerry Rubin.
Left: Stew leading
Pigasus, Chicago, 1968.*

Above: Second Yippie convention, New York, 1969 (Author is in the fur hat.). Right: Stew Albert for Sherrif, 1970.

On the front cover of the Berkeley Tribe, *1970.*

Do Xuan Oanh, Vietnamese poet and diplomat.

Photo by Judy Gumbo

Top: Meeting Russian Hippies in Moscow 1970.
Bottom: From left: Genie Plamondon, Nancy Kurshan, and
Judy Gumbo outside the U.S. Embassy in Moscow on their way
back from Vietnam, June 1970.

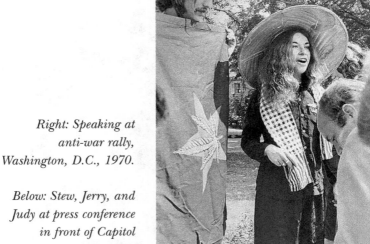

Right: Speaking at anti-war rally, Washington, D.C., 1970.

Below: Stew, Jerry, and Judy at press conference in front of Capitol May 1971.

Special Mayday Issue

QUICKSILVER TIMES

VOLUME III, NUMBER 7   APRIL 14-27, 1971   WASHINGTON, D.C.   25¢ IN TOWN, 35¢ OUT OF TOWN

Women attack Pentagon

Judy Gumbo and Linda Evans at Mayday.
Washington, D.C., 1971

Top: Judy and Stew at their Catskill cabin, Winter, 1974. Right: William Kunstler, Stew, and Judy after finding an FBI tracking device, 1975.

Judy and Stew at wedding, Beaverland Estate, near Woodstock, NY, Mayday, 1977 (with Jerry Rubin, behind).

Jessica (child), Stew Albert, Judy Gumbo, and Abbie Hoffman,
family photo, 1980.

All Photos © Copyright Judy Gumbo Albert, personal archives

CHAPTER 14:
FREE OUR SISTERS, FREE OURSELVES

THE TRIAL RECESSED OVER CHRISTMAS, 1969. Stew and I left town. We flew youth fare back to Berkeley.

The lure of fame is catching. I was not immune. In Berkeley, I achieved my own fifteen minutes of fame—I became a poster person for women's self-defense at a time when such classes were forbidden to women on the Berkeley campus. The January 16–23, 1970 edition of the *Berkeley Tribe* featured a front page cover photo of me, dressed in a white karate-gi, knees bent, my feet wide apart, my peasant calves a mat of liberated leg hair to let the world know I, a free woman, rejected mainstream standards of beauty. My right fist extends in front of me, I punch with "two big knuckles" as my karate instructor advised, to smash whatever or whoever impeded me. Karl Marx wrote that revolution is rooted in changing your material conditions. My front-page photo demonstrated to the world, to me, and especially to Stew, that women could change the material conditions of our bodies. Ourselves.

My pride in making the *Tribe's* front page did not pass untainted. On that same front page, a text box appeared in the top right-hand corner above and to the right of my image. One line read, "Napoleon's Penis" and then directed readers to page two:

Several weeks ago, a Paris auction house auctioned off $72,000 worth of Napoleonic relics including a death mask and a packet of hair from various parts of Bonaparte's body. But nobody wanted to pay $40,000 for his penis, described as "a small dried-up object" in the sale catalog.

I hated that headline. It diminished my moment of glory.

Fame and notoriety often arrive together: In January 1970 I earned fifteen minutes of both. Had I known, I would have felt flattered. The FBI now awarded me a highly exalted status—*Key Activist, Priority I* on their *Security Index.* If President Nixon had instituted a national emergency, under an FBI plan that targeted me along with 11,000 others, I and the rest of us "Key Activists" would have been rounded up and incarcerated—without a trial. Luckily for me, Nixon did not. But from then on, the cover page of my FBI files looked as if a person with multiple personality disorder was sending out a bizarre wedding invitation:

JUDITH LEE HEMBLEN, AKA
JUDITH LEE CLAVIR
JUDY CLAVIR
MRS. DAVID HUGH MILNER HEMBLEN
JUDY GUMBO
"GUMBO"

I would have been flattered had FBI followed up with:

INVITES YOU TO WITNESS
THE BREAKUP OF HER RELATIONSHIP WITH
STEW 'THE SEXIST' ALBERT

* * *

SHORTLY AFTER WE RETURNED AND THE Trial had resumed, Stew again left Chicago for California to guide the *Berkeley Tribe* through a crisis. Without him, and compounded by the Trial's escalating stresses, the gender-based competition between Jerry and me erupted. Jerry issued orders or ignored me; Nancy stayed silent while I seethed. So, I left. I moved in with defense attorney Lenny Weinglass's legal team, where I first became friends with Micki Leaner, the Trial's legal assistant.

In Stew's absence, and un-coupled, I started to exaggerate Stew's flaws. Was my mild-mannered lover as insensitive as his good friends Jerry and Abbie? Had Stew absorbed that same "it's all about me" self-centeredness which came to dominate Jerry's behavior as his fear of jail closed in? By then the siren song of women's self-empowerment had arrived. I decided that all men— and especially unrepentant men like Stew, Abbie, and Jerry—were to blame for every wrong ever done to any woman throughout time. My evidence was Stew's condescending attitude toward me. Nonetheless, and despite Stew's and my increasingly frequent flare-ups, I was unwilling to relinquish my desire for the comfort of Stew's body at night or the privileges that accompanied being a partner of the mildly famous Stew Albert.

In January 1970, a clandestine message arrived at the Trial office. A delegation from America's "enemy," North Vietnam, wanted to meet the Conspiracy defendants in a town outside Montreal. For peace activists like me to meet North Vietnamese, who our movement considered heroes, was the crown jewel in the pantheon of anti-war privilege. I speculated as to motive and decided our Vietnamese visitors likely wanted to update the defendants on the War and be themselves updated on the Trial. I wondered if they'd ask for the defendants' help to repatriate American POWs, as Conspiracy Trial defendants Dave Dellinger and Rennie Davis had already done. The defendants quarreled; they fantasized about leaving the country, but crossing the Canadian border would have violated their bail. Saner lawyers prevailed. The Chicago 8 defendants did not go. I, a Canadian citizen, could—and did.

A Trial supporter named Frank Joyce accompanied me to Montreal. He was a boyhood friend of Tom Hayden's, founder of the once large but still famous radical organization Students for a Democratic Society. Frank was a white, anti-war, anti-racist working-class organizer from Detroit. Frank represented the serious, peacenik faction of the Trial defendants, while I was a Yippie counter-culturalist. My thrill at being part of the trial of my generation expanded into a greater thrill—representing Yippie interests to America's "enemy"—the heroic North Vietnamese.

In a small town outside Montreal, our Canadian host ushered us—one American, one American wanna-be (me), six Canadians, and three Vietnamese—through a hotel lobby decorated with ostentatious gold trim into a banquet room that, in its high-end cheesiness, reminded me of Niagara Falls decor of my childhood. I was the only woman present. A waiter in a white jacket sat me in a brocade chair around a formal U-shaped table set with crystal.

"What entrée do you prefer, Miss, steak or fish?"

I chose steak. Every other Westerner also ordered their personal chunk of charred red meat. The food arrived. The Vietnamese all had fish on their plates. I had, to my shame, selected the side of war-mongering carnivores when my heart lay with the fish-eaters! Our balding host stood and, in that flat Ontario cadence I'd worked so hard to overcome, he welcomed us on behalf of the Canadian Peace Committee. 475,000 American military personnel had served in Vietnam with close to 40,000 U.S. soldiers plus untold numbers of Vietnamese killed in action, or so our host made clear. We had been invited, he declared, to exchange views on what he called a disastrous international situation.

As I listened, slightly bored, it came to me that I'd abandoned indirectness, passivity, and being one step removed from the action, just like I'd discarded my cheating first husband when I found him in Toronto in bed with that other woman. Now Judy Gumbo, international border-crossing ambassador from a world-famous anti-war trial, had returned to her native land triumphant, entrusted to take greetings from the Conspirators to representatives of a country the Conspirators idolized. It felt as momentous as one could get in the anti-war movement, and made being chased and tear-gassed in Chicago the year before all the more worthwhile.

Our host ushered the leader of the Vietnamese delegation to a brocade chair next to mine. The man's gray pants, white shirt, and black hair combed back made him look as if late 1950s dress style was still in vogue. The man turned his head away as if shy, then reached out to shake my hand. He spoke his name. It consisted of two syllables that sounded so exotic I didn't dare repeat them back.

Rushing in my nervousness to get the correct words out of my mouth, I said, "My name is Judy Gumbo. I am very pleased to meet you. Jerry Rubin and Abbie Hoffman send their warmest greetings. It was too risky for them to come here. They could have had their bail revoked—or even gone to jail."

The delegation's leader replied, "These men of the Conspiracy are very precious to us. They understand U.S. administration has no business in Vietnam. Making war in my country is wrong. They help U.S. people act to put an end to such crimes."

As the offensive meat disappeared tasteless into my mouth, the delegation leader revealed that this was not the secretive, high-level, urgent diplomatic mission about which the Conspiracy defendants had fantasized. My seatmate was just doing his job: bringing thanks and gratitude from the people of Vietnam to those he considered heroes of the North American peace movement. In Vietnam, veneration of heroes extends back millennia. I was not alone in admiring the men who sat across from and beside me. Hundreds of thousands of anti-war activists like me considered the North Vietnamese and their compatriots, the National Liberation Front of South Vietnam (or Viet Cong, as the media called them) as noble Davids doing battle against the high-tech killing machine of the American Goliath. To our movement's way of thinking, the chant "Ho, Ho, Ho Chi Minh, the NLF is Gonna Win" was not wish fulfillment; it was inevitable.

The words my seatmate spoke sounded clipped and musical, as if a tiny gulp of air accompanied every diphthong. I could not help but notice the fresh scent of his hair and what I thought was his uncanny grasp of English. He stood up. I was pleased to see he was short like I am, exactly my height.

He said, "We have much to discuss. Can we meet tomorrow? For breakfast?"

I felt as if Che Guevara, the handsomest man ever to grace the stage of world revolution, had just asked me out. Except, next morning, it was an Asian Che who sat across a pink Formica table from me. The predilection I have for blonds evaporated in an instant. I have no idea what I ordered but I'm sure it wasn't steak. Suddenly our balding Peace Committee host, red and green shirted arms on his hips, appeared at the foot of our table.

"May I please speak with you a moment, comrade?" he demanded, positioning his Paul Bunyan back squarely in my face. The Vietnamese man stood. I smiled politely. The pair moved out of earshot. I giggled as our Canadian host, almost a foot taller than my Vietnamese friend, waved his arms in the air like a tartan windmill. My companion sat back down, paused, traced a line with his fingernail on the icy window next to our table then spoke as if to give me news of great import.

"Our friend came to warn me I should be cautious with Women's Lib. I thought the man to be quite rude."

We Canadians have our norms of proper social decorum. Being *rude*—except at hockey games—is not among them. Astonished at our host's behavior and that this representative of war-ravaged Vietnam understood Western jargon like "women's lib," I responded with jargon in the hope I would sound like a sophisticated diplomat.

"Perhaps his sexism is exacerbated by anti-Americanism. Anti-Americanism is a powerful current among Canadian progressives, you know."

"Perhaps our host belongs to some dogmatic and male-chauvinist institution," my new friend replied.

"Yeah, like the Canadian Communist Party," I asserted, then rebuked myself for being an idiot. In my desire to impress, I'd spoken without thinking and I'd disparaged the global communist movement of which my new friend had to be a part. With that, aspiring diplomat Judy Gumbo picked up her first lesson in diplomacy—know when to keep your mouth shut.

My companion appeared unaware of my discomfort. He looked directly at me, his black eyes sparkling. I flushed. He pulled a pen and striped green index card out of the front pocket of his shirt and made a quick sketch of a daisy, under which he wrote the words "Dieu Ly."

"Ju-dy," he said. "In Vietnamese, Judy may be pronounced as Zio-lee. In Vietnam each word has five tones, and each tone gives the word different meanings. Your name has the meaning Divine Orchid."

I was born Judy Clavir. The FBI identified me as Judy Hemblen long after I had rejected my unfaithful first husband and his hateful last name. Eldridge Cleaver, friend, best-selling author, and Black Panther Party Minister of Information, called me Gumbo, because, for Eldridge, Gumbo went with Stew. To become an independent, self-determining woman, I had renamed myself Judy Gumbo. So, there I sat, Divine Orchid Judy Gumbo, in that glorious Montreal hotel.

As my new friend and I bantered back and forth, I felt my body give off those familiar sparks. Even in that era of a new sexual freedom, I understood that to take what I was feeling any further was improbable, impossible—no, inconceivable. And inappropriate. This man was a senior member of Vietnam's diplomatic corps—and I did not even know if he was single or married. That evening, my new friend walked me to my room. I did not hesitate to ask him in. He sat next to me on my rose-colored bedspread. Our fingers touched. For an instant I, Judy Gumbo, Yippie ambassador, thrower of paint at police cars, was seized by an unaccustomed restraint.

Then, as my friend so quaintly e-mailed decades later, "Judy and I became a couple."

One week after the Montreal conference, I received this letter from Paris. It was written on thin blue stationary in all caps:

IT WAS IMPOSSIBLE FOR ME TO HAVE A QUIET NIGHT SINCE THE STORM BROKE OUT, AS IF SKY AND EARTH HAD TURNED UPSIDE DOWN. PEOPLE TALK SOME TIME ABOUT SPIRIT REMOULDING, I THINK IT'S CORRECT. LET ME SAY IT AGAIN: MIRACLE.

Storm. Earth. Sky. Miracle. My world too had been upended. After his first letter, my lover wrote to me three times in the following two weeks.

Comfort and inspiration come along with your letters.
A miracle again.

I felt no need to justify my actions or excuse myself by labeling what I had done free love. My boyfriend Stew, with his foibles and familiarity, his curly blond hair and famous friends, had simply lost the battle for my affections. I had found myself a new hero, a man who embodied the pinnacle of my ideal of what it meant to be a fighter for truth, justice, and a revolutionary way.

* * *

I RETURNED FROM MONTREAL IN LATE January, 1970. I told myself I was no hypocrite, nor did I feel remorse for having "betrayed" Stew by sleeping with my lover. Stew was close and comfortable but my lover, while distant, was heroic. For me to make love with a resistance leader from a country I and my compatriots idealized gave me a secret confidence I'd never previously known. All I had to learn, or so I thought, was how to manage this new romantic contradiction.

By Friday February 13, 1970, Stew and I were back in Chicago to hear Bill Kunstler make his closing arguments at the by now world famous Trial of the Chicago 8.

You can crucify a Jesus, you can poison a Socrates, you can hang a John Brown or Nathan Hale, you can kill a Che Guevara, you can jail a Eugene Debs or a Bobby Seale. You can assassinate John Kennedy or a Martin Luther King, but the problems remain.

Indeed they did. With my new romance as a catalyst, Stew's and my problems escalated. I recall Stew storming into our bedroom, his blue eyes emitting those Zeus-like bolts of anger only he could summon. In one hand, he waved a crinkled copy of a late January issue of the *Rat*, a New York City underground newspaper.

He yelled, "Look where your punk-ass women's liberation shit has got us now!"

To find myself on the receiving end of such misogynist verbal abuse felt as if Stew had betrayed the ideal human being I thought he was. I felt the muscles of my hands tense into a karate fist. I grabbed the newspaper from Stew's hand, almost tearing it. Former Yippie Robin Morgan had published a rant. In it, she denounced the Conspiracy defendants, the male counter-culture, environmentalists, and ultimately every man on the planet for their patriarchal domination of women. Robin blamed Abbie for ditching his first wife Shirley like any philandering movie star. She castigated Jerry for cashing in on media celebrityhood while Nancy remained unknown. She condemned Paul Krassner for joking about an instant pussy aerosol can and reeled off names of Movement women Paul had slept with. Robin ended with this slogan printed in capital letters

FREE OUR SISTERS! FREE OURSELVES!

Robin then named names of women she believed must declare *"Goodbye to All That"*—as she'd titled her rant. Robin's list included many of my friends: Kathleen Cleaver, Anita Hoffman, and Nancy Kurshan, among others. Robin also called out a woman I knew only by reputation—Valerie Solanas, who had shot the famous artist Andy Warhol for, or so a *Daily News* headline proclaimed, being too controlling. My eyes scrolled down the *Rat's* type-heavy page as if I was a search engine. Then I saw it: "Free Gumbo!" I confess—I felt relieved. Had I not made Robin's "A" list of women who needed to free ourselves, I would have wallowed in that same distress about being second tier that I'd suffered during the Conspiracy Trial.

Every woman, Robin wrote, will experience a moment of "insult so intense that she will reach up and rip off the amulet of madness she wears around her neck on a thin chain of fear." Stew's "women's liberation shit" remark was for me an amulet moment. I stood up on my mattress to give myself height equal to Stew's and, quoting Robin as my authority on all things misogynist, screamed at him.

"You see my name there? You know what that means? You're an asshole sexist pig and I need to free myself. So there!"

Then I rushed over to Stew and hugged him; I was that confused. Like Frantz Fanon wrote, I was no different from any oppressed person unwilling to admit the fundamental truth of their oppression. Despite the thrill of my new romance, I was not yet ready to do as Robin advised—to free myself.

* * *

ON FEBRUARY 18, 1970, FIVE OF the seven Conspiracy defendants—Abbie, Jerry, Dave Dellinger, Rennie Davis, and Tom Hayden—were convicted of intent to riot. They, plus Bill Kunstler and Len Weinglass, were also sentenced to up to five years for contempt of court. In 1972 the convictions would be overturned on appeal, and all contempt charges dropped.

I blended my hatred of the charges with joy about my new lover and a romantic desperation to see him again. Shortly after the verdict, I wangled an invitation to update a famous British rock star in London on the outcome of the Trial. Secretly, I was hoping for a lover's tryst across the channel in Paris where peace talks to end the war in Vietnam were being held. The rock star sat across from me at a conference table in an office that I recall was painted black. It was two months after the debacle when the Rolling Stones had played at Altamont and a young Black concertgoer was killed—but to me the rock star did not appear saddened or depressed. I know now that celebrities are trained to put on a happy face; at the time I had no way to judge the man's mental state.

Dressed in my defiant Judy Gumbo leathers, I told him, "All the defendants in the Chicago Conspiracy Trial were acquitted of conspiracy. But the jury convicted five of them—Abbie Hoffman, Jerry Rubin, Dave Dellinger, Rennie Davis, and Tom Hayden—of intent to riot."

I went on, my voice more emphatic and packed with outrage: "They, plus their two lawyers Bill Kunstler and Len Weinglass were sentenced to up to five years for contempt of court! Judge Hoffman is sending them to jail. For riot! And 175 counts of contempt of court."

Mick Jagger grinned his famous Cheshire Cat grin.

"Contempt?" he interjected. "That's appropriate. I liked that bit when they appeared in judge's robes. Saw that one on the telly."

I one-upped Mick by telling him that, to denounce the verdict, Anita, Nancy, and Dave Dellinger's daughter Tasha had dressed as witches and set judge's robes on fire. Theirs was, I announced, a fabulous Yippie act. The rock star paused and waited, as famous entertainers will, for me to continue entertaining him. Pleased the man had heard about Jerry and Abbie's stunt of wearing judge's robes to satirize Judge Hoffman, I went on to tell Mick Jagger how next day thousands of people across America and in Europe took to the streets to protest the Trial's verdict with a rapid response tactic we called The Day After or TDA.

As years passed and I have watched that rock star's face become even more iconic than the single time I met him, I asked myself why I did not feel nervous at the man's global fame. My answer is that Yippie chutzpah empowered me. Delighted that I had not acted like a deferential groupie under Mick Jagger's thumb, from then on I refused to be intimidated by celebrity.

* * *

1970 TURNED OUT TO BE A year in which the magnitude of Yippie influence exceeded our wildest dreams. Yippie groups sprouted like psychedelic mushrooms on campuses and in cities across America and Europe. On April 22, 1970, twenty million people across the globe rallied to oppose climate change and advocate for ecological sustainability—our planet's first Earth Day. By then Keith Lampe, who'd carried Abbie's small, cute pig to Chicago's Bandshell two years earlier, had become a dedicated environmentalist and changed his name to Ponderosa Pine.

We Canadians also seized our moment: not only had the photo of me in my karate-gi dominated the front page of the *Berkeley Tribe*, but, in May 1970, one hundred Yippies from Vancouver, Canada invaded the United States to counter President Nixon's invasion of Cambodia. With such defiance, my home and native land redeemed itself in my eyes.

Meanwhile, Stew ran for sheriff of Alameda County to protest brutal conditions at our local jail. He ran against Sheriff Frank Madigan, who had sent the Alameda County Sheriffs we nicknamed Blue Meanies—from a Beatle's song—into People's Park. Stew's campaign slogan was "People's Pig, 100% True Blue Commie Rat." On his poster, Stew's head of curly hair is framed by a cartoon rifle and a hookah embellished with this slogan: "If Madigan Dies, Stew Albert Will Win for Sherrif." Perhaps it was the misspelling but no one, including Sheriff Madigan, took the poster as a genuine threat instead of what it was: a Yippie send-up. Stew did not win public office but he did receive a huge 65,000 votes and carried the city of Berkeley, as well as North and West Oakland.

In August 1970, San Diego Yippies invaded Disneyland to protest the war and Disneyland's dress code that banned beards, long hair, and miniskirts. In September, 1970, with the help of the Weather Underground and facilitated by Stew and others, Timothy Leary broke out of a minimum-security prison in San Louis Obispo after being convicted of two 10-year consecutive sentences for marijuana possession. Leary would emerge in Algeria as Eldridge's guest—a well-intended effort that, according to those who participated, turned into a truly divisive mismatch, because, or so I later heard, Leary angered Eldridge by treating Algerians like servants.

The majority of late 1960s women protesters I knew—myself included—were both free agents and helpmates who supported men. Still, the Trial of the Chicago 8 gave me a key experience—I learned to stand my ground, to fight back, and to resist. All of which I needed to become a free woman.

Equally good, the show trial envisaged by President Richard Nixon, Attorney General John Mitchell, and FBI Director J. Edgar Hoover to "harass, disrupt, and neutralize" the new left achieved its opposite: Jerry's *Do It!* and Abbie's *Woodstock Nation* and *Revolution for the Hell of It* became international best sellers; *Mademoiselle Magazine* voted Abbie one of the four sexiest men in America.

I still enjoy imagining how President Richard Nixon and FBI Director J. Edgar Hoover must have suffered when, for one brief moment in American history, "Yippie" became a household word. And I understood for the first time the meaning of *schadenfreude*, the pleasure you experience at the misfortune of your opponents.

CHAPTER 15:
THE AMERICAN GIRLFRIEND

MY NORTH VIETNAMESE LOVER AND I met each other in person only six times, all during seven months in 1970—my year of living romantically. We rendezvoused in exotic capitals of countries sympathetic to the anti-war cause: Stockholm, Paris, Prague, Hanoi, and Havana.

For decades after we met, my lover insisted I never speak of our affair or publish anything he wrote. I happily complied. I kept our affair secret. Jerry Rubin's partner Nancy, who was with me on numerous occasions when my lover and I were together, told me she suspected. Tom Hayden, SDS founder and Conspiracy Trial defendant, found out; when and how I do not know, but Tom always had deep sources. The FBI, completely clueless, missed it—my FBI files contain no reference to a high-ranking North Vietnamese official. The CIA missed it too. My lover's directive not to disclose was clear; I can only guess at the personal and professional risks he must have faced from his side had he come clean about our relationship:

> "Things might be interpreted in the wrong sense and I don't want to get complications . . . We might both be labelled as 'perturbative and worthless elements.'"

But on March 16, 2008, I received an extraordinary e-mail. Aging alters perspective; I now had my lover's approval to reveal a secret I had kept for forty years.

"Go ahead with your writing about anything we shared in the past. What matters is we can re-live the most wonderful time that made our life significant while providing the world a reason to think and act."

I do so for the first time now.

My lover's name was Do Xuan Oanh—pronounced like "wine" in English but with a nasal intonation and *nnnng* at the end. Musician, politician, diplomatic emissary for the North Vietnamese government, poet, intellectual, artist, painter, and translator—everyone from the inner core of the U.S. peace movement knew him. The literary icon Susan Sontag writes about Oanh in her 1968 book *Trip to Hanoi* as having a "personal authority, (he) walks and sits with that charming 'American' slouch, and sometimes seems moody or distracted."

From my experience, I'd say Oanh's moodiness originated in what he told me as we lay together under a dusty bedspread our last night together in Montreal. Oanh revealed that he was married, the father of three sons. He confided that his wife, the daughter of a doctor, had been arrested by the French in the early 1950s and imprisoned at the Maison Central, a concrete building in downtown Hanoi that would become infamous to Americans as the Hanoi Hilton. Oanh's wife suffered chronic headaches and fainted if she saw a snake. Only when I visited Vietnam in 2013 to help celebrate the 40th anniversary of the Paris Peace Accords did I grasp the import of Oanh's story. On the wall of the War Remnants Museum in Ho Chi Minh City, I saw a painting in subdued watercolors of a woman being held down by two burly, bare-chested men who were raping her with a snake. But when I first met Oanh in Montreal, I chose to deny the inconvenient truth of his marriage. To me Oanh's wife was a distant, tragic figure, not of my world. I could not help her.

I did not see my lover in February of 1970, but by the end of March, Oanh had arranged for Nancy and me to meet him at an international peace conference in Stockholm. I booked a single room. In keeping with the clandestine code of our relationship, Oanh would appear in my doorway, smiling, but only after midnight. We'd make international peace under thick blankets on a narrow mattress on a bed of blond Scandinavian wood. I easily accepted Oanh's explanation that, unlike his first letters, his recent reticence to express his love for me on paper was, given the delicate stage of peace negotiations, now a necessary diplomatic caution.

In Stockholm, Oanh, Nancy, and I decided to organize a conference between American "cultural workers" (our free-form translation into Vietnamese commie-speak of the word Yippie) and those to whom our movement gave the greatest moral hegemony—Vietnamese guerrilla fighters. Such a gathering, on the island paradise of Cuba, would legitimize Yippie in the more strait-laced anti-war community as political hippies with principles. Oanh said Nancy and I ought to visit Vietnam first, to plan. The thrills just kept on coming.

On April 30, 1970, one week prior to our departure for Vietnam, the world learned that U.S. and South Vietnamese Army troops had invaded Cambodia, a neutral nation and Vietnam's next-door neighbor. It did not cross my mind to cancel my trip. In truth, if I had to risk my life to see my lover in a country I idealized, I would have done so in a heartbeat.

* * *

ON MAY 4, 1970, IN THAT same week Nancy and I arrived at Moscow's Sheremetyevo airport, four students protesting the war were shot to death and nine wounded at Kent State University by members of the Ohio National Guard—an event I found out about only on my return. Nor did I learn at the time about the killing of two Black students and wounding of twelve at Jackson State in Mississippi, eleven days after the carnage in Kent, Ohio. At the Moscow airport, Nancy and I were greeted by a stout matron in a drab, military green uniform. The matron informed us that our visas, arranged in Vietnam but funneled through layers of non-lethal but obstructive Soviet bureaucracy, had been delayed.

To please my father, as a young teen I had learned to speak tourist Russian: *"zdrastsvetsye"* (hello), *"dosvedanye"*(goodbye), *"tovarisch"* (comrade), *"spaseebah"* (thank you), *"mir i druzbah"* (peace and friendship), plus two especially valuable phrases: *"Gde tualet"* (Where is the toilet?) and *"Sobranye nye vosim ab shest."* (The meeting will be at six instead of eight.) To annoy our official nanny, once every thirty minutes I poked my head out of the airless room in which we waited, to demand, *"Zdrastsvetsye Tovarisch. Gdye tualet spaseebah?"*

We were eventually informed our visas would arrive in a week. Or two. Or, who knew, perhaps never? Our official nanny ferried us to the Hotel Ukraine, a four-story monstrosity that looked like a Stalinist prison disguised as a wedding cake. A kindly cook in a deserted kitchen offered bowls of cabbage borscht. Nancy and I settled in our room and, as good Yippie women must, called the press. I spoke as if I alone possessed the power to influence international events. I have no idea how I managed such a call, long distance, but I know that I got through since the FBI reported, in all caps for emphasis, that I'd told the press,

WE DON'T TRUST PRESIDENT NIXON AND THE THINGS HE IS DOING, WE ARE GOING TO HANOI TO TALK WITH OUR NORTH VIETNAMESE FRIENDS AND TELL THEM JUST THAT.

To kill time, I strolled with Nancy down the cobblestone streets of Red Square, marveling at the psychedelic red, blue, gold, and green spires atop St. Basil's Cathedral. Muscovites stared at us: to them were must have been alien creatures given how we looked with our blue jeans, open-toed sandals, ponchos, beaded purses, and our pink-on-purple Yippie buttons. A young man whose straight blond Slavic hair seemed shaggier than most approached me with a group of friends.

He introduced himself, saying, "Ve are heeppies. You heeppies too?"

"How did you learn to speak such good English?" I responded.

"Ve listen records. Creedence Clearvater. Rollink Stones. Jeemi Hendrix. Ve hate the peegs."

Such was detente Yippie style. An entrepreneurial young woman offered me a clothing exchange: my brown suede vest with its foot-long fringe strung with multicolored beads for her Ukrainian sheepskin jacket embroidered with alternating rows of red, blue, and green swirls on front, back, and sleeves. As we traded, I heard a Russian shout at us. Our new friends translated, "Cut your hair and join the Russian Army!"

In the United States I'd heard the bigots yell, "Go back to Russia where you belong!"

In Moscow's Red Square, at the height of the Cold War and U.S. anti-hippie sentiment, I discovered a truism about which Russians and Americans apparently agreed: a taste of Stalinist discipline would bring us long-haired hippies to our senses.

* * *

ONLY 174 PEOPLE FROM THE UNITED States visited the former North Vietnam while the war still raged. I was one. Visas in hand, Nancy and I flew in a four-propeller plane out of Moscow down ancient routes of nomadic traders past the fabled cities of Ulan Bator, Tashkent, and Karachi. Our vintage Aeroflot shook like a bird in a headwind as our stocky flight attendant stomped her way down the aisle. In Calcutta I saw, through the plane's windows, ragged women and children who lived in corrugated iron huts less than a hundred yards from the runway. I found a woman in a yellow sari begging for change in the airport restroom. These sights dented but did not dampen my mood.

We arrived in early May, 1970, at Hanoi's jungle encrusted airport, where I caught a glimpse of Oanh on the tarmac surrounded by schoolchildren with red, yellow, and pink gladioli waving hand-painted banners of welcome. I was almost too exhausted to care. Oanh smiled and shook Nancy's and my hands, telling us he'd take us to our hotel and had arranged for us to see a performance that evening. Two minutes after I eased myself down into the theater's worn velvet seats, I fell into a deep sleep.

Next morning, I heard a knock on my door. It was Oanh. I felt refreshed, alive—and as turned on as if I was Ingrid Bergman greeting Humphrey Bogart in the movie *Casablanca*. Oanh entered. I shut the door, alone finally with my lover, expecting him to take me in his arms. A gentle breeze from a ceiling fan rustled the muslin curtains encircling my bed. But Oanh retreated. I took one step forward, Oanh took two steps back. Forward, back. Forward, back, as if he and I were practicing the most awkward of tangos. Oanh stopped just before we reached a room that housed an ancient but functioning bidet. He put one hand on each of my shoulders, his arms stiff in front of him. Uncomprehending, I asked what was wrong.

"Nothing to worry," he replied. "I am extremely happy you are here. Now we must meet outside the hotel."

He smiled, turned his back on me, and left.

I collapsed onto my bed, my only companion the soft whirr of the ceiling fan. At first, I blamed myself. What had I done wrong? I went to worst-case scenario: I decided Oanh didn't love me anymore, then dismissed that as ridiculous. I would not believe the man who'd written such romantic letters would reject me without explanation. Next paranoia took hold. Did Oanh suspect his government had bugged my room? After minutes during which eight out of ten of my no longer bitten fingernails met their painful end inside my mouth, it came to me that I'd ignored the obvious. Oanh lived with his wife and three sons in Hanoi. I was but a visitor to his world.

Shortly after I returned to the United States, I was interviewed in a colorful but short-lived psychedelic magazine out of Detroit called *Sundance*. By then I'd decided that a gap existed between the more traditionalist Vietnamese sexual mores and my counter-cultural expectations of free-form romance. I wrote:

You wouldn't see couples walking hand in hand in the streets of Hanoi. It was much more delicate. You'd see a man with a woman behind him on a bicycle, and you could just tell, like maybe she had her hand around his waist, that they were most likely lovers. Or you'd be walking by a pagoda and you'd come across this couple, just two people together, sitting or squatting and they wouldn't even be talking, they'd just sort of look at you and smile and you'd look back at them and smile, but it was a very delicate, fragile, beautiful thing.

With the exception of short walks, always in view of others, and one sweet, brief, secret touching in the warm silky blue waters of Sam Son Beach on the South China Sea, during my entire trip to North Vietnam, Oanh and I had no alone time. To my surprise, I did not feel disgruntled. Rather, my longing for sexual intimacy faded as I became more and more enamored of the country and people of Vietnam.

* * *

GENIE PLAMONDON, MINISTER OF INTERNAL AFFAIRS for Michigan's White Panther Party, a Yippie affiliate, joined Nancy and me in Hanoi. Genie towered over me, Nancy, and almost every Vietnamese person we met. We became a women's delegation of three. With her broad Midwestern farm-girl face and long straight brown hair, Genie's persona of a working-class tough girl with a heart of gold felt distant from the ironic, fast-talking, New York City planet from which Nancy and I hailed. Frictions occasionally bubbled up between us, then vanished into the emotional tsunami which engulfed all three of us in Vietnam.

That first morning, after I'd pulled myself up out of rejection, I stepped into a dilapidated dark green school bus with the number 4709 stenciled on its windshield. It waited on Ngo Quyen Street outside our hotel, the former French colonial Hotel

Metropole, now named Reunification. In the seat next to me, Oanh's leg briefly brushed mine in reassurance. With stops, starts, fits, and bumps, our bus ferried us and three Vietnamese guides—two men and a woman—through waves of bicycle riders in conical straw hats, women in black silk trousers and white blouses, men in white short-sleeved shirts like Oanh's, three hours south until we crossed the Ham Rong Bridge in Thanh Hóa province. The bridge did not resemble a bridge at all; instead it looked as if a deranged spider had spun a web out of gouged steel girders. A hole in the bus's rusted floor afforded a view of muddy brown river water rushing mere yards under my feet. Oanh told us the North Vietnamese army moved war material by train, oxcart, bicycle, and foot across this bridge to the South. U.S. planes had made at least 400 sorties over this bridge, each one laying down a carpet of anti-personnel bombs.

"Every day this bridge is demolished," Oanh explained, "Every night it is rebuilt. The courage of the peasants is a local legend."

I could not grasp what it meant to live such a life.

On my right, a mountain loomed. At its base, a mass of broken railway cars lay as if in a graveyard. One half of the mountain's top had been sheared away as if an industrial-sized backhoe had strip-mined giant bites out from it. I made out the words QUYET THANG carved into the mountain's top. I asked Oanh what the words meant.

He replied, "Determined to win. So American pilots will see this as they fly over."

I have asked myself for 50 years why Oanh believed American pilots could translate this slogan and make sense of it, until I realized mine was an American-centric point of view. The purpose of the slogan was to inspire defiance among those peasants being bombed rather than act as a deterrent to U.S. pilots.

By the time the bus stopped, I was feeling no small measure of guilt and remorse, as if I was in some way personally responsible for the destruction I'd just witnessed. A woman in a stained light-weight patterned shirt, visibly pregnant, ushered us through a narrow passage into a low-ceilinged cave hollowed into the mountain's core. Bare bulbs attached to wires flickered orange; tons of mountain earth above us tamed Vietnam's humidity and heat. An image of Stew's and my sunless Greenwich Village cellar intruded. Our cellar felt luxurious compared to this. I saw seven or eight women and men bent over lathes that resembled oversize sewing machines. Despite daily bombings, this munitions factory had remained in continuous production.

Events can remold your spirit. I'd learned neither empathy nor compassion growing up, but in that moment, I felt I had acquired both. I do the best I can to avoid rhetorical writing, but if Oanh and his compatriots could make a life amid such losses, I vowed then and there to re-make myself, to behave more like my revolutionary heroes, Che Guevara, the Trưng Sisters, Mme. Binh, and Emma Goldman. I'd become less self-centered! I'd learn empathy, determination, and compassion for others—and for myself! The vows I made in that factory cave seem utopian to me now, but at age 27 they felt genuine enough to change my understanding of myself and thus my life.

I recall shivering, not from fear or from my cooling skin but because the air around me felt infused with such resolve I could not help but sop it up. Suddenly the machines stopped. The cave fell silent. I heard a faint *ping ping* of dripping water. The woman began to chant, a bird-like, trilling sound. I could feel Oanh's body heat beside me as he translated line by line:

> *If you love me come back to this beautiful province with me*
> *I stand on guard at this bridge, for seven years strong here*
> *Through cold and rain*
> *I stand looking at the yellow star flying in the flashing light*
> *And each call that I hear from the South tears into my heart.*

* * *

As we departed Thanh Hóa province, our bus passed rice paddies dotted with water buffalo in which three-sided boxes like painted dollhouses stood on poles. Chi, our female guide who was almost as tall as Genie, told us these boxes marked the graves of ancestors, which allowed deceased members of a family to remain close to their relatives and their fields. Nancy, Genie, Oanh, and I, plus Chi the and other guides, bounced our way along a ragged road until we saw a ferry made of planks. We boarded, serenaded by a man whose notes rose from a four-foot-long flute made of bamboo rods. Alongside him, two local peasants each shepherded gigantic water buffalo strapped to an oxcart filled with rusted metal gallon drums. Americans, flute player, peasants, and water-buffalo were ferried together across a lake outlined by mountains. I breathed in Vietnam's familiar heat and humidity but also picked up a minty odor. Peace might smell like this if peace came bottled as perfume.

We stopped at a hut in a village of Vietnam's Thai Noir minority. The hut's bamboo walls were worn and slotted, its ceiling made from spiky palm fronds piled thick and weathered brown. The hut itself was built high on stilts, Chi told us, to keep the family safe at night from tigers. Forty or fifty barefoot villagers stared at us, never having seen white women before. Despite it all being so new to me, I felt it would be impolite for me to stare back. We three Americans climbed a ladder into the hut's interior. Two village elders, petite, female, shorter even than Nancy or me, stepped forward to greet us. Each had wrapped herself around with a long strip of black cloth with hand-woven blue, white, orange, and magenta stripes. As they spoke, I noticed that their front teeth were stained red brown. I later asked Chi to explain. It was, she said, not tooth decay but betel nut, a sign of beauty for their generation and also a preventative of tooth decay.

Oanh sat behind me on a low wooden bench to translate. Along with Nancy and Genie, I took my place of honor on a woven brown bamboo floor mat. In those quiet intervals between translations—English to Vietnamese to a language I could only guess at—I told myself how fortunate I was to be sitting here, in revolutionary Vietnam, drinking sweet tea out of a miniature white enamel cup.

A villager offered me a water pipe, hollowed from a single piece of round bamboo and stained deep brown. Oanh translated.

"We call this thuốc lào, a Vietnamese tobacco. Be careful," he said and winked. "It is strong."

I covered one end of the two-foot-long pipe with my hand and breathed in deep and slow, as if I was smoking pot. Wrong. Spicy, tart, hot smoke filled my mouth and traveled up and out my nostrils. For a moment I felt dizzy. My mouth watered, my nose ran, I could not control my cough. I, the foreign visitor, turned bright red, provoking smiles and giggles from my audience.

"Well, that was quite a buzz," I managed to get out.

The next instant, I heard a boom in the distance as if some hellish creature tromped the ground with monstrous footsteps. A series of deep bass bangs and rolling thunder followed. It was the sound of falling bombs and heavy artillery fire coming from the nearby DMZ.

* * *

I TOOK A PHOTO IN THANH Hóa province of eight women lined up in formation, four abreast. Each wears a pith helmet and those ubiquitous black silk pants. They are a platoon of artillery gunners. They appear as tall as I am and look about my age. One is barefoot, the others wear black sandals recycled from used rubber tires. Behind them I saw a six-foot long gun barrel pointing toward the sky. A second photo shows me, my hair in braids to ward off the heat, seated in a Russian anti-aircraft machine gun mounted on what looks like a two-wheeled tractor spattered with mud. The women in the photo appear stern yet puzzled. I recall Chi, our woman guide, introducing the three of us.

"These are American friends come to observe what we do to liberate our country."

I can see myself now, in my pink and blue tie-dye tank top, climbing into the gun's metal swivel seat and staring out through its elongated sights into a clear Vietnamese sky. The actor Jane Fonda had her picture taken in this same model machine gun when she visited North Vietnam two years after I did—an act Jane says she now regrets. Jane's right-wing enemies branded her a traitor; even her friends said the fallout from that photo made the task of winning over mainstream Americans to the anti-war cause more difficult.

I have never regretted looking through those gun sights, but I do remember feeling like a fraud. My life was one of privilege. How could I compare my life to that of a woman for whom making it through one day meant pulling the trigger on an anti-aircraft heavy machine gun mounted on a tiny tractor to shoot an airplane stuffed with lethal weaponry out of the sky?

Overwhelmed, I murmured, "You are an inspiration to me."

"No, no," the barefoot soldier replied, Chi translating. "You, dear friend, inspire us. You help in your country to end war."

Another barefoot soldier handed me a small, gray-green ball made of metal: half of a bomblet destined never to detonate. It was round, hollow, two-and-a-quarter inches wide, and three-quarters of an inch deep with a jagged hole in one side as if a single tear had burned like acid through its metal casing. This unexploded U.S. pellet bomb, or "pineapple," had once contained 250 steel ball bearings, still caught like pomegranate seeds inside its metal skin, holding a lethal promise of a weapon designed to shred the flesh of any human being or animal unfortunate enough to be in range. I'd later learn that "mother" bombs dropped by B-52 Stratofortress bombers contain 37 million pellet bombs like mine. A single B-52 could drop 1,000 pineapples over a 400-square-yard area.

My bomblet is now antique, but even today many remain buried in the soil of Vietnam where they rise like ghouls, unbidden and undead, to kill or maim children who mistake the bombs for playthings. For all the effort my compatriots and I put in to ending war, I'm still appalled that the United States continues to pollute our planet with the most technologically sophisticated military ordnance imaginable.

I kept my bomb fragment for decades, then donated it to the University of Michigan Labadie Collection for all to see.

* * *

I ALSO KEEP THIRTY OF OANH'S letters in the 1950s turquoise vinyl carrying case where I store my keepsakes. Oanh's letters are handwritten or typed single-spaced and double-sided, as if scarcity in Vietnam demanded he cram every word onto blue onionskin or unlined paper. I believe most are from 1970–73, dated only by day and month so I regard those few with actual written years like edge pieces of a jigsaw puzzle which allow me to fill in how our relationship evolved. No letter I wrote to Oanh remains.

Oanh advised me as if he was a therapist of revolution:

> *I found a mixture of almost everything in your letter: confusion, self-critical, uptight, depression, anxiety etc. If such was the case, those are the characteristics of people who are "easy to turn on, quick to turn off." You always deserve my trust and confidence. Forever.*

He'd reassure me I was not alone in feeling lost:

> *You know, Judy, sometimes I too had the feeling that my bowels are topsy-turvy and I hate myself for being so powerless in the face of events. You know that the flame inside you is burning with much greater heat than ever before, yet you feel weak, isolated, and that makes you crazy, mad, silly. There are moments like that in life. How can things be that unjust and absurd?*

I've fantasized about but never completed turning Oanh's letters into a self-help book. Had I done so, I would title it *Lessons from America's Former Enemy* and center it around these sayings:

Any disease in this world can be cured except the one that is hypocrisy.

If you feel it impossible to bear a small uneasiness, it would be hard to imagine how you could stand the whole burden.

Gold must be tested by fire and strength must be tested by hardship.

Temperament is human. When you're sure of yourself, you don't need to prove anything.

When you feel like proving something, you're more or less not sure of yourself.

Just figure you're crossing a minefield. With battle-mates walking beside you. This is the time to keep your head cool, but your heart warm. The test will be a long and hard one, but life insists that you should overcome.

I'd read and re-read Oanh's letters whenever I'd feel vulnerable or insecure. They gave me strength. I'd quote them to friends who needed help in hard times or put my favorite quote from Oanh—the one I find most relevant to politics today—as a message at the bottom of my e-mail.

Be good to friends who are good to you; also, be good to friends who are bad to you, for only friends will go with you on the long road to revolution.

What this means to me is: be tolerant of political disagreement; keep your long run goals in mind; don't bitterly attack your friends or destroy friendships, even if those friends say or do things you strongly disagree with. I still try to follow Oanh's advice, but sadly, as with any self-improvement program, I often relapse and revert to being just an ordinary person.

* * *

BEFORE GENIE, NANCY, AND I LEFT Hanoi, Oanh and his compatriots organized a farewell dinner for us. Oanh dressed for the event in his standard 1950s style gray pants and short-sleeved white shirt. Our women guides wore ao dai's of faded reds and blues. I knew the Vietnamese population suffered war-related food shortages, yet the dinner in our honor felt sumptuous, a traditional gesture of gratitude. On the banquet table I found spring rolls fried a delicate brown, bright red prawns, steaming bowls of pho with fish braised in brown sauce, plus a beige vegetable I did not recognize cut in fantastical shapes. A dessert of ripe yellow pineapple came accompanied by slices of a white fruit, its flesh speckled with tiny black seeds as if Mother Nature had created a pellet bomb of peace and friendship just for us.

In his farewell speech, Oanh instructed Genie, Nancy and me on how to live our lives as Yippie revolutionaries. "You must," Oanh advised, "keep the long view in mind." He ended with a story told to him by his father when he was a child.

"You must not wait until the score is achieved to know who is the real hero."

Then, speaking directly to us as if we too were members of his family, Oanh concluded, "I would not wait until revolution is achieved in America to know that you represent the future."

I could not have asked for a more loving and inspirational farewell. Be patient, Oanh was saying, but at the same time never quit. By then I felt so certain of my life's path it was as if I'd reached a plane of moral certitude beyond any carnal need. My romance with Oanh, and my time in Vietnam, had stoked my determination to go for broke. To let my extremist flag fly. I would do everything I could, according to my abilities, to stop this war.

* * *

I LANDED IN MONTREAL FROM HANOI on June 6, 1970, two and a half weeks before my 27th birthday. The government of Canada held no affection for this wandering Canadian, nor for Nancy and Genie who arrived with me. A customs official yanked my suitcase open. He was flanked on either side by twin Sergeants Preston of the Yukon, scarlet red jackets and leather knee-high jackboots—the traditional uniform of the Royal Canadian Mounted Police.

The agent extracted a paperback children's book from my bag. On its cover, smiling cartoon yellow honeybees swarmed around fleeing U.S. soldiers. To me the book was a metaphor for an inevitable Vietnamese victory; the official muttered, "Communist propaganda," and declared he'd have to seize it. One kids' comic, two opposing views; that's the way it is with wars.

In that severe, Harriet-like tone I knew spelled trouble, the official asked, "Would you be so kind as to hand me your purse?"

I flinched. Amidst the chaos of my brown leather bag, in addition to half a bar of Parisian chocolate, now melted, the blue plastic case that held my diaphragm, and a stash of metal rings engraved with the number 1000 recycled from downed U.S. planes, I carried a packet. It was wrapped in brown Manila paper and tied with twine. It contained 143 letters from American pilots who had been shot down, captured, and imprisoned in Vietnam. At our farewell banquet, Oanh had taken me aside and asked me to deliver this packet to Cora Weiss in New York City. Cora's Committee of Liaison with U.S. Servicemen was the only reliable route at the time for uncensored mail from American pilots detained in Vietnam to reach their families in the United States. I understood Oanh's request for what it was: a privilege he bestowed only on those he trusted.

Determined not to let Oanh down, I announced in my best Harriet in high dudgeon morphed into Her Majesty the Queen voice:

"I am a Canadian citizen. This is my personal property. I am entitled to bring it in."

Four hours later I was released from airport detention, my rings intact but sans letters, children's books, and my subversive conical straw hat. Nancy, Genie, and I held our standard Yippie press conference to protest our treatment. I called a lawyer friend from college days who had connections to a Canadian Member of Parliament. I felt no compulsion to call Stew. By day's end, I had reclaimed my children's books and my packet of letters, unopened as far as I could tell. But not my straw hat.

Next day, back in my parent's home in Toronto, the *Toronto Daily Star* landed on that same porch I'd crossed a lifetime of seven years ago to marry Hemblen. Its headline read:

"Letters from U.S. prisoners seized from Yippies in Canada."

Perhaps in keeping with the *Star's* perception of newsworthiness, or a bias that all things American belonged together, the paper printed our Yippie/POW letter headline just below a photo of famous singer Barbra Streisand, a Cleopatra look-alike in a polka dot designer dress with matching turban. Barbra was, at the time, dating Canada's Prime Minister Pierre Trudeau. I too had revived my dating game—I'd stayed over the previous night in Montreal with my high school friend Normie Cook. And, as if to make up for lost years, I'd slept happily with Normie for our first time.

I was not especially sad to leave Oanh when we bid each other farewell in Vietnam that June. Oanh and I were to meet again at the Yippie conference of "cultural workers" in August, a short two months later. How could Cuba with its permissive Latin culture and iconic Che Guevara not offer us opportunities for intimacy? But during the flight from Toronto back to San Francisco—and to Stew in Berkeley—my inner announcer staged a wrestling match inside my head.

"Laaaydees and Gentlemen," she proclaimed, "In one corner we have 'Judy Gumbo,' independent woman inspired by her Vietnamese lover and committed to an arsenal of Black, women's, queer, and national liberation theologies. In the opposite corner we have 'The Bitch,' a drama queen whose confusion about Stew is compounded by her conviction that she still loves him."

By the time the airplane landed, both sides were winning. In Vietnam, I'd been so focused on learning to live my Judy Gumbo life that I'd stuffed Stew into a corner of my mind and left him there. I had to face him now.

* * *

"HEYYYYYY GUMBY," I COULD HEAR THE pleasure in Stew's voice as he opened the front door, now painted red for revolution, of our Ashby house. Stew looked the same, still wearing that by-now threadbare paisley shirt with curlicues he'd worn when I first met him. His long arms enveloped me. He planted a wet, sloppy kiss on my lips and muscled his tongue between my teeth.

"Hey Stewie," I said, stepping back.

"It's great to see you. How was Vietnam?" Stew cocked his head to one side like a blond, curly-haired owl, a touch of worry in his blue eyes. Stew, an empath, found it easy to pick up dissonance in personal interaction, although he'd never appeared curious about the paper-thin blue envelopes that arrived from Paris.

"It's great to see you too," I replied truthfully, comforted by Stew's girth and the familiar, slightly sour smell of his body. Stew and I made love in the late afternoon California sun surrounded by the orange glow of our Buddhist curtains of peace. Stew's big chest weighed on me like a rock. His rough beard scratched my face, his untrimmed toenails scraped my leg. I could feel him move inside me in short grunts. I told myself I still loved Stew, so I allowed my external self to go through the motions while, in my imagination, I was responding to Oanh's gentle touch. Perhaps I should have felt guilty; instead, having a secret lover gave me a sense of superiority I had never previously known. I thought all I had left to learn was how to negotiate this new romantic contradiction.

* * *

IN JULY 1970, A MONTH-AND-A-HALF AFTER I returned from Hanoi, and thanks to the generosity of an anonymous donor, I abandoned Stew to visit Oanh in Versailles where he functioned as support staff to the Paris peace talks. But I first met leaders of the French student protest movement who introduced me to their personal hero, the five-foot tall philosopher Jean Paul Sartre, a member of the International War Crimes Tribunal. I identified with Sartre's existentialist philosophy—that in an absurd world, humans must exercise their free will and make life choices for themselves.

That same evening, Oanh and I sat together in the sitting room of his small hotel. His Vietnamese compatriots might arrive at any moment. After Oanh said that American hippies represented the spirit of true freedom—a claim with which Sartre might have agreed—I decided to test Oanh's limits. The French students had gifted me a joint. Provocateur that I was and still remain, I moved aside the room's green curtains to open a window, brought out the weed, struck a match then teased, "Try this, Oanh."

Oanh later wrote:

> You are a wonder in many things but a Psych Out, if I may say in some ordinary matters.

At the time he ran his hands through his hair, squinted at me, and inhaled.

Suppressing a cough, Oanh said, "I find it not as enjoyable as thuốc lào, that water pipe tobacco you smoked at the Thai Noir village."

Later, as if contrite and perhaps fearful for contradicting his official duties, Oanh's playful mood dissolved. He challenged me and my Yippie pals to give up marijuana.

"Marijuana is harmful to both mind and health while not being a real incentive for freedom fighters."

Much as I adored Oanh, I knew I would refuse. Smoking pot was a freedom upon which we Yippies had founded Woodstock Nation. Oanh and I could not make international peace about the politics of smoking marijuana. Both of us stayed stuck on opposing sides of our "Take a Toke of thuốc lào" diplomatic exchange.

* * *

I MET OANH FOR THE FINAL time in August 1970. I had no idea this meeting would be our last. Nancy and I had arrived in Cuba, the advance team for our conference of Yippie "cultural workers."

That conference never happened. The Cubans called it off. Not as permissive as their reputation implied, I later learned the Cuban government disapproved of us marijuana-smoking Yippies. Disappointed Yippies from across the United States—including Stew—stayed home.

(INFORMANT NAME BLACKED OUT) recently traveled around the country to recruit people associated with the Youth International Party (YIP) and other movement people to travel to Havana Cuba with Judy Gumbo. These people believe that considerable tension would develop on the Cuban ship between the members of the Venceremos Brigade (VB) and Gumbo's group. The VB are going to Cuba primarily to pick oranges, while the other group is going to Cuba to meet with a North Vietnamese on a cultural exchange program. It is felt that the VB, which will be made up mostly of "third world" individuals, would resent the other group which is made up mostly of white people.

Thirteen and a half years before my visit, Fidel and his guerrilla army had marched into Havana, set up headquarters in Room 2324 of the Hilton, planted their muddy combat boots on expensive leather sofas, and replaced photos of Conrad and Mrs. Hilton and their guests, who dressed in black tie and floor length ball gowns, with the red and black flag of the 26th of July Movement. They changed the hotel's name from Havana Hilton to Havana Libre. **INFORMANT BLANK** had a point. Had I been a Black or Latinx member of the Venceremos Brigade, I too would have resented picking oranges or harvesting sugar cane under a sweltering Cuban sun while privileged white Yippie women met with Vietnamese heroes in the luxury Havana Libre hotel.

* * *

My Caribbean vacation with my lover at my personal Club Med could not hide war's cruelty. One afternoon, as Oanh and I entered the atrium of the Havana Libre after an afternoon of lovemaking, I recognized a woman I'd met in Hanoi at the Vietnam Women's Union. When I was there in June, she'd looked immaculate, no gray hair out of place. Two months later, her face framed by unruly wisps of hair as if no force on earth could offer her stability, she clutched the railing of the angular staircase that links the Libre lobby with the second floor. Thanks to Castro's revolution, the Havana Libre, a former vacation spot for American gangsters, now provided rest and rehabilitation to Vietnamese freedom fighters. Oanh picked up on my dismay, explaining, "Her condition is from the war. My wife suffers the same illness."

I hated how despicable it was that prison guards had likely raped this woman, as they had Oanh's wife.

On what would be our final afternoon together, Nancy and I sat with Oanh at the far end of the Libre's massive swimming pool, as far as we could get from the muscular Russians—mostly men with large round bellies—who lounged on deckchairs getting drunk on mojitos. Oanh began a conversation unlikely to be heard at any other Hilton on the planet. He leaned in toward Nancy and me, his tone serious.

"This New Nation stuff, for how long can it be new? It is time for you Yippies, my dears, to change from spontaneity to calmness and lucidity."

Oanh continued, "Your claim of a directionless and leaderless youth movement is absurd. It betrays the hopes and desires of people thirsty for a change."

"And why is that?" I asked, fully aware of my confrontational tone.

"Such a thing will disintegrate and your ideas about revolution will vaporize as quickly as they are formed."

The music in Oanh's voice hid the severity of his message: we improvisational Yippies needed to create organizational structure, overcome our individualism, and learn the art of compromise. Oanh went so far as to suggest we work in coalition with the uber-serious Tom Hayden, who denigrated all things counter-cultural.

Taking the title of Abbie's latest book, *Revolution for the Hell of It* in vain, Oanh concluded, "No one is making revolution with 'the hell' in mind. This is basically reactionary."

In the 1970s the word reactionary meant coming from the far right, not, as some confuse the word today, reactive. I refused to believe that Oanh believed that no one makes revolution just for fun, and that he'd chosen what he must have known would be our final hours together to label Yippies as ideological reactionaries—a biting critique from any communist, let alone my lover.

It would take decades for me to appreciate that Oanh had made an important argument about Yippie self-identity. Much as I hated it, there are times to confront ideological purity and times to go along with a majority to achieve a greater goal. But at the time, I dismissed our differences as a lover's quarrel to be suffered through and then forgotten. So, as it turned out, did Oanh. Memory can single out both the painful and the positive; when I asked Oanh years later what he recalled about Havana, he wrote, "Both of us had in Havana the most wonderful moments for exchange of ideas and emotion. Everything happened like in a fairy tale."

And so Yippie princess Judy Gumbo and her North Vietnamese prince allowed their fairy tale romance to triumph over ideology. In October 1970, three months after we'd said farewell in Cuba, Oanh wrote:

> *Just remember that wherever I'll be and what I'll do, you're in my mind. And I always hope, who knows, we'll see each other again celebrating more beautiful days. Take care my dear. This kiss waiting for the day we'll see again. Me.*

I never got that final kiss. Still, I took Oanh's words as a promise and kept the faith. I never saw Do Xuan Oanh again, but we continued to communicate by letter and subsequently e-mail.

To this day I consider our affair a microcosm of the Great Romance my cohort and I had with Vietnam. But I've come to believe that Oanh's and my consummation of what our peace movement called "people to people diplomacy" was unique. And, like many of the world's great romances, ours did not end in tragedy—it evolved from love to friendship.

CHAPTER 16:
GIRL DUMPS BOY

SHORTLY AFTER I RETURNED FROM CUBA, Stew and I separated by default. Stew remained in Berkeley, I moved to Boston. I no longer wanted to be Mrs. Stew in any guise.

My first big act of liberation was to buy myself a bright blue 1962 VW Bug. I named her Lindequist, after I found the name Lindequist embossed in raised letters on a strip of metal tape stuck to her dashboard. I purchased her, used, in Boston, with money "donated" by my father. Lindequist was an extension of me—small and perky. To name her humanized her and made her my accomplice. Lindequist gave me freedom to travel when and where I chose. And, of course my car had to be a she.

On September 22, 1970, a coalition of anti-war groups invited me to speak at a press conference in Washington D.C. South Vietnam's Vice President Nguyen Cao Ky, a fop of a man whose mustache made him look like a turn-of-the-century villain, a man who spoke publicly of his admiration for Adolf Hitler, was to appear at a pro-war rally organized by Carl McIntire, a fundamentalist Christian preacher. An FBI agent commented:

```
McIntire predicted that his rally would
attract 500,000 people. Now, however,
District of Columbia security officials and
police are beginning to fear that a large
percentage of that group will be protesters,
not sympathizers.
```

Such a glorious opportunity to sway the mainstream press fed my ego in a genuinely Yippie way—I'd expose establishment hypocrisy. I'd already achieved one minor press success on my own: a photo of me, Nancy, and Genie outside the U.S. Embassy in Moscow had appeared in global media after my trip to Vietnam. Now I'd hit the big time. I, Judy Gumbo, Ameri-Cong, dressed in black silk pajamas, sandals recycled from rubber tires, conical straw hat, and a ring with the number 2000 made from metal of a downed American plane, announced to the media, or so the *New York Post* reported:

> *I come on behalf of young people living in free communities who oppose the Nixon Administration and this terrible war. Nguyen Cao Ky is a fascist. He is personally responsible for incredible murders, tortures, and hangings of innocent Vietnamese people. A hundred thousand Yippies and freaks will come to the Washington Monument to make a people's arrest of Ky.*

No longer a couple, I felt free from Stew's oppressive caution. And competitive with him. I'd take this opportunity to create my own myth bigger than reality, or at least one bigger than Stew's. According to the FBI:

> This anxiety was heightened yesterday by a YIP spokesman who told reporters at a news conference here 'we declare the rally to be a free-fire zone.'

> The spokesman, Judy Gumbo, who took part in the Chicago demonstrations, declined to go into any details about what weapons might be used. She promised that her group, among others, would try to disrupt the rally.

I had no direct knowledge that a free-fire zone is a military term for exactly what it sounds like: an area where anyone can be a target. I was so caught up in the theater of the moment it also did not occur to me that my free-fire statement—spontaneous, defiant, and unfiltered—went beyond the bounds of Yippie ridicule, let alone the First Amendment. Nor did I fully comprehend the degree to which words have consequences. Ky canceled his appearance; I celebrated my victory.

But within nine days, the FBI created a myth of their own which was also bigger than reality. They disseminated a report to every FBI field office, the CIA, foreign legations, and the United States Army that I was to be considered **ARMED AND DANGEROUS**. In the eyes of the FBI, I was not palling around with terrorists—I was one. At the same time, the FBI complained in capital letters about what they considered an equally subversive act. The FBI also claimed I'd advocated that **SEX DEVIATES, MEMBERS OF THE GAY LIBERATION FRONT, A HOMOSEXUAL ORGANIZATION, UNDRESS AND PARADE IN THE NUDE DURING THE DEMONSTRATION.**

More likely I suggested a nude march, but the homophobic term "sex deviates" is 100% FBI-Speak.

To my surprise, Stew had shown up in D.C. at my anti-Ky press conference. He nattered on about how Leary's escape was a victory for the counter-culture, that he'd come to D.C. especially for my press conference but that he absolutely *must* get to New York City to consult with Abbie and Jerry about an appropriate Yippie response to Leary's prison breakout. I felt indifferent to Leary's fate but guilty enough about the state of Stew's and my relationship that after the press conference I allowed Stew to ride with me up the New Jersey Turnpike back to New York City. The presence of a young male hitchhiker I'd picked up in D.C., who now sat in Lindequist's back seat, did not limit my behavior. In order not to hear Stew pontificate, I'd turned on Lindequist's radio, but the moment Carole King began to sing "It's Too Late," I started in.

Carole's song gave me permission to cut loose. Releasing all that anger I felt about Stew that I'd previously repressed, I belted the song out at full volume along with Carole.

Stew turned his head away from me to gaze out Lindequist's window, as if any hidden message in Carole's song would be swallowed up by the poisonous smoke from factory chimneys that lined the New Jersey Turnpike. I turned on Stew in that same manner I'd learned by being on the receiving end of alcoholic tirades from my mother—without compassion.

I began not with a single defining incident in our relationship but with what I considered Stew's long chain of usurpations and abuses, both real and imagined—a playlist I'd replayed over and over in my mind. I began with the general:

"Why do you always expect me to do what you want?"

"Oh Gumby, give it a rest."

I'd said all this before. Stew had not listened.

I moved on to the specific. I chose domestic servitude as my battleground. As a young boy, Stew had learned to do only one chore—take out the garbage. Beyond that, he had no domestic skills. No cooking, no dusting or tidying, no washing floors or dishes, no making beds, no nothing. Stew's gendered division of household labor clashed so strongly with my expectation of equality in a relationship that I felt completely justified in my rant.

"I'm glad I'm free from you, Stew Albert. You know why? You never cook. You don't even set the table! You don't wash dishes. I do your laundry. I'm the one to clean the toilet, not you. You leave the place a pigsty. You leave piles of what you say is your 'important' shit scattered all over the house! I type your articles. How many times have I had to type your articles? You never even learned to drive! I have to drive you everywhere! What do you think I am, your chauffeur? I AM NOT YOUR SERVANT!" I ended, my voice rising to a shriek.

All my complaints boiled down to one thing—control. I needed more of it. Despite our love for each other and the rebellious history we both shared, neither of us had the ability to communicate with each other in a way that would resolve our differences. But I also knew Stew had learned the trick of how, initially, to stay calm in a crisis.

"Judy, you're being ridiculous. You're freaking out."

Perhaps I was. If so, I felt any freak out from me was justified. But I also noticed red streaks begin to run up Stew's neck—a telltale sign he was about to lose his temper. The more intensely I berated him, the more Stew's face turned beet red under his curls; that familiar vein in his forehead began to pulsate. But I would not be silenced.

"You expect me to do everything for you. Just because I'm the woman, right?"

The tension in my voice reflected that I had arrived at Stew's most egregious sins.

"Why don't you ever fuckin' listen to *me*? Why can't you take *me* seriously, Mr. High and Mighty friend of Jerry Rubin and Abbie Hoffman? Who's going to show up when the history is written—you, Abbie, and Jerry, that's who! What about us women? What about *me*? Who do you think I am, a nobody? I'm a political person too!"

I needed Stew to acknowledge that in everything that mattered he ought to treat me as his equal—and that he did not.

Instead, by now incensed, he yelled back, "I'll tell you who you are, Judy. You're a cunt. A stupid, stupid cunt."

To me the c-word, then and now, is hate speech. It denigrates a woman's sexuality with an insult no woman should endure. Stew had used that same c-word for me that Jane had confided *Barb* editor Max Scherr had called her when he demanded she cook weekly dinners for *Barb* staff without giving her any money. Max may have treated Jane like an indentured servant, but Stew had never sworn at me with such aggressive bitterness before. Any conflict-avoidance I once had vanished into the pollution outside Lindequist's window. Violating my own prime directive to keep personal arguments private—an agreement I'd adopted with myself after observing my alcoholic parents verbally abuse each other in public—I proceeded to spit out the most vituperative string of feminist insults I possessed.

"You're a self-centered, patronizing, oppressive, macho, patriarchal, misogynist domineering, condescending, male chauvinist pig!"

"Jesus Christ! What the fuck is going on with you, Judy?"

"The women's movement. That's what's going on."

"Is it because the Cuba conference didn't happen?" Stew paused. His blue eyes narrowed. "Are you having an affair?"

"No, of course not." The lie came easy.

"Are you sure?"

For me, this was a true Robin Morgan amulet moment. I understood that, I—Judy Gumbo—could control the outcome if I gave myself permission to jump headfirst into interpersonal confrontation.

I shot back, "I'll tell you what I'm sure of. I'm sure I'm sick of you, Stew Albert. You go live wherever you want. I'm moving to Boston."

"Fine," Stew said.

"Fine," I replied.

Hypocrisy, that ideological contradiction between the egalitarian ideals we both believed in and the Stew Albert I'd experienced, did us in. The more I saw Stew as unwilling to treat me as his equal, the more I perceived inequality in his behavior. I gazed across the gap between Lindequist's two front bucket seats to see my golden Stewie shape shift into a scraggly-haired hippie in a frayed yellow shirt with streaks of black crud under his un-manicured fingernails. I did experience a twinge of guilt after I caught a glimpse of the hitchhiker's sad face in

Lindequist's rear view mirror. But I did not feel depressed; I felt fortunate. Even though we lived more than 8000 miles apart, disagreed politically in fundamental ways, had a marriage, sons, and a twenty-plus year age gap between us, I had my sweet Oanh to fantasize about.

Happy to know I'd be rid of Stew and the hitchhiker when I dropped them off in New York City, I downshifted, stepped on the gas, and heard a satisfying *vroom* from Lindequist's sewing machine-on-steroids engine.

* * *

IF I ADD HO CHI MINH'S maxim that *nothing is more precious than independence and freedom* to Sun Tzu's adage *know your enemy and know yourself, in a hundred battles you will never be defeated,* stir in the feminist mantra that *the personal is political* and apply that combination to my relationship with Stew, my way was clear. I no longer needed Stew to give me love, admiration, power, or prestige. I'd have my own adventures and make my own mistakes. My hair fell in waves down to my chest; my butt attracted women as well as men. I numbered among my favorite possessions Lindequist and my embroidered sheepskin jacket from the Ukraine. I had come into my own as Judy Gumbo—feisty, confident and unrepentant. A twenty-seven-year-old adventurer who aspired to be the hero of her own life.

Free from me, Stew spent some months homeless, occupying a living room couch at the Upper West Side apartment of Weatherperson Brian Flanagan and book editor Sylvia Warren. Stew then took up with Phyllis Vanik, daughter of a member of Congress. I didn't get exactly what it was that Phyllis saw in Stew, except perhaps his curly blond hair. Nor could I comprehend what attracted Stew to her, until it came to me: Phyllis was Stew's version of sleeping with the enemy.

Years later Stew confided to me that, in his heart of hearts, he'd always hoped that he and I would get back together. Not so for me.

My job description in 1970 was "national Yippie traveler." I'd fly youth fare around the country or drive Lindequist to nearby college towns where I'd agitate against the war and for the liberation of women. Even though Yippies professed to have no leaders, I was treated like a minor celebrity when I'd arrive in town. Men, and the occasional woman, hit on me. I recall waking up one morning in a sun-lit loft after a delicious one-night stand with a dark haired, bearded anarchist in Ann Arbor, Michigan. Out from under Stew's yoke, I was having more fun than I'd imagined, although the occasional outburst of hostility—especially from women—surprised me. It shouldn't have. My cohort was beginning to embrace an egalitarian ideology of anti-leadership while I was playing, as Phil Ochs warned me not to, the "Chords of Fame." I hadn't yet learned to look out for myself; this girl just wanted to have fun.

* * *

WHEN I WASN'T ON THE ROAD, I lived in Boston with my roommate Marion Feinberg. In 1971, our telephone kept ringing; I never knew for whose relationship it tolled. Nancy had called it quits with Jerry after she and I returned from Vietnam. She could no longer stomach Jerry patronizing her.

"He put me down. He belittled me. He badgered me into doing things I didn't agree with."

Anne Weills left Tom Hayden. Jane Scherr left Max. Betty Dellinger left Dave. Genie Plamondon left Pun. My former Keith Street roommate Miche Hittleman left Walter, took the baby, and relocated to a rural commune south of the Oregon/California border. Rosemary Leary left Tim. Artie and Bobby Seale separated. Kathleen stuck it out with Eldridge until she could no longer take it.

Anita Hoffman was also on her own, but for another reason. When Anita and Abbie's son America was just a toddler, Abbie was arrested and charged with selling cocaine. Abbie went underground, leaving Anita a single mother on welfare who used her Yippie experience to organize others in the same circumstance.

It was break-up city everywhere.

For a time in 1971, as in 1968, even Abbie and Jerry no longer spoke to each other. FBI Director Hoover seized the advantage, instructing his New York office, in a typical COINTELPRO operation, to **anonymously mail a leaflet to selected New Left activists designed to broaden the gap between Abbott Howard Hoffman and Jerry Clyde Rubin, co-founders of the Youth International Party (Yippies) hopefully to split this scurrilous and completely unprincipled organization.**

Yippies, scurrilous? Perhaps, but unprincipled, never! I have no idea if Abbie or Jerry received such an anonymous leaflet but by then it was too late. Like so many cisgender couples I knew, the two most famous Yippies also split up.

CHAPTER 17:
HANDS UP!

By March 1971, I lived wherever protest took me. I took up temporary residence in a tiny back bedroom of a house at 2226 M Street, near Georgetown, in Washington D.C. Chicago 8 defendant Rennie Davis, who I'd last seen at the Conspiracy Trial, had called a demonstration in coalition with student and anti-war groups. The Nixon Administration refused to end that terrible war, which meant the escalating conflict in Vietnam demanded an escalated response. Both countries were drowning in blood. The time had arrived for an emergency distress call: Mayday! Mayday! Mayday!

"If the Government Won't Stop the War, We'll Stop the Government!" Mayday fliers announced.

Rennie asked me to come help. How could I stay away?

As a member of the Mayday Tribe, I called on my *Barb* and *Tribe* experience to help Rennie and his cohort put out a Mayday manual, which gave tactical advice to demonstrators about how and when to block twenty-one of the nation's bridges and intersections with acts of massive, non-violent civil disobedience. I also did my best to put out a full color Mayday newspaper with a traffic light on its cover and the headline, *"Washington! May! Go!"* I told myself and any other Mayday confederate who would listen that I wanted a symbol to encourage demonstrators to take action: Red to stop traffic, Orange for caution, and Green for Go—to Washington.

Rennie nixed my idea. Son of a government official—now relieved of duty based on Rennie's anti-war activities—Rennie was no Yippie. By then, the ongoing American atrocities in Vietnam had raised Rennie's scale of earnestness from single-minded to magisterial. Non-violent blocking of traffic across Washington D.C. was provocative enough for Rennie. No image more extreme, even by implication, would make the Mayday cut.

I decided to lighten things up, to introduce some traditional Yippie medicinals into this serious Mayday effort. Paul Krassner enjoyed telling me that I was addicted to pot. I'd deny it—even though I knew Paul qualified as an expert, given his LSD meltdown at the Conspiracy Trial plus the honey laced with hash oil he may or may not have handed out in Lincoln Park four years earlier. I could accept that I was addicted to cigarettes. I'd roll my own out of a green and white Macdonald's tobacco tin, leaving behind a trail of brown tobacco shards wherever I went. Ads for Virginia Slims cigarettes assured me I'd "come a long way baby," a slogan which this Yippie took to mean that marijuana, like tobacco, was as suitable for women as it was for men.

By the time I was helping Rennie out with Mayday, Stew and I had lived apart for seven months. I had discarded, or so I hoped, the insult of him calling me a cunt on the New Jersey Turnpike. I was a free woman; that incident was old news. Stew didn't sound surprised to hear my voice when he picked up the phone in his New York City apartment. I went straight to the point.

"Hi Stew, um, this is Gumbo. Um, listen, I'm here in D.C. working on Mayday and, I uh, I don't have any . . . you know . . . um . . . stuff . . . the stuff our friend in New York gets for us?"

"Why are you asking me? Aren't I the arrogant, patronizing, male chauvinist pig?"

He hadn't forgotten our scene in Lindequist.

"Well, yeah, but I need you to come down here. I need you to do this one thing for me. Not just for me; for everybody, OK?"

"OK," Stew said, confirming I could still count on his compliance. Stew most often did what I wanted when I asked.

"Thanks, honey," I replied. The "honey" word slipped out. Followed, like any girlfriend, by unsolicited advice.

"Take the bus. I don't want you to get busted."

I picked Stew up in Lindequist at the Washington Greyhound station. With his brown Frye boots, a green army surplus knapsack slung over his leather jacket, and shoulder-length curly blond hair now washed and clean, Stew looked as desirable as he did when we first met. Even the black gunk under his fingernails seemed as faded as my rage. Back in the bedroom of 2226 M Street, I lifted the donation from our sympathetic New York City lawyer out of Stew's knapsack as if it was an offering. I thought the package weighed a kilo, but we all know pot exaggerates. Stew wrapped his long, familiar arms around me. We kissed.

I don't recall feeling ambivalent about sleeping with my former lover. It was March of 1971. By then, what the Age of Aquarius had labeled free love and what some in the women's movement advocated as freedom from male domination had been re-defined as "smash monogamy," a promise of sexual liberation to any person willing to adopt its polyamorous dictates. At least according to the Weather Underground, formerly Weatherman, now underground and for many of us a self-styled vanguard of all things politically correct. I used a Judy Gumbo version of smash monogamy to justify sleeping with Stew. I was horny. I could have—or could not have—sex with whomever I chose! That's what "smash monogamy" meant to me, and what I believed free women did. Just as my anger had once transformed Stew into a patriarchal pig who patronized and dominated me, the pot aroused in me a longing for his solid, familiar, albeit still misogynist, body.

Early next morning, Monday, March 1, 1971, the telephone rang in M Street's front office. Still groggy from sex and pot, I left

Stew's arms to answer it. The voice at the end of the line contained a shrillness unusual for Leslie Bacon, a nineteen-year-old whose angelic blond hair disguised her caustic wit. Leslie had arrived in Washington to work on Mayday as a way, I imagined, to rebel against her wealthy Republican parents. Leslie and I had bonded over our mutual commitment to marijuana.

"They bombed it! They bombed it!"

"Bombed what? Who bombed what?"

"The Capitol! The Weather Underground bombed the Capitol!"

The Weather Underground had exploded a small bomb in the Capitol Building. They'd issued a communique beforehand, alerting the Capitol police to evacuate the building. Their warning was ignored. No one was killed or injured, but the bomb did demolish a men's restroom, overturn tables in the Senate dining room, damage a portrait of George Washington, and ruin a Congressional barber shop.

Rennie was incensed. He and the majority of the Mayday Tribe, as well as the mainstream peace movement, immediately denounced the bombing. They rightly felt such an act undermined Mayday's strategy of non-violent civil disobedience and would frighten protestors away.

I was an outlier. An informant described me as **exultant**—which matches my own recollection. After I hung up the phone, I felt exhilarated, irrationally exuberant in fact. Given my penchant for extremism, combined with the horrific destruction I'd observed in Vietnam when I'd visited the year before, my sympathies lay not with Rennie but with the David who had struck back at a far more powerful Goliath.

I yelled out the news, ran to 2226 M Street's front porch and grabbed Stew, Colin Neiburger, and Michal Tola, two members of the Mayday Tribe who also lived at M Street. Together, we kicked our legs in the air in a can-can chorus line of Yippie resistance. I placed us deliberately in full view of a round, black camera lens on the second floor of a red brick fire station across the street, a surveillance I had previously joked about and then ignored.

> *It is also noted that the Washington Field Office maintains a look-out on the May Day Collective and obtained photographic evidence of the presence of persons whom the source alleged were at this location on 3/1/71.*

To break the tension that day of the bombing, Stew and Leslie decided to walk to Lafayette Park, directly in front of the White House. I disapproved. Despite our having slept together the night before, Stew could instantaneously provoke my wrath with any misstep I considered macho. But Stew and Leslie returned unscathed. I had decided the time had come to get the hell out of Dodge.

Stew, Colin, Michael, and I piled into Lindequist like clowns in a jalopy. Leslie chose to stay in D.C. Stew took his usual place beside me in the front passenger seat. I drove up to Dupont Circle then screeched my car to a halt and announced, "We gotta go back."

"You gotta be kidding," came a chorus from the front and back seats.

"I forgot my hat."

The way you dress is never neutral; what I wore defined my Yippie identity in opposition to the mainstream. No FBI surveillance could force this Yippie fashionista to abandon her hat—a fisherman's cap made of beaver fur with a matching leather brim that my grandmother Ida had sent me from her Hat Shoppe. I sped around Dupont Circle and charged up M Street's front steps to find my hat curled up in the center of my bed like a lost puppy. Alex Pacheco had yet to form PETA to inform me that a cute Canadian beaver had sacrificed its life to become my hat.

Our gang of misfits roared out of D.C. to the haven of Colin's parent's home in a modest suburb of Baltimore. Colin's mother fed us Jewish comfort food—roast chicken, salad, and iced tea. Under a night sky five hours later, when my companions and I were close to the entrance to the Pennsylvania Turnpike, I leaned down to wiggle the brown plastic knob to brighten Lindequist's headlights. Suddenly, behind me, beside me, and in front of me, red, white, blue, and orange lights turned a dimly-lit state highway into a surrealistic airport.

A man's voice distorted by a loudspeaker commanded, "Pull over! Stop your car!"

Followed immediately by, "Get out of the car with your hands up!"

In what must have been the greatest jolt of either macho fool-hardiness or denial I have ever accomplished, Judy Gumbo, mistress of exaggerated cool, announced to her companions, "I'll take care of this!"

I opened Lindequist's door and slammed it shut behind me. Pump-action shotguns pointed at me, confronting me with a reality I could not deny. I raised my hands above my head. Two state troopers grabbed me tight under each arm, marched me to their patrol car, spread-eagled me against it, then did the same to my companions. My breath hung in front of me, in the cold March air.

"Stew?" I managed to exclaim. "What the fuck is going on?"

A hand shoved me into the cop car's back seat. The door slammed shut. The backseat had no inside door handles. Through the wire mesh of a metal screen that separated front from back, I watched Stew, Colin, and Michael get frog marched into a separate cop car ahead of me. A man who I later learned came from a U.S. Army Demolition Team extracted Lindequist's back seat and laid it upside down, ungently, on the roadside gravel. He then penetrated every corner of my car with his flashlight. Outraged, fearful, and not yet knowing how to relieve stress by focusing on my breath, I discovered a particle of cuticle on my thumb, put my thumb inside my mouth and tore at it. I assumed our Yippie antics on M Street's front porch had pissed off the authorities, although I could not imagine how one confrontational can-can could provoke such an exaggerated response. After what felt like hours, a helmeted highway patrolman—pistol clearly visible at his waist—yanked open the door of the police car that imprisoned me.

"You're free to go," he announced.

Safely back in Lindequist, I noticed that her back seat had been re-installed as if it had never been removed. My companions were also shoved inside, but before any of us could speak I heard a knock on Lindequist's window. I jumped so hard I almost hit the roof then rolled my side window down. A helmeted patrolman handed me an oblong piece of yellow paper.

"Got to give you this ma'am."

It was a ticket. A ticket for a bald tire. Someone had signed the ticket "James Bond." It took my traumatized brain a week to get the joke.

My companions and I hightailed it back to New York City. Bill Schaap, our marijuana-donating lawyer, gave us the explanation I'd been seeking: A *New York Times* reporter had alerted Bill that the FBI had put out an all-points bulletin for Lindequist, with a warning that she might contain explosives. The *Times* reporter requested an interview with Stew and me. Bill, an attorney with strong Yippie tendencies, had agreed. I considered the opportunity to be quoted in America's national newspaper of record a golden moment. I assured the reporter that I had no knowledge of any explosives.

Then I declared, "This is the kind of harassment to which those of us opposed to the war are subjected by the Government."

To his credit, the *Times* reporter wrote that Stew and I denied any involvement "firmly." Concurrently, the Special Agent in Charge of the FBI's Washington Field Office wrote:

TO: DIRECTOR, FBI
FROM: SAC, WFO
CAPBOM

As a result of extensive investigation being conducted into the bombing of the U.S. Capitol Building 3/1/71, the following individuals have been identified as prime suspects: STEWART EDWARD ALBERT (BLACKED OUT) (BLACKED OUT) JUDITH LEE HEMBLEN a.k.a JUDY GUMBO (BLACKED OUT) (BLACKED OUT) (BLACKED OUT)

Their status as prime suspects is based on the following information:

All of them are quite capable based on their background and prior activities of engaging in senseless violence of this type.

All of them are known to have been in Washington prior to and subsequent to the bombing.

* * *

IN APRIL OF 1971, 500 OF my closest women friends and I marched down Washington D.C. streets at the Women's March to the Pentagon. Under a deep purple banner I and my roommate Marion had made from a bedsheet with a slogan that read *Janis Joplin Brigade,* we used the moment to revive the insouciant spirit of our favorite woman rock star, now six months dead from an overdose of heroin and alcohol. No matter that our women marchers were small in number, we were a fresh wind that blew against a hated empire; we reveled in our collective power, determined to disrupt a racist war machine with witchy curses, chants, and yells:

> *We are going to the Pentagon on April 10 to serve notice to our enemies that women are moving against them. Our urgency and our fury at the expansion of the Indochinese war and our rage at the repression of our Black and Brown sisters and brothers needs expression right now.*

We enjoyed ourselves; I believed we had succeeded. Eight days later, a group twice our number—one thousand plus Vietnam Vets Against the War (VVAW), mostly men—camped on the Washington Mall, some in full dress military uniform, others in jeans, headbands, and tattered green army jackets. Their number included a long-haired future senator, presidential candidate, and Secretary of State, John Kerry. The vets threw military medals and ribbons over a fence newly erected in front of the Capitol building to keep out dissenters. That the vets had arrived shortly after our women's march was pre-planned. They were part of what we called our Spring Offensive. Still, I chose to take the VVAW actions as an affirmation that gender-based protest works.

I learned recently that not one but two women's marches occurred at Mayday—the April 10th march, well known among us protestors, and another march, on May 2nd, 1971, that women in town for Mayday had pulled together at the last minute the day before. These women were met by a wall of D.C. riot police, but managed to break through and continued to protest in the streets. Except for one. Abby Kaplan, a Barnard student, was clubbed on the head by D.C. cops, arrested and jailed. Abby died a few weeks later as a result of her injuries. Women's history is often sidelined or forgotten. Abby's was the only death I know of that I can attribute directly to police violence at Mayday. I offer Abby's story to you now.

* * *

THAT MAY, TWO DAYS BEFORE THE scheduled start of Mayday protesters stopping D.C. traffic, the Beach Boys played in front of 100,000 people, many of whom—myself included—were stoned. In his book *Mayday 1971*, Larry Roberts has me stomping onto the stage, grabbing the mic from lead singer Mike Love, and giving an impassioned speech about women's liberation. I have absolutely no recollection of doing this but if I did, I'm proud of me. By the time I awoke Sunday morning, D.C. police had stomped on tents and tear-gassed concertgoers. There was a rumor President

Richard Nixon had issued the order. Sunday night I drove to a supporter's house and, as if to prove Paul Krassner right, I once again smoked weed—but with the rest of my affinity group. I had convinced myself I was leading by example.

Demonstrators were to assemble at 6 a.m. next morning, Monday, May 3, to commit acts of non-violent civil disobedience by blocking traffic at previously specified intersections. My new boyfriend, Harvey, from Boston, tapped me on the shoulder at 5 a.m.

"Lemme sleep," group leader Gumbo muttered.

"Are you sure?'

"I'm sure. We'll get there in plenty of time."

Judy Gumbo and the Slackers reached their designated intersection around 8 a.m. I saw no protesters or police. Traffic flowed as freely as the Potomac River. My affinity group wandered off in search of protest. I did not follow. I walked D.C.'s quiet streets alone, not a cop in sight, questioning how I dared to call myself a revolutionary after so forfeiting my activist credentials. Nor was I among the 12,000–14,000 Mayday protesters to be rounded up and imprisoned in a field behind a barbed wire fence or locked into cages at various locations in our nation's capital over the next few days. Stew helped Abbie crawl underneath that fence and escape. Stew stayed inside the fence with Jerry, *Pentagon Papers* leaker Dan Ellsberg, and famed radical professor Noam Chomsky. I, however, left Washington. I told myself I did not want to risk deportation by getting arrested, but that was a cover up—I was painfully embarrassed. So, I fled.

I did not consider myself a "dope addict" as President Nixon called all Mayday protesters, or addicted to pot as Paul Krassner liked to claim. But I did begin to question my Yippie commitment to unfettered use of marijuana. Out of my self-hatred came a discipline I still practice: Use cannabis as medicine, smoke pot for relaxation, but don't inhale the strong stuff right before a major protest.

* * *

MAYDAY MAY NOT HAVE STOPPED THE U.S. government as Rennie hoped, but its non-violent civil disobedient tactics worked. FBI files reveal a paranoid President Nixon complaining to H.R. (Bob) Haldeman, his stern White House Chief of Staff, that he could not escalate the Vietnam War as he wished since, if he did, he'd have demonstrators climbing over the White House fence, out to get him.

For myself, being in Washington D.C. to work on Mayday had put me in the right place, but at the wrong time. Dancing in a chorus line in clear sight of FBI agents to celebrate what today we call an act of domestic terror certainly did not help. I now faced a new dilemma: when you know with absolute certainty you are not guilty of a crime, how do you persuade authorities, skeptics, mainstream reporters, and even your friends to believe you?

CHAPTER 18:
I DIDN'T DO IT BUT I GOT
SUBPOEANED ANYWAY

AFTER MAYDAY, I BECAME A KNIGHT who zig-zagged across the East Coast using Yippie/feminist politics as my strategy to win. I'd moved some months earlier out of Nancy and Jerry's St. Marks Place apartment where, for no reason I could fathom and without any attendant privileges, the FBI had labelled me *President of the Yippies*. I now lived at the top of a twisting flight of stairs in a two-bedroom apartment at 2 Albemarle Street in Boston. To protect ourselves from evil, my roommate Marian Feinberg and I had painted a Yippie coat of arms—a green marijuana leaf emblazoned atop a red star—on the front door of our Apartment #3. Under it we painted the logo of the Weather Underground—a blue, red, green, and yellow rainbow pierced by a lightning bolt.

Each apartment in our three-story building had its separate entrance. I hadn't met my neighbors until two students knocked on my door. They said the FBI had offered them rooms in a "nice hotel" if they would vacate their apartment, so, I had to assume, agents could listen into mine. The young male students, impoverished and ready to party, told me they'd agreed to leave. I, a woman dedicated to defiance, stayed put.

Our telephone rang one afternoon when Marion and I were repainting our living room, covering a gentle Easter egg lavender with high gloss Janis Joplin purple. It was Stew. He sounded worried. The Feds had kidnapped Leslie Bacon, forcing her to appear before Judge "Maximum" John Sirica (soon to be of Watergate fame). Stew told me federal authorities had imprisoned Leslie in a Seattle hotel, questioning her about the Capitol bombing. They permitted Leslie to speak only to her lawyers. Like the individual who brings their workplace frustration home and takes it out on their family, I immediately laid into Stew, blaming him for Leslie's predicament.

"You're an idiot. Why the fuck did you take Leslie on that walk to Lafayette Park right by the White House? How provocative could you be, for chrissake?"

I heard Stew inhale his breath followed by, "Yeah. Right. I'll talk to you later."

Stew hung up. Even though we were estranged, I was unaccustomed to what I saw as Stew's lack of concern for Leslie—and for me. I wanted to have my cake and smash it too. Instead, Stew made me furious. Later that week, Leslie's mother, a Republican homemaker, took a different tack. She calmly told members of the press camped out on the lawn of her home in Atherton, a wealthy Northern California suburb: "I don't see why everyone is so upset about someone blowing up a building when the government is blowing up people."

* * *

ON FRIDAY, MAY 21, 1971, TWO months and twenty days after I was stopped and searched on the Pennsylvania Turnpike, I opened a Boston newspaper to find a photo of Stew grinning like a madman. He was burning his subpoena to a grand jury as if it were a draft card. Stew gazed at a flaming piece of paper in his hand with that same combination of affection and glee he once reserved for me.

Three days later, on Monday, May 24, 1971, I heard a knock on my own front door. I wondered if our next-door neighbor FBI agents had decided to visit after they overheard Marian, her friend Alvin, and I discussing whether or not to take mescaline. We must have, since when I answered the door I saw—or hallucinated—a pile of dog poop next to the thick, black soles of an agent's shoes.

I do recall one agent saying, "Miss Gumbo? Miss Judy Gumbo?"

I replied with all the arrogance I could muster in my stoned state that "Miss" bore no relationship to "Gumbo."

"Where is your husband?" The other agent asked.

I replied, "I have 1000 husbands!"

I was too high at the time to remember the stern admonition I'd given Stew:

"Never under any circumstances talk to the FBI."

An agent handed me my very own subpoena.

The FBI visit shocked me into sobriety. My Yippie marijuana leaf and Weather Underground rainbow had not protected me—I was alone.

From: Director FBI

Although the Bureau's extensive investigation of the bombing of the U.S. Capitol 3.1.71 has developed suspects and Federal Grand Jury action is pending concerning some of them, the importance of this case dictates that we continue to press and expand our investigation in a way to develop additional information of value. The time lapse, nature of crime and revolutionary proclivities of likely subjects make it absolutely imperative we drive hard toward an early solution. The most logical suspects at present are New Left activists with recidivist tendencies—the longer they remain free, the more encouraged and bold they might be to perpetuate other similar crimes. At present Bureau's most likely suspects are the following:

1. Stewart Edward Albert, SM-YIP (EXTREMIST) KEY ACTIVIST . . .

5. Judith Lee Hemblen, aka Judith Lee
Clavir, Judy Clavir, Mrs. David Hugh Milner
Hemblen, Judy Gumbo "Gumbo" SM-NL
(EXTREMIST) KEY ACTIVIST.

Urgency of Investigation: All leads, whether
relating to CAPBOM or individual suspects,
are to be assigned immediately and afforded
continuous investigative attention. SACs
are being held personally accountable for
implementing these instructions.

Within an hour of the FBI visit, our telephone phone rang. *The Washington Post* was on the line.

"It's a total frame-up," I told them, in a shaky, un-Gumbo-ish voice. Newspaper headlines across the country proclaimed:

"Judy Gumbo Not To Answer Questions!"

"Activist to Face Grand Jury Probe!"

"Girl Peacenik Called in Probe of Bomb Plot!"

As a Yippie, I reveled in this media coverage. I especially appreciated "Girl Peacenik"—a Soviet-era word which revived my communist roots. But getting subpoenaed to a grand jury forced Stew and me together when we should have been apart. We'd disagree in public with such ferocity our friends gossiped about how difficult we were to be around.

"You surround yourself with sycophants. Weak minded people," Stew commented like a disapproving uncle. I found no validity in this, but Stew was onto an intransigence in me I didn't want to recognize. Instead, as usual, I lashed back.

"Give me a fucking break, asshole. Who the fuck do you think you are, criticizing me?" I would not be mollified. But had Stew and I been together when I overslept at Mayday, he would have cared enough to do the right thing—to wake me up.

* * *

To ALLEVIATE MY STRESS BEFORE MY grand jury appearance, I switched my cigarettes from roll your own to Marlboros, both for quick accessibility and to cultivate a macho female image. My Yippie sensibility, plus my lawyers, convinced me to appear with Stew on New York public television. Stew and I sat next to each other on plastic chairs in an airless television studio. Such an opportunity to denounce government repression overcame my distrust about appearing in public with my former partner.

As I'd expected, Stew's turn on air came before mine. He began to rant about how lousy it felt to be framed, then resorted to his brilliant but untrained legal mind.

"The old statute," Stew said, "was called total immunity. We face a new statute—use immunity. Anything you say can be used by the government against you—as long as their evidence doesn't come directly from your own testimony."

Stew then launched into a complex peroration on the legal differences between total and use immunity. I didn't want to hear it. Stew noticed I was antsy. He turned to me and murmured, "Gumby, we could face twenty years in jail."

I ignored him. Judy Gumbo would never concede to fear. Our interviewer asked,

"And how do you feel about being called to a grand jury, Miss Gumbo?"

I let both "Miss Gumbo" and Stew's expectation of more jail time slide.

"It's annoying." I said. "Uncool. But our lawyers will take care of it. Nothing to worry about."

My tongue was numb, my brain ran slow; those were the only words I could make come out of my mouth. I had moved from feeling terrified to paralytic non-emotion—a state of being I could not acknowledge—especially to myself. I went with what was easy—let others handle it.

To hold up my feminist end of Stew's and my break-up bargain, I chose not to reveal any more weakness to Stew. Instead, I wrote what I could of my distress about being subpoenaed to Oanh in Paris. Within two weeks, that familiar thin blue envelope appeared in my mailbox.

> *This is going to be a hard time for you. Be very cautious, also prepare for the worst, but don't be depressed. The sun never sets once. When water overflows, it sprays. If things are "heavy" on one side, there is room for the other side to "mount." I have had several times in life, when nothing like hope was left, but I knew that depression never helped, so I did not give it a damn chance to harm my guts.*

Oanh's words broke through the way an external voice, especially of someone you idolize, can wake you up. If those peasant women I admired in that bombed-out North Vietnamese mountain cave could stand up to the most formidable enemy on the planet, so could I. The Yippie way. I'd take my grand jury summons as an opportunity for self-promotion. I'd call a press conference. To publicize my innocence. I can't say distress drained from me, but I certainly felt better.

Even though we were estranged, I asked Stew to participate. I justified my request because Stew was a companion subpoenee; it was easier than admitting to myself I needed—and wanted—Stew's support. Stew agreed. Besides, no good Yippie passes up such a golden media opportunity. My attorneys, a well-regarded Park Avenue firm who used their profits from selling their souls to corporate overlords to help resisters, also approved. They agreed to defend us pro bono.

I dressed as if I was having a job interview to be a Janis Joplin roadie. I wore a turquoise chenille sweater with puffy Edwardian sleeves and a necklace of red, green, and blue glass beads that my mother maintained the Dutch had given to Indigenous (not her word) Americans in trade for commodities such as, say, Manhattan. By the time I arrived at the Capitol building, my inner Yippie had kicked in. If this had been an actual job interview, I would have aced it. Until I saw Stew, walking across a green lawn close by the Capitol with Jerry Rubin's stocky frame beside him.

Dumbfounded, infuriated, livid—I was all of these. How dare Stew invite Jerry without first asking me? Still, when women take our rightful places in the world, positions can reverse—Mr. High and Mighty Jerry Rubin had now become a Yippie hanger-on, just as I once was. I, former naive Canadian, was now in charge. I ignored Jerry. I stood on the western steps of the Capitol of the United States of America, a Weather Underground rainbow painted on my forehead, an orange woman's liberation symbol on one cheek and yellow, red, and blue NLF flag on the other, green marijuana leaf on my chin. Cowgirl style, I hooked my thumbs into my two-inch-wide leather belt, settled my hips down into a karate stance and from this position of female empowerment I made my announcement.

"My name is Judy Gumbo. I am a WITCH. From the Women's International Terrorist Conspiracy from Hell."

In the before times you could use the word terrorist as satire without fear of surveillance, arrest, or being cancelled by your peers. WITCH headquarters were located in the brain of former Yippie Robin Morgan. I identify with witches. As with the Yippies, any woman who chose to could call themselves a WITCH. Witches threaten the established order; witches have been persecuted and murdered for practicing our craft from time immemorial. To call myself a member of the Women's International Terrorist Conspiracy from Hell gave me an identity independent from Stew and Jerry. It also linked my persecution by Guy Goodwin, the Justice Department official responsible for our grand juries, to Cotton Mather, that infamous preacher who inflamed his fellow Puritans into hanging innocent women in 1690's Salem.

I rehearsed for the press conference beforehand. I'd affirm my and Stew's innocence but also defend the Weather Underground bombing as a theatrical act of property destruction prompted by a barbaric war. Why did I feel upbeat about endorsing what today would be branded domestic terror, when placing a bomb is something I would not do or ever did myself? My answer is threefold: to avoid human casualties, the Weather Underground had issued a warning before the bombing. I looked on it as a non-lethal act destruction not comparable in effect to 54,000 American lives lost, at least three million dead in Indochina plus millions more, Americans and Vietnamese, poisoned by toxic chemicals that persist to this day. I'd publicly and repeatedly engaged in extreme speech, but extreme speech does not a bomber make. Finally, being a bomber did not feel like fun. For me, it was far too serious and disciplined an effort to be a Yippie act.

After my rousting by the cops on the Pennsylvania Turnpike, I felt able to speak on behalf of every young person who'd protested peacefully but in vain to end that bloody war. I began by quoting a communique released to the media by those who claimed to be the actual bombers—the Weather Underground. The press reported:

> *Miss Gumbo said the predawn blast was done to freak out the warmongers and bring a smile and a wink to all the kids in this country who hate their government.*

I went on to speak my truth:

"We didn't do it, but we dug it."

I'm often asked in present time what I would say if I could have a re-do. Here's my answer: If I could be twenty-seven again; if I could time travel back to 1971 and even be harassed by the FBI, I'd still say: *"We didn't do it, but we dug it."* To say otherwise would falsify my own history. I dug it—but I didn't do it. Nor would I. Nor did I have the technical expertise. To me this act by members of the Weather Underground was a tiny response to oppose the horrific death and destruction caused by a war perpetrated by President Richard Nixon and the United States Government. I said at the time and have continued to repeat many times over as the decades pass—David had struck back at Goliath.

* * *

Ten days before my twenty-eighth birthday, June 15, 1971, I appeared before a grand jury. It was two days after the *New York Times* began to publish portions of Daniel Ellsberg's *Pentagon Papers*, which revealed Johnson and Nixon's perfidy in waging the war in Vietnam. I don't recall feeling nervous but again that may be denial. Or lapses in my synapses from having smoked too much pot. I do remember feeling arrogant. And cocky. As I strode between the fluted white columns of New York City's Federal Courthouse, I spotted Guy Goodwin, architect not just of my personal persecution but also that of Stew, Leslie Bacon, and perhaps 400 others summoned to grand juries across this nation. With his gray tailored business suit and short, neat brown hair slicked back by the perfect amount of product, I might as well have swapped Goodwin for a mainstream politician seeking re-election, rather than the evil Inspector Javert out to pursue and punish I knew he was.

Women friends from Boston and the April 10th March on the Pentagon accompanied me to the courthouse. I wore a floor length green silk dress with a black velvet vest that skimmed the sidewalk. But Stew stole the fashion show. He appeared as a "cross-dressing female terrorist bombshell, glamming to the nines in an utterly fabuuulous rainbow-striped minidress with the name 'Bernardine' stitched in sequins across the bodice," or so a journalist friend wrote. Bernardine Dohrn was the public face of the Weather Underground. My supporters wore a T-shirt bearing the face of our hero the guerrilla fighter Mme. Nguyen Thi Binh, now chief negotiator for South Vietnam's National Liberation Front at the Paris peace talks. But a volunteer designer had squished a portion of our silk-screened shirt so that on at least one run of T-shirts "Live Like Her" had become an embarrassing "Livelikker." Even so, this T-shirt came to define my brand and that of many more of my compatriots.

No matter the outcome, I would refuse to testify.

* * *

I WALKED DOWN A CORRIDOR OF paneled wood into a grand jury room accompanied only by my trepidation. Grand jury rules do not permit an attorney to be present with those summoned to this form of inquisition. High above me, sunlight streamed through narrow, oblong windows. On my right, three rows of older women and men, both of color and white, stared at me with suspicious eyes. In front of me, a woman with mousy hair sat bent over a machine—just like in Judge Hoffman's courtroom but without an audience. Prosecutor Goodwin and two clones in business suits sat behind a wooden railing on my left.

"State your name," a suit asked.

I replied, "I refuse to answer on the advice of my attorneys. I invoke Amendments 1, 4, 5, 6, and 9."

These numbers are engraved into my consciousness to this day—though I omitted Amendment 14, "due process under the law," which I forgot—perhaps because I wasn't sure if this amendment applied to me, a non-citizen, or only to "native born" Americans. These numbers are engraved like inscriptions in my consciousness to this day. Goodwin put his well-coiffed head together with his fellow attorneys, whispered briefly then turned to me, his voice flat.

"You're dismissed. You may be recalled."

Guy Goodwin found no evidence of wrongdoing. That aged guard who testified he spotted Stew walking with a blond woman at the Capitol must have extended the footprint of that historic building into Lafayette Park.

With that, the explosion in my life imploded. Three weeks later my subpoena was quashed. As was Stew's, Leslie Bacon's, and that of Colin Neiberger, whose mother had served us comfort food before we were stopped on the Pennsylvania Turnpike. Also dropped, or so I heard, were subpoenas to Ken Kelley and Skip Taube of the White Panther Party in Detroit, Carole Cullum,

Noreen Banks, and other members of the Mayday Tribe, including Tucson Tom Miller, Jim Retherford, and Walter Teague, activists from Vietnam Veterans against the War, the Catholic priest Rev. Phil Berrigan and the nun, Sister Elizabeth McAllister. These are only the names I recall out of the 400 anti-war activists targeted by Goodwin's grand juries.

I cannot speak for others, but my assessment that Stew's and my innocence had freed us turned out to be completely off the mark.

On June 29, 1971, Assistant U.S. Attorney John H. Doyle III, Southern District of New York, advised that subpoenas issued to ALBERT and others to appear before the Federal Grand Jury at New York City had been set aside "to avoid litigating the issue of electronic surveillance in connection with the issuance of the subpoenas.

In other words, what in 1971 I'd dubbed the United States Department of Injustice had dropped our subpoenas so as not to expose their illegal wiretapping.

CHAPTER 19:
THE GUEST LESBIAN

I WAS AND STILL AM AN outlier on many issues: one is my belief that feminism can and should be fun. When I was not traveling around America giving speeches and getting laid, I spent my time in Boston at the Women's Center, a run-down building at 888 Memorial Drive in Cambridge—a building owned by Harvard University but occupied without permission by women on March 6, 1971.

I didn't fit the puritanical Boston mold. I believed with all my being that the Boston women were ideologically correct—yes, to struggle against misogyny *was* both critical and serious. But when I called myself a Yippie, the label "male-identified" stuck to me like tear gas you could smell but couldn't see. The cartoon character Lenore Goldberg with her super-sized breasts was considered pornographic, her cartoonist R. Crumb a misogynist male who objectified women's bodies. I agreed. Crumb's misogyny was obvious, but for me Lenore possessed great courage and leadership. Lenore fought back.

At the Boston Women's Center I did my best to absorb the practice of non-violent consensus decision-making. Ideally, everyone got a chance to speak, power was equally shared, speakers were respected not interrupted, and everyone listened. Women of color and lesbians, who had once occupied the lowest rung in the hierarchy of the oppressed, were now being accorded the highest position of respect. I concurred. At least intellectually. But then, I was informed by conference organizers I was not invited to attend a conference in Canada with Vietnamese women fighters I'd befriended on my 1970 visit to Vietnam—since having met them once defined me as a leader. Places at the conference were scarce, leadership must be democratized, women of oppressed races and genders fully represented. In theory I agreed; in practice, I was marginalized. I took it personally. Then a woman I'd barely met railed against me at a public meeting for being male identified. I was, she claimed "on a bullshit ego trip just like your idols, Abbie, Stew, and Jerry." I was crushed. Another woman excoriated me for wearing my favorite silver ring with a large, raised circle in its center surrounded by twelve smaller circles.

"Egocentric," the woman announced.

Secretly, FBI agents joined in:

> GUMBO is a very intelligent and well orga-
> nized individual, but would be more
> effective but for personality defects.
> GUMBO was an extremely irritable, bad tem-
> pered person who was not very well liked
> by "Movement" people. She made herself
> extremely hard to like. She was well versed
> in Maoism. She was also a smoker of grass
> (marijuana).

Women have been scarred by millennia of oppression. I whole-heartedly believe that irritability, grumpiness, and raging anger are justifiable prerequisites of our women's revolution. And exaggerating a negative personality trait is a time-honed trick to discredit any opponent. I see now that the rejection I experienced as coming from the Boston women's movement came equally from me—and perhaps, although I hated to admit it, from the lack of compassion I'd learned from my mother. I had no idea how to act if I could not be a Yippie "leader." I decided to escape rather than confront; I'd flee Boston to discover once again the free-form Yippie life that I assumed women's liberation demanded of its heroes.

* * *

BY FALL OF 1971, I'D HEAR my Mayday friends echo Rennie's words that our protest movement was done. As if to prove Rennie right, my letters requesting advice from Oanh in Paris became more and more sporadic. As were his letters back:

J. Dearest,

> *It was like unreal getting your word again. Guess you're in quite another mood after a long while of silence. Farewell to politics, demo, mass activities, organization, and embark on something else innocuous. If such is the case I sure can understand, and it's normal, you're not to blame. Each year may have several seasons, but each human life can only have two springs, the first and the last. You are being between two springs, both having a nostalgia of the former and longing for the next. There are always insoluble problems, but no one can help but ourselves. Take care my dear. Love. Me.*

I was for sure nostalgic about protest but to do "something less innocuous" was not exactly what I had in mind. In a seminal—no, germinal—article (to use a 1970s woman-centered phrase) Anne Koedt argues that the sole function of a woman's clitoris is female sexual pleasure. Vaginal orgasm is a myth of domination maintained by men to satisfy their basest needs. Penetration is irrelevant; a woman doesn't need a man to get off. Which means Stew and the entire male species were redundant. So informed, I made a conscious choice to abandon Woodstock Nation for what Jill Johnson was about to label a Lesbian one. I decided, as many women did, to be both liberated and politically appropriate. I'd re-invent my sexual orientation.

I didn't come out as a lesbian. I did visualize women's bodies when I masturbated. Then I got lucky. At the April 10th Women's

March on the Pentagon, I'd met a woman named Linda Evans. Linda was my type: curly blond hair, blue eyes, physically strong, politically radical, a smart cookie with a broad smile and guttural laugh; perhaps, I realize now, a female incarnation of Stew.

Shortly after the Women's March, a full-page photo of Linda and me graced the front cover of *Quicksilver Times,* D.C.'s local underground newspaper. *"Women Attack Pentagon,"* the paper's headline read. In the photo, Linda's blond curls rise above my darker, unwashed tresses; both of us are smiling, our silhouettes framed by red, white, and blue balloons. Linda, who wears a leather jacket, has placed her arm possessively around my shoulder as we gaze with love into a heroic, socialist-realist future.

Like me, Linda had visited Vietnam. Unlike me, she was a Weatherwoman. Linda had grown up a mainstream Girl Scout in Dodge City, Iowa. By the time I met her, she was on probation for conspiracy to incite a riot at Weatherman's 1969 Days of Rage. Inspired by outrage at Dee Brown's tale of white mistreatment of Lakota Sioux, Linda and I decided to make a pilgrimage together to the Black Hills of South Dakota. As stars exploded across a dark Dakota sky, Linda and I chased each other in circles, rolling together down small inclines, our bodies separated by inches. I felt filled with lust but could not get up the nerve to consummate. Nor could Linda. We knew only masculine ways to do it; neither Linda nor I had figured out which one of us should be on top.

Six months after Linda's and my non-consummation in the Black Hills, I jumped in Lindequist to barrel down Highway 30 toward the Texas/Arkansas border. I went on the road to visit Linda, who now played in an all-women's band in a rural commune outside Austin, Texas. Two dented, dingy loudspeakers blocked my view out of Lindequist's rearview mirror—speakers so gigantic in those days before miniaturization that they occupied the entirety of Lindequist's back seat. The excuse I gave myself for delivering these speakers to Linda hid my real objective—to re-ignite Linda's and my relationship.

I heard a rattle. Followed by a bang. Lindequist's engine had cut out. I watched gray & white smoke rise up out her exhaust. Once again, my car had betrayed me, only this betrayal came from my beloved Lindequist, not some janky cop car. I coaxed my car over black asphalt and rolled her to a stop by the side of the road. I turned Lindequist's ignition key. I heard only the buzz of panic in my ears. My trusty steed was as dead as the armadillo whose gray shell her wheels had just crunched to bits. To paraphrase the French radical theorist Régis Debray's *Revolution in the Revolution*—a must read in my cohort—I had desolation in the desolation. Luckily for me, Sandy Wardwell, my friend and sister subpoenee to a Guy Goodwin grand jury, had "borrowed" a gas card from her mother and passed it on to me. I told myself I would survive. I put on my head my straw Stetson cowgirl hat I'd purchased for this journey in my favorite Greenwich Village hat store and, now appropriately attired, I began to walk. Eventually I saw in the distance a faded red star of a Texaco station with *Repairs All Makes All Models* painted in homemade letters above the auto bay. That sign filled me with such relief I almost cried. A Marlboro Man with sun-browned face drove me in his pickup past fields of peanut plants a mile and a half back to Lindequist.

The mechanic looked my Volkswagen up and down then drawled, "We don't work on them there critters."

I took this as an omen. I was about to enter a world the likes of which I'd never known.

The counter-culture rescued me. The mechanic's son, a clone of his father except for his pungent aroma of pot, managed to find and install a new exhaust valve. Equally fortunate for me, Sandy's mother had not yet stopped payment on her card.

Two days later, I turned off a two-lane highway onto a dirt road outside the central Texas town of Bastrop, seventeen miles outside Austin. Three steel electrical towers of Texas-sized proportions stood like twisted Christian crosses in front of me; even from a distance I heard the tower's electrical wires hum. I drove through an open barbed-wire gate, past a stand of scrub oak and mesquite which looked other-worldly to this Canadian, and glimpsed a metal A-frame in a field of peanuts with a beat-up stove and red-handled water pump rusting out front.

My first look at the cowgirl angel with a pixie face whose right hand rested casually on Linda's shoulder made it clear to me that I'd arrived too late. Linda put her arms around me, hugged me, then stepped back.

"Gumbo, this is Laurel."

"C'mon in," my rival said and strode inside the A-frame. Dismayed, I followed. Two dogs—one wolf-like, the other a black Afghan hound—bounded up in welcome. Three women materialized out of the shadows.

I heard one say, "Hi. I'm Trella. This is Nedra. And Goose."

"Thanks for the new speakers. You'll sleep here," Laurel commanded, her voice curt, as she pointed to a single mattress, a prison bed without the bedding that lay on a ragged Persian rug in a far corner of the A-frame.

"Linda and I sleep upstairs. In the loft."

Such an unrelenting combination of rejection and The New might cause a more rational person to say, "Well, I tried," then turn her car around and drive off—but not the intrepid Judy Gumbo. Disappointed and disillusioned by Boston, I became more determined than ever to make the leap into lesbianism. In truth, I had nowhere else to go.

In re: Airtel to Bureau 2/18/72; it was requested through appropriate sources, that an attempt be made to identify the Anti-Male Lesbian Women's Collective in Austin at which subject JUDY GUMBO reportedly has been residing and if successful attempt to identify subject's associates at the collective. Name GUMBO is alias for suspect HEMBLEN.

* * *

LAUREL WAS OUR DIVA-IN-CHARGE, A CHARISMATIC creator of her personal myth bigger than reality. I recognized her type—like Yippie men, Laurel motivated the rest of us through force of will and her own ego. We lived the way poor folks are often forced to do. With Laurel at the wheel, we'd drive to Bastrop, buy 25 lb. burlap bags of rice, pinto beans, dried lentils, and onions, load them in our ancient Ford and, back at the commune, boil them up to eat. We'd heat water in a bucket and scrub our clothes with an ancient glass washboard, like the one my grandma Ida used to own. We'd scavenge in our scrap heap to find that perfect piece of rusty metal so Laurel could take the lead in fixing whatever broke last week, only to have it break again the next.

I felt like I had moved into a nunnery with benefits. But I had not yet proved my worth so, without a sexual relationship with Linda, I was ineligible for sexual perks. Before I arrived, Laurel had been in a relationship with Trella. Now it was Laurel and Linda. Goose had been with Nedra. Now Trella and Nedra were a pair. Once again, I felt marginalized as my companions chattered on about who was sleeping with who and which woman had hurt another's feelings. Since sexual musical chairs appeared to be a way of life in this community, I'd ask myself why I had to be the last woman standing.

As a former Red Diaper Yippie, I based my grasp of how women ought to love each other in Marxist notions of equality to which I added sexual freedom. If I put in according to my ability, I expected I'd receive according to my need. I was wrong.

I made a play for Nedra, a thin woman with dark hair and an abundance of energy. My mistake. My advances were as clumsy as a pre-pubescent boy. To no one's surprise but mine, Nedra rejected me. I put my attempt at lesbianism on pause, then snapped at Nedra's lover Trella.

"You're too individualistic. Don't you understand the word *share?*" Outburst over, I slunk away.

Most evenings we'd get stoned on weed. We'd lie on sleeping bags beside a campfire under brilliant Texas stars. While a natural orchestra of crickets and the beat of croaking frogs accompanied the drone of nearby electrical wires, Linda and Laurel improvised on their guitars. Laurel would predict, her cheekbones angular and foxlike in the firelight, "We're all going to die. From cancer. From the towers. It's a true fact. I can feel these things."

A single anecdote does not a "true fact" make. I decided Laurel's words held as much validity as politicians who today oppose science by claiming God speaks directly into their hearts. Then, decades later, a sister-in-law of mine who had lived for thirty years 100 yards from an electrical substation died of brain cancer. Laurel and our commune also lived close by electrical towers—and, Linda told me years later, Laurel had also died of cancer.

Laurel persisted, "Maybe we should blow the towers up. Just like in the Tarot deck."

Laurel's eco-terrorist suggestion held no appeal for me: as a suspect in an actual bombing, I'd had enough of that drama in real life. I told them no to such an act, but I stayed.

Telephonic inquiry established new registration for a nineteen sixty-four Volkswagen two door sedan with VIN 6062655 Texas tag KMF 443 registered to Judith L. Clavir, 502 West 15th Street Austin Texas, for reason of "blown-out" engine, which was replaced in HEMBLEN's VW. Records indicate engine blown in Texarkana, Texas. No criminal record located for her at Texarkana, Texas. Clavir stated the Austin address was somewhat temporary and she would also be residing in San Diego, California, and New York City.

* * *

LINDA TAUGHT ME TO READ TAROT cards—not so much to predict the future, but as a process of self-discovery, a form of instant therapy. A tool to put my emotional cards on on a real table in a real world. A century ago, Tarot divination was the provenance of Carnival magicians, mostly men, skilled in legerdemain, until reading Tarot was appropriated by female fortune tellers who passed its rituals on, one woman to the next.

I was overjoyed when Linda offered to read my cards for the first time; it was a rare opportunity for the two of us to have alone time. We sat opposite each other on a tattered rug that lay next to my mattress inside the A-frame. Linda used a wick from a kerosene lamp to light a joint, inhaled, then passed the joint to me. She took a battered box of Tarot cards out of a fringed and beaded leather pouch she kept tied around her waist, shuffled her deck, then opened it face-down into a fan-like formation.

"This first card represents the underlying foundation of your personality," Linda began. "Pick a card, any card."

Linda held the Tarot deck out to me, careful to keep each card face down so I could not see their illustrations. I ran my fingers over the cards, trying to absorb any emanation dislodged by my stoned state. Without seeing the card's face, I chose: an illustration of a lithe young person of indeterminate gender appeared. They wore a green and yellow flowered tunic and balanced a white rose between their thumb and index finger.

Linda said, "This card is the Fool. The underlying foundation of your personality. About to leap off a cliff into the unknown."

I couldn't believe that I'd managed to pull such an accurate card to represent me. Embarrassed, I covered my incredulity with a joke.

"Naturally," I said. "What else would I pick?"

My sarcasm made me homesick. I had to be the only Jew for miles. But Linda's response was serious.

"Now, ask the cards a question. You can either say your question out loud or keep silent."

"What the fuck am I doing here?" I thought.

Linda cut the cards, then turned another one over.

"This second card is your cover. It represents the way you present yourself to the world."

I had to admit the cards had done their job—I did see my inner self as a risk-taking Fool who jumped off cliffs, but for my cover, for how I presented myself in an actual world, I became The Magician—a long haired, gender-neutral person who stands beneath a symbol for infinity. One hand extends toward the heavens the other reaches toward the earth. Which made it clear my job in Texas was to unite my private lust for lesbianism with my public persona as a straight person.

The next card was my obstacle—that which prevented me from achieving my heart's desire. A fierce, charging Knight of Swords revealed the obvious. My obstacle was Laurel. I decided I'd forget Oanh's dictum in her case. I was justified in hating her.

Linda dealt a closing vertical line of cards all at the same time. The Tower, with its apex struck by lightning and on fire, stood for transcending subconscious fears. I had no doubt—the burning Tower represented the Capitol building, the lightning strike came from the Weather Underground. With this destructive act over which I had no control, I'd become that female figure tumbling off the Tower's right side. I must either go beyond myself or perish. Before Linda placed my final future card on the carpet, she'd explained that whatever future that last card foretold became, by virtue of its placement, no longer final or my future. The Hanged Man card materialized in front of me—a beardless, Christ-like figure, balancing on a tree trunk. And so, Judy/Jesus appeared, martyred by a love that, in 1971, had just begun to speak its name.

"I am so fucked," I told myself, and immediately felt better.

I'd later invent an alternate persona for myself. Her name is Mme. Gumbo. She dresses in a floor length cloak and hat with feathers; she has silver rings on every finger and even owns an antique crystal ball which, to her mother's great disgust, Mme. Gumbo purchased with a gift of $60—from her mother. Mme. Gumbo appears just once a year, on Halloween, to read Tarot cards, for free, to anyone who asks.

Mme. Gumbo gets it: there is a final future in a Tarot reading but, as in life, when that final Tarot card appears on the table, the magic of that card is spent. When Linda placed the Hanged Man card onto the rug in Bastrop, Texas as my final future, she moved my unrequited love for her into my past. The future I'd look forward to would change.

* * *

JUST AS TAROT READINGS OFFERED INDIVIDUAL insight, playing music together was our commune's spiritual practice. Laurel played lead guitar. Linda accompanied her on guitar or with low notes coaxed from her harmonica. Trella played keyboard, Nedra bass, and Goose played drums. But Laurel was the talent. I was the spectator. The band's rehearsal cabin where my speakers had landed was the only building on our land wired for electricity—a compromise between musical necessity and the evil towers. Laurel also sang lead, often without words; the other women harmonized with wild and haunting melodies, neither hard rock nor jazz but their own ethereal melodies that flowed outside our tiny cabin freeform. At first I watched but did not join in.

Laurel, however, was too much a band leader to ignore my presence. Not even the pillow I'd put over my head at night to muffle the sounds of Laurel and Linda's lovemaking suppressed my jealousy—or my worry—over how I could contribute to making music. When I was a child, I'd learned only a single musical skill from my father: If I held a soup spoon against my cheek and banged it with a second spoon at the same time as I moved my cheeks in "O" formations, discordant tapping noises emerged. Mine was not a talent, it was an embarrassment.

After I'd lived on the land for about a month. Laurel asked, "So, Gumbo, what instrument do you play?"

I fessed up. I couldn't play an actual instrument. But I did have a plan.

"I've heard you say you want the band to perform in public. How about I become your manager?"

I was arrogant enough to believe you can choose to do whatever you like no matter your skill set. Or perhaps I'd just bought into the myth that strong intent alone creates a winner. I booked the band a gig in Dallas; I don't remember how. Laurel had informally named our band "Women's Experiential." I used my preferred name for the booking—"The Texas All Girl Country Band."

When I walked inside the red barn of a nightclub, trailed by five lesbians who carried guitars, an electronic keyboard, microphones, amps, and my two gigantic speakers, the pony-tailed manager in cowboy boots looked me up and down.

"You're the first all-women's band we've ever had," he said, "Do you want your ladies to go on first or second?"

I'd absorbed enough about the rock scene from Abbie and Jerry, two of my generation's better-known promoters, to know that the lesser band opens for the greater. I chose the second option. Boys with long hair took the raised stage standing, legs apart, knees bent as they shouted out their masculine beat. My women started dancing, legs pumping, arms and hips thrusting. Out. In. Up. Down. Like avatars on speed.

"What the fuck are you doing? You'll use up all your energy to perform!" My objections were ignored. Even if I got through the mob to try and stop them, my women would not listen. The all-male band played on.

By the time Laurel, Linda, and the others took the stage, I was sweating Texas bullets. Laurel's chords began, with that hollow, haunting, free-form melody, just like in our private music house. But within minutes their music petered out. The crowd shuffled in place. Laurel looked down at her guitar as if it was a guillotine, with an invisible blade poised above her head.

"More! Go on! Play more!" The audience shouted their encouragement.

Laurel, Linda, Nedra, Trella, and Goose started up a second time. Their instruments performed a melody for what felt to me like thirty seconds—of pain. Laurel's guitar again fell silent, as did Linda's, followed in turn by keyboard and bass, leaving only Goose's lone drumbeat behind. The crowd began to jeer. Male and raucous. A Lone Star beer can sailed close by my head. It suddenly dawned on me that Laurel's name for our band, "Women's Experiential," predicted such a final future. For Laurel, the goal of playing was to play. Without notes. Or music scores. Or even a chord pattern. And never to rehearse, or play the same thing twice. My women exited the stage, their heads bowed.

It's rare for a band leader to choke as Laurel had. But as a Lesbian Band Manager Wannabe, I felt terrible and as I often did, I blamed myself. I'd made a neophyte decision as to order of appearance, one based in custom rather than my direct experience with and understanding of the experimental nature of the Texas All Girl Country Band.

Decades later, Linda and I sat close together on my green, and brownish red paisley couch in my Berkeley home. Apart from being surrounded by more comfortable, newer furnishings, we might as well be reading Tarot cards on my mattress in the A-frame. We talked about what Linda now titled the "Debacle in Dallas."

"We were untrained. I felt so intimidated I could barely play. No wonder people booed."

With these words, Linda absolved me of any guilt I felt for misreading what lay behind the Texas All Girl Country Band—aka Women's Experiential.

I departed Texas shortly after the Debacle in Dallas. I wasn't a lesbian, nor was I nonbinary, trans, or queer—or by then even questioning. My attempt to sexually re-program myself had flopped. I was, as Trella put it, a "guest lesbian." By now I'm fully comfortable identifying as cisgender. Sadly, unlike Jerry, Abbie, and my father Leo, my career as a promoter had foundered on the shoal of first round knockouts. But I've learned that even if I dislike a person in charge, I'll be at ease with myself if I can listen to and act on what that person is trying to tell me. I remain dear friends with Linda.

Meanwhile, Stew had spent our time apart with Jerry, Abbie, and Rennie Davis in John Lennon and Yoko Ono's bedroom. They had concocted a plan to mobilize young people across America with a rock and roll extravaganza starring John and Yoko. Thanks to the FBI and Justice Department, that tour never happened. As exciting as hanging out with John and Yoko must have been, I would not trade it for learning to read Tarot cards, or even for my interlude at Women's Experiential—where I learned the difference between performing for self and performance in public. I now stick with the advice Mme. Gumbo offers—in matters of love, follow your heart.

CHAPTER 20:
MY BODY, MYSELF

IN ADDITION TO BEING A CHILD of communists, an immigrant, a pot-smoking Jewish Yippie, a friend to Black Panthers, a woman who slept with America's enemy, a prime suspect in a famous bombing, and a woman who tried to bend her sexual boundaries, I've also had an abortion. With that, I'm no longer an outlier—so have at least one third of women in the United States.

Some months after the Debacle in Dallas, I drove Lindequist to San Diego. Jerry and Abbie, with typical Yippie exaggeration, had boasted that a million young people would occupy that city at the 1972 Republican National Convention to protest the Vietnam War. I too was seeing red—the bloody kind. By then more than three million Indochinese had been poisoned, burned, maimed, or killed, and more than 50,000 Americans had sacrificed their lives. The war at home raged on.

In March or April of 1972, I arrived in the offices of the anti-war San Diego Convention Coalition to this news: Paula Tharpe, a 22-year-old spokesperson for the Coalition, had been shot and wounded that January. City officials confirmed to the New York Times that "right-wing vigilantism has plagued San Diego's small radical community for several years, and that no arrests have ever been made."

The person who told me this was a wiry 40-something man who wore a white clerical collar beneath his prominent Roman nose. The Reverend Paul Mayer had been born a Jew, rejected

Judaism, spent eighteen years as a Benedictine monk before being ordained a Catholic priest, then left the priesthood. Like Stew, Reverend P. had been named an unindicted co-conspirator, in his case for an alleged plot to kidnap Secretary of State Henry Kissinger. I recognized my type—male Movement celebrity. Given my failure to change my sexual orientation combined with what I thought were Reverend P's decades of celibacy—he did not disclose to me he had been married—I figured both of us might enjoy making up for lost time. It was easy to begin a casual affair.

After a month or so of off-again, on-again sex with Reverend P. in my bedroom of the stucco house I shared with four activists, I awoke one morning to find an army of bile invading my throat. My stomach heaved. Fifteen minutes of queasiness passed, only to return with flu-like persistence the next day. And every morning for the following week. No tell-tale red arrived to stain my morning sheets. It dawned on me I must be pregnant. Pregnancy tests were not yet on the market. I figured I was at most six weeks along.

My control issues emerge most strongly when they involve decisions about my own body. I did not question for a millisecond that I would have an abortion. In 1972, my confidence in that decision could not be undermined by being forced to wait a mandatory 24 hours to reconsider, listen to a fetal heartbeat, view a black and white image of cells inside my womb, have a cold wand thrust inside my uterus to perform an ultrasound against my will, or walk through a line of picketers, faces distorted with hate, yelling at me that if I went through with an abortion I would kill my baby, a sinful act I'd regret every day for the rest of my life.

I did, however, excoriate myself—not Reverend P.—for getting pregnant. It was my sense of self-importance that did me in. I'd spent too much time on the road protesting wars to waste my time seeking out a doctor willing to prescribe contraceptives, even though I'd heard that, earlier that year, the Supreme Court had legalized oral contraceptives for all women—not just married ones. After Texas, my need to find a doctor to prescribe oral contraceptives wasn't strong. I delayed, I procrastinated, I was lazy. It was easier to stay loyal to my diaphragm with its gooey contraceptive gel. But diaphragms can fail.

Even in San Diego, that staunchest of Republican cities, abortion was available by 1972, but not until January 1973 was it declared legal. I needed only to get a word-of-mouth recommendation from my sisters in San Diego's anti-war movement. As soon as I realized this, my panic ebbed. But given who the father was, I did, however, allow myself an uncontrollable fit of laughter. Here I was, Judy Gumbo, impregnated by a lapsed Jew and former monk who had been ordained a priest then left the Church.

Only a Yippie Goddess of Absolute Absurdity could have concocted such a stunt!

As a recent arrival in San Diego, I had no close women friends or relatives to accompany me to my appointment. In fact, except for Reverend P., I felt independent but also isolated, a feeling I was now ready to accept after Boston and then Texas. Lindequist was my closest female friend in San Diego. I told myself it was no big deal to have an abortion alone; I was, after all, a woman of courage determined to live my life as I chose to live it. And pay whatever consequences that entailed.

A young receptionist smiled at me from her desk inside a rundown, single story, Spanish-style building on a four-lane San Diego street roaring with traffic. She asked only for my name, address, and payment. The $30 I handed her came—again, and as usual without their knowledge—from my parent's less and less frequent infusions of cash. I had no second thoughts. Leo had once told me the money he gave was for the revolution. This was my personal revolution. For my body. Myself.

I removed my canvas sandals, shorts, and underpants in a room whose casement windows let in enough San Diego sunshine to color its walls with a greenish jail-like tinge. I counted on my

Yippie sense of the ridiculous to get me through. The gurney I climbed up on took up almost the entire room; I crunched my butt down so I could fit my toes into cold steel stirrups and stretched my knees apart. The young receptionist draped a green cloth over my knees and bare vagina. A man entered. I assumed he was the doctor based on his white coat. The man did not introduce himself. Nor did he offer any sedative except to say, "This won't hurt much."

Yeah, right, I thought, unnerved by the man's indifference. No humor here: Was I taking this abortion stuff too lightly? Then I remembered. Although Stew and I were now miles apart, emotionally and in real time, my mind jumped to Stew's tale of how he and Joanne, his about-to-be first wife, had traveled to Tijuana in the early 1960s. Their procedure room was cramped and dirty. Instruments lay uncovered on a dingy wooden side table. Stew waited on a lobby bench while Joanne screamed. Back in Berkeley, Joanne developed a raging fever; they both feared she would die. That was serious. I was lucky. No matter how ridiculous I felt, how impersonal the manner of this man in the white coat, his instruments were covered with white, sterile gauze. The black and white floor on which my gurney rested was clean and shiny. Such modernity reassured me, the buzz of overhead florescent lights calmed me, I shut my eyes until a loud *whrrrr* startled me out of drift. I looked up to see the reassuring presence of a plastic yellow sunflower—strategically placed—dangling above me from the ceiling.

An impressive sucking noise started from what sounded like an electric motor. A hard tip at the end of a plastic tube entered my vagina. My cramp was immediate, sharp, and deep. The tube withdrew, the cramping stopped. Then started up again. A few spasms more, each as painful as the first. Those cells inside my body brought together by accident now were gone. My first trimester abortion took no more than ten minutes.

I walked out of the clinic elated, my nausea evaporated, my entire body relaxed. My recovery was that quick. I felt neither sadness nor regret, just the opposite. I felt free.

In a paroxysm of gratitude and relief, I grabbed Lindequist's steering wheel and, oblivious to a police car positioned outside the clinic, made a joyful and illegal U turn across four lanes of San Diego traffic. Given my euphoria, the traffic citation I received felt less absurd than the ticket for the bald tire signed by James Bond that I'd been given in Pennsylvania. Once again, I had my life back.

* * *

IN BED IN OUR SAN DIEGO house the following evening, before Reverend P. and I had sex, but not until after I'd engaged in a one-woman monologue with myself about whether or not to confess to this former Catholic priest that I'd had an abortion, I decided to be honest.

I blurted out, "Paul, there's something I need to say to you."

"What's that?" Reverend P. replied in all innocence, his hands stroking my back in a way that made me tingle as if I was being caressed.

"You know how I've been saying I wasn't feeling well? Turns out I was pregnant. I went to a clinic yesterday and had an abortion."

Then, as if to rationalize my behavior I added, "It didn't feel like such a big deal."

I watched Reverend P's face change from pink to white as he sat up and said, a wobble in his voice.

"Why didn't you tell about this before you did it? Why didn't you ask me first?"

There are reasons women have abortions without informing the father. Every woman has one—most frequently rape or physical abuse. My dominant reason was ideology.

"It's *my* body. It was *my* decision, not yours," I replied, defensive but unbowed.

Reverend P stood up, turned his naked butt to me, slipped on his pants, and silently left the room. He also left my life. I would not see him again until decades later, when we greeted each other as old friends, him sitting on the grass surrounded by his wife and children at yet another rally against yet another imperial war.

Often, on Yom Kippur, the Jewish Day of Atonement, I will attempt to seek spiritual enlightenment not through LSD or weed but by attending an uber-liberal, Reconstructionist synagogue. The service provides me a mechanism to enter my personal holy of holies and repent my sins. Neither guilt, remorse, nor shame ever arose in me about my abortion. My sin was to have avoided confrontation by dismissing Reverend P's religious convictions out of hand. I lacked the empathy and likely the courage to involve Reverend P. in a decision I considered mine alone. I knew Reverend P. to be a staunch believer in equal rights for women and minorities, so I took the easy route. I assumed but did not ask.

Today I am a mother and a grandmother. I am forever grateful I had access to abortion care when I was 29 years old, single, broke, and employed without pay in the service of ending unjust wars. This I know: had I allowed those cells to grow, my life's course would have altered in a manner unfair to any unborn child and untenable to me. In 1972, that year before *Roe v. Wade* became law, having an abortion wasn't a sin, it wasn't a crime, and it wasn't a baby.

CHAPTER 21:
WHO CAN I TRUST?

SHORTLY AFTER BUT HAVING NO RELATIONSHIP to my abortion, the Republican Party relocated its convention across the continent from San Diego to Florida. They did this to create distance between the Party and a corruption scandal in San Diego involving ITT (later to be absorbed by AT&T) and the Republican National Committee. But Jerry and Abbie, who'd been derided in the local San Diego press as "long-haired sissy, commie freaks," took credit for that move, claiming the Republicans had fled because Yippies would foment protest. With this move Miami, Florida became the host to the 1972 conventions of both of America's major political parties.

I walked into a pink stucco house on SW 10th Street in Miami desperate for a shower, to discover I was in a house inhabited by cave men. Its single bathtub was filled with slimy water, now re-purposed as a breeding ground for mosquitoes.

"Clean this shit up NOW!" I demanded of the occupants, all men, then wondered if this bathtub was an omen—would our protests against Republicans and Democrats end up as rotten as this swamp?

Now a committed feminist, I chose to work not with the Yippies but with the Miami Women's Coalition. Aging former furriers and communists, survivors of the Russian Revolution now retired, visited our office on Alton Road to recount their stories and by so doing pass on to my generation the anti-fascist causes to which they had devoted their lives. Elderly women arrived bearing pots of chicken soup or ruffled white café curtains, faded numbers visible on their arms. Their appearance was to me a way to give our demonstrations the support of traditional Jewish mothers. Their presence also reaffirmed my view that President Nixon was indeed a fascist.

Despite our homey ruffled curtains, inside the offices of both the Miami Women's Coalition and the broader-based Miami Conventions Coalition, Conspiramania reigned. I define paranoia as catastrophe coming at you, even if the actual probability of such an occurrence is less than 0.001%. Conspiramania is a higher form of paranoia—worst-case scenarioism, a belief that, no matter what, everyone around you has joined together in a surreptitious, covert effort to do you—and your cause—harm.

I'd resist Conspiramania, then get seduced. I was right to do so. An FBI agent reported that:

> JUDY or JUDITH HEMBLEN, who is known as JUDY GUMBO has been associated with the Miami Conventions Coalition (MCC) and the MCC has been resisting a take-over by the People's Coalition for Peace and Justice (PCPJ). Very little constructive work has been accomplished.

What about John and Sheila, a couple previously unknown but now ubiquitously present? Or the stern woman who'd volunteered to act as office receptionist, and grilled me with a relentlessness worthy of Joe McCarthy as to exactly where I had been? Her job was to manage mailing lists. Could she be reporting names and addresses to the local Miami cops? Whatever happened to the tall blond woman who'd stuck to me like glue while I beat out a da-da-da on my wooden drum as we marched side by side down Collins Avenue, the front line of a demonstration under a hand-lettered orange banner that read *Women in Revolt?* She'd disappeared. Should the cleanliness of her straight blond hair have made me wary? Rumors followed her—was this woman under contract to the CIA? And what ever happened to my friend Carol, a Southern belle from Atlanta, a demonstration stalwart with long black hair who I slightly lusted after but whose commitment to our cause I did not doubt. Was Carol an informant as some claimed, or, after Miami, had she simply left the movement, got married, and changed her name? What might I have believed had I known that, from 1967 to 1971, the FBI maintained a secret Security Index, later renamed ADEX: a list of over 100,000 people to be investigated as subversives in the event of a national emergency? And that my name appeared on it? Or that Nixon operative G. Gordon Liddy had, with his Operation Gemstone, hoped to kidnap dissident leaders in Miami and imprison us in Mexico until after the conventions? Could my name on the ADEX list be my personal version of an Academy Award of Protest? The U.S. Justice Department seemed to think so.

When I learned that Stew, Jerry, and Abbie were also in Miami Beach, I decided to reject Conspiramania in favor of a familiar, comforting sexism. I spotted my buddy George Katsiaficas at the unofficial Yippie headquarters at Miami Beach's Albion Hotel. George was a stunningly handsome radical, a former frat boy of Greek extraction. I'd first met George in Boston after he'd dropped out of MIT and taken on a career he considered far more sacred than any Greek letter lifestyle. George advocated— incessantly—that the U.S. accept the 7 Point Peace Proposal of South Vietnam's Provisional Revolutionary Government.

I stood in the entrance to the Albion Hotel's green and pink art deco lobby while George filled me in. A group of street-fighting 20-something men who called themselves Zippies had arrived in Miami to, as they put it, put the "zip back in Yippie." They'd invaded the Albion to throw a retirement party for Abbie, Jerry, and Stew.

"They've told the local media they are the true Yippies," George declared. "Abbie couldn't stand it; he's already left town."

By 1972, Stew was 33, Jerry 34. Jack Weinberg's formula from the previous decade, *"Don't Trust Anyone Over 30,"* now applied. Yippie chickens had come to roost, a new generation come to depose the old. Both the hotel and its Yippie occupants looked to me as if they'd seen better days. The sunburn on Jerry's face almost obliterated his freckles as he paced the Albion's art-deco lobby. Sweat had flattened Stew's blond curls against his head; the brown settee on which he sat looked as worn out as he did. It shocked me to see Stew, always a non-smoker, now dangling a cigarette between the fingers of his right hand.

Again, George whispered, "This stuff with the Zippies is gonna kill Stew. I think he knows it. He insisted that the only way he'd leave this planet is if I absolutely promise him that I'll protect you if you need me."

The cliche goes that when you're in your teens and twenties you feel immortal. I was 29, too close for my liking to that dreaded age of 30. Could I no longer be trusted—mostly by others but also, I wondered, by myself? Deciding that it was craven for me to need reassurance from any man—not what a liberated woman ought to do—I said goodbye to George without approaching either Stew or Jerry.

I retreated instead through Flamingo Park, past an army of long-haired members of Vietnam Veterans Against the War who had bivouacked under palm trees like those both of us—former combatants and peace activists—had seen in Vietnam. Occasional wolf-whistles from the vets annoyed but did not deter me. If the vets took my frayed jean shorts and blue work shirt as provocative, that had to be their problem, not mine.

But it did dawn on me for the first time since Stew had called me a cunt in Lindequist that a world without Stew Albert would feel out of balance. When I got word two weeks later that Stew had been admitted to a New York City hospital, I panicked. I flew to him using the youth fare to which I was still entitled. Even the airline industry had decided that after I reached age 30, I'd be trustworthy enough to pay full freight.

* * *

My rapprochement with Stew did not go well:

> ALBERT PRESENTLY IN PROGRESSIVE CARDIAC CARE UNIT, LENOX HILL HOSPITAL, NEW YORK CITY, UNDERGOING EXTENSIVE TESTS FOR EXTREMELY SERIOUS HEART CONDITION, PROGNOSIS FOR RECOVERY NOT FAVORABLE AND ALBERT WILL UNDOUBTEDLY NOT ATTEND CONVENTION.

As was their way, the FBI exaggerated. Perhaps it was wish fulfillment, but they predicted a negative outcome for Stew's hospitalization. I didn't help.

"Hey Gumby, what're you doing in this place?"

Stew asked this after I discovered his room. The IV in his arm displayed a blue line that ran like an erratic earthquake across a heart monitor next to his bed. I sighed, at a loss at what to say. I found it hard to explain to Stew—and equally to myself—why I had felt compelled to hop on that airplane after Jerry had called me urgently from the Albion. Jerry had sent Stew to New York on some Jerry Rubin errand, but once there, Stew had collapsed.

With a smile so broad I could see his incisors under his beard, Stew told me, "It's not a heart attack. The doctors' call it mitral valve prolapse."

The blue eyes that stared at me from atop his pillow held that same twinkle I once adored. Stew told me mitral valve prolapse was no death sentence. He confessed: Lola, Carole, and Coca, three Yippie women friends of Stew's who lived in New York City, had just visited. Stew called them his Sisters of Mercy, after the Leonard Cohen song. His Sisters of Mercy had unhooked his heart monitor, hitched his IV to a rolling stand and walked Stew, naked butt visible to the world, onto a hospital balcony—where all three snorted cocaine. This get-well gift may have given Stew a sense of instant immortality and helped deaden his dismay that the protest movement that had given meaning to both our lives was ending—but my resolve to make nice to the sick guy vanished as fast the cocaine Stew had put up his nose. I found no mercy in such a gift. So, like everyone whose first take on medical news goes immediately to worst case scenario, I overreacted.

"You did what?! How could you be such a fuckin' idiot?"

Then, in my best Mother Harriet The Vicious voice, I lit into Stew: for endangering his health, for wasting both the money and goodwill of Michael Rater, a sympathetic lawyer from New York's Center for Constitutional Rights who'd paid the hospital bill for uninsured Stew, and for every self-destructive act any man in the Yippie universe had ever been arrogant enough to commit.

The Yippie infiltrator who'd sat on Stew's lap at Yippie head-quarters in Miami, as if she was Marilyn Monroe flirting with President Jack Kennedy, reported back to the FBI that.

The easygoing Stew Albert put up with the verbal abuse of the ill-tempered Judy Gumbo.

I no longer question whether this informant was onto some-thing about my temperament. In this case, the FBI was right. If provoked, I for sure can be ill-tempered. I did not give up my anger until I was on a plane back to Miami, when I realized that my outburst could only have compounded Stew's stress. In com-parison, the Zippie youth rebellion seemed like a terrific bargain.

CHAPTER 22:
JUST BECAUSE YOU'RE PARANOID . . .

LOOKING BACK, I'M NOT ESPECIALLY SURPRISED that I was targeted by the FBI and the Justice Department. By the 1972 protests in Miami, and despite the predominance of patriarchal men, I'd become recognized as a leader or "heavy" in an extremist, feminist/Yippie wing of the anti-war movement. My "fame" began with my speech at the Black Panther rally in San Francisco in May 1969. It grew after I returned from Vietnam in May of 1970, when I travelled around the country agitating for women and against the war. I relied on grassroots movements and the press to disseminate my feminist/Yippie message. In September 1970, I told the press that I'd organize a "free-fire zone" to greet the far-right leader of South Vietnam. In 1971, I helped organize Mayday's massive non-violent civil disobedience. After my car was stopped and searched, I escalated my media presence by publicly supporting the Weather Underground—as a WITCH. In 1972 two photos from Miami bear witness to my ongoing notoriety: I lead an anti-Republican march accompanied by a living symbol of Republicanism—an elephant plus trainer; and, dressed in shorts and beating a drum, I'm in the front lines of an anti-war Miami women's march in front of a banner that reads *Women In Revolt*. And, although I had no knowledge of this at the time, the U.S. Justice Department did my ersatz celebrityhood one better.

Of the individuals connected with the anti-war movement going on in Miami Beach, Florida, the subject JUDY GUMBO is considered to be the most vicious, the most anti-American, the most anti-establishment, and the most dangerous to the internal security of the United States.

I enjoyed my reputation as a Yippie and a feminist, but I also doubted it. Given my experience in Boston, I no longer aspired to be a recognized "leader" like the men.

I was, however, forced to admit to myself that, sometime after the inevitable police vs. protester violence in Miami, but before Richard Nixon's equally inevitable electoral victory in November 1972, the anti-war movement had begun to fade. My prominence faded along with it. I moved into a spare room in a two-bedroom, one-bath apartment at 158 West 81st Street in New York City. This apartment, once occupied by the marijuana-donating lawyer Bill Schaap and his partner Ellen Ray, was now empty. Ellen and Bill had departed for Japan to help anti-war American GI's solve their legal problems. I stayed on, to live once again in a rent-free New York City apartment, this time uptown and not a cellar on Bleecker Street.

By winter of 1972, I was starting to feel lonely. I had tired of the FBI hunt and of the chase. Oanh and I were no longer in touch, but Peace Accords were signed in Paris on January 27, 1973. With our help the war had ended; an important part of our movement had succeeded. The day the Peace Accords were signed, the Selective Service announced that there would be no further draft calls. My friends in the anti-war movement from which I drew my self-worth began to disperse into a myriad of protest movements or embarked on careers that allowed them to prosper without having to relinquish their radical ideals. As a hybrid—a Yippie, a feminist, and an anti-war activist—I found it hard to find a home that fit.

I based my solution to this new situation on old expectations—I asked Stew to move in with me. Within a month he had. Perhaps Stew's incarceration in Lenox Hill Hospital had helped heal the hidden injuries of gender we'd inflicted on each other that prompted our break-up. Without fanfare or much forethought, I slept with Stew again. It was easy to fall into old patterns. As with Mayday, I was horny enough to let physical desire take over; I once again felt comforted by Stew's familiar body. Most importantly, I began to differentiate my feelings—dealing with Stew the Sexist no longer felt equivalent to confronting the FBI.

As for the Yippies, by 1973 we might as well have crumbled what remained of our legerdemain into a pot pipe and smoked it. Still, the FBI neither forgave nor forgot. Their bureaucratic machine kept up its harassment. FBI agents arrived at my West 81st Street apartment with monotonous regularity. I'd grab the four-foot-long steel rod that braced a deadbolt into my floor and, in my most irate Judy Gumbo voice, berate the agents from behind the safety of my black metal door.

> *Attempts have been made to interview JUDY GUMBO, however, during these attempts GUMBO, inside her apartment, was able to avoid facing the interviewing agents and made the statement, "See my attorney" through the door. Another attempt will be made to interview GUMBO at New York. This attempt will take place while GUMBO is on the street or getting in to a car. A face to face confrontation is deemed worthwhile.*

Fed up with such a vigilant life, Stew and I surrendered to our counter-cultural impulses. We quit New York City, determined to take a vacation both from our public lives and the FBI. In early summer, 1973, we rented a cabin in New York's rural Catskill Mountains. Our landlord was a well-known local chiropractor and the father-in-law of Hal Jacobs, a friend from

SDS, now professor of Sociology at the State University of New York at New Paltz.

Our rental cabin was located two-and-a-half hours north of New York City, just outside the pre-revolutionary town of Hurley, a half-hour drive from the famed counter-cultural enclave of Woodstock. Our cabin perched on a mountain's edge surrounded by a green Catskill forest. It was up a hill on a dirt road behind a trailer-home now occupied by the cabin's previous owners, Ted and Mae Heath, two elderly alcoholics. Class differences were so great that I could not admit to any similarities between the Heaths—white, lanky, and poor—and my middle class yet equally alcoholic mother.

Our cabin's exterior was white, chipped, and worn. Its oblong porch led into a kitchen, a sun porch, and a living room which the Heaths had wallpapered in 1930s beige florets and never updated. The cabin's heat came from a wood-burning kitchen stove installed in the living room, its cold running water from a nearby stream. I could not have imagined a more idyllic setting in which to reconcile with Stew, yet I approached my new environment with a combative attitude that applied initially as much to that kitchen stove in the living room as to Stew's and my possible reconciliation: Warning! Approach with caution or get burned!

The peace of my first summer in the Catskills gave me the mental space to create a home. I was happiest recycling found objects. In the center of a shed attached to the cabin, a twenty-foot-tall pine tree grew happily out of a ramshackle roof. I discovered in that shed two 48" round silver cathode ray tubes that, in a former life, had produced images on TV screens. I adored those tubes—magnificent artifacts from a bygone era of black and white TV. I rescued them, attached an electrical cord, socket, and light switch to each, added fabric lampshades as beige and ancient as my wallpaper, balanced the tubes screen down on circular gray grinding stones, and presto change-o I had lamps. Fearful visitors to our cabin warned me the tubes could contain poisonous chemicals that might explode—especially if exposed to heat from light bulbs. "Screw that," I told myself and placed my matching lamps on top of sawed-off tree trunks two feet tall—my side tables.

To complete my rustic re-creation of our Greenwich Village cellar, I wallpapered our sun porch with curtains of beige and ruby stripes that Kate Coleman, a journalist and original Yippie, had rescued from a garbage can on New York City's tony Upper East Side. But I was not yet ready to abandon urban Yippie living. Inspired by an article in the Arts section of the *New York Times,* which I'd pick up every Sunday in the nearby town of Hurley, I named my style of decorating "Trashed Palace."

* * *

IN THE MIDDLE OF A WARM October 1973, I spotted a line of hunters in plaid jackets emerge out of the forest outside my cabin. They marched in military formation, shotguns at the ready, over fallen oak leaves the color of mahogany.

"This is private property!" I yelled. "No hunting allowed!"

"Pardon us, ma'am," the trespassers replied, and tromped on down my hill.

I could not admit to myself that these men might be anything but hunters.

When fall's frost began, I took it as a sign to do as local residents advised: I used my personal hammer and nails to practice carpentry and shore up the cabin's glass storm windows against any January blizzard. Stew—taller, male—held the storm windows in place while I hammered. I also ordered eight cords of seasoned firewood from our friendly local cop and general fix-it man named Johnny Hasenflu.

But I did begin to wonder why Hasenflu began to knock so frequently on our cabin door.

"Need more wood?" he'd mumble through misshapen teeth.

Still, I had no proof. Until one day a James Dean look-alike in a black leather jacket roared up to our cabin on his Harley to inform on his mother. She worked, he told us, in the Old Guard House, a grey stone building from the 1700s that functioned as the Hurley post office. The mother was close friends with Jack Lupton and George Twadell, both resident FBI Agents in the Bureau's nearby Kingston office. I wondered if the mother had gone so far as to steam open our mail before she put it in our box—I would find out she had. Our James Dean's mother had, according to my FBI files, not only monitored our mail; she'd willingly supplied Lupton and Twadell with *more information about the subjects than that which would be requested under a mail cover.*

In revenge, I revived my WITCH-y identity and did what I could to put a hex on her. I glared as I turned the worn brass knob of Stew's and my P.O. Box #36 while I chanted rhythmically under my breath the box's prescribed combination—6-24-36. But as is so often the case with appeals for supernatural intervention, my hex did not work, at least on the FBI. Their surveillance continued.

The subjects were observed (BLACKED OUT) leaving the US Post Office, Hurley, NY proceeding on foot in the direction of their residence. HEMBLEN is now wearing her hair in braids.

I was not alone in my suspicions. By 1973, many of my friends suspected they were under FBI surveillance. It may have been true. It may have been that the myth of being surveilled revived our sense of self-importance at a time when our power to change the world was ending. A woman friend, a community college teacher, hightailed it out of New York City during a drug scare instigated by New York's Governor Nelson Rockefeller—that same governor who, in 1971, had authorized state police to shoot and kill twenty-nine prisoners and ten guards to quash a rebellion at Attica Penitentiary. Rockefeller then informed President Nixon that the state troopers had done "a fabulous job."

My friend left us with a green plastic garbage bag half-filled with low-grade marijuana. I buried her gift under a wall of flat gray stones that some forgotten pioneer had piled one atop another to mark our property line. Rip Van Winkle, or so the story goes, had fallen asleep in these very mountains. I told myself I hid the weed in the off-chance Rip woke up looking for a toke. Still, after my friend's visit I revived my New York City habit of listening for suspect clicks on our party-line country phone.

* * *

THAT FALL OF 1973, I'D SIT on a brown cushion of aromatic pine needles which was the lawn outside our cabin, roll a peaceful joint, turn on a radio, and cheer each time I hear the hoot owl voice of Senator Sam Ervin say "Ah'm just a simple country lawyer," as he led the Watergate hearings that took the Nixon Administration apart. A balmy October seduced me with its warmth and a leafy downpour of red, yellow. brown, and gold. On October 10, 1973, Vice President Spiro Agnew resigned.

> TO: DIRECTOR FBI (100-451802)
> FROM: SAC NEW YORK
> CONFIDENTIAL
> JUDITH LEE HEMBLEN (SM) EXTREMIST
>
> NEW YORK OFFICE (NYO) DETERMINED IN THE FALL, 1973, THAT BOTH HEMBLEN AND ALBERT WERE MOVING TO AN EXTREMELY RURAL AREA IN THE CATSKILL MOUNTAINS OF NYC. IN PARTICULAR, INVESTIGATION ASCERTAINED SUBJECTS MOVED TO 252 JOHNSON HILL ROAD, HURLEY NEW YORK. THIS ADDRESS IS AN ISOLATED CABIN THAT IS HIGHLY INACCESSIBLE BEING LOCATED AT THE DEAD END OF A ONE LANE DIRT ROAD. THIS LOCATION, LIFESTYLE OF THE SUBJECTS AND
>
> THEIR EXTREME PARANOIA DICTATED THAT EFFECTIVE COVERAGE OF THEIR ACTIVITY COULD ONLY BE ACCOMPLISHED BY SURVEILLANCE TRIPS TO THE AREA.

Despite hunters and that visit from the Postmistress's son, the bucolic setting in which I now lived gave me comfort enough to say to Stew, "Let's not leave. Let's buy this place."

Stew and I had little income. Still, we managed to buy the cabin that November for $10,000—considerably less than the $100,000 in bribes Vice President Agnew was accused of taking. Jack Soltanoff the chiropractor and property owner vouched, perhaps foolishly, for Stew's and my financial stability. Our mortgage payments were $80 a month. I panicked after we signed the papers, questioning whether owning property meant I had become my parents. Had I given up living according to my values, no matter how run down and decrepit our property? Had I joined the ranks of the bourgeoisie? How could I remain committed to my feminist Yippie ideals?

I must confess: Life among the Catskill pines was not as idyllic as I have made out. Cooped up in our cabin, Stew and I argued and got on each other's nerves. Our telephone kept ringing with calls from friends in need. My cohort and I all faced a similar dilemma—how to make a living and at the same time overthrow capitalism. Money became scarce. Laurel, Linda, and the Texas All Girl Country Band arrived, asking for a handout. Still jealous that Linda had hooked up with Laurel instead of me, I declined their request. David Hilliard, former Chief of Staff of the Black Panther Party, showed up also looking for a handout and reeking of alcohol. I handed David $20 then felt guilty for not supporting Linda. Jerry Rubin visited, now short-haired and ill at ease among the pines in his button-down beige shirt and light green sweater vest—an incongruous urban sophisticate in our rural setting.

"I'm trying to change my attitudes about money. But I'm worried. What if I share my money and no one else does? I'll be the nice guy who loses."

Jerry asked Stew to edit a book of letters he'd received from younger Yippies.

I knew Stew would jump back happily into his role as Jerry's support system. I could have predicted his reply.

"Don't worry, Jerry. You're still famous. You still inspire young people. This book is a Yippie way to make a living and at the same time not sell out."

Stew completed Jerry's letters book. It was never published.

I, however, caught a break. By then I'd wrangled my first "real" job. Once a week, I'd drive two hours down from the Catskills to Essex County Community College in New Jersey, where I, a white woman, guiltily taught Sociology to Black people who rightfully hoped that a community college degree would help them out of Newark's poverty. I also had an affair with Andy, a colleague at the college. Why did I sleep with Andy—Lust? Expediency? "Why not?" I told myself. In the days I was away, Stew had his own affair with Peggy, the editor of the *Woodstock Times,* our local newspaper.

Being monogamous felt as unreal to me as owning property. Much as I tried to deny it, I hated Stew's affair. But I was not yet willing to give up my freedom to smash it.

One night a Catskill storm crept in with cat-like tread. Stew and I moved our mattress from the cabin's glassed-in sun porch to its warmer living room. We made love sandwiched between two electric blankets.

Afterwards, I said to Stew, without much forethought, as was my way, "You know I'm sleeping with this guy in Newark, right?"

"Yeah, I knew that. And you know I'm sleeping with Peggy?"

"Yeah. It's OK," I lied. I was just beginning to formulate for myself what would become a guiding truth for me about managing intimate relationships—hidden secrets spell doom. At the time I could articulate this reality only in half-truths and non-offensive terms:

"We *should* sleep with other people. Just be honest with me when you do it, Stewie. I mean, I need to know not really who you're doing it with but what it means to you."

"Peggy's cool," Stew answered, then asked only that I tell him of any other affairs I might decide to have.

"Andy's nice," I said, circumventing any necessity to confess about Oanh—long out of touch. An announcement that earth-shattering would have to wait. But the more I turned our cabin from a house into a home, the more my feelings began to undermine my commitment to abstract feminist dogma about what I should or should not do. I set the circular dial on my side of our dual control electric blanket to high, Stew set his dial to medium, then we turned our backs to each other and failed to fall sleep.

* * *

I MARKED THE CHANGE OF SEASONS—DEAD deer slung over hoods or roofs of passing cars meant fall; the slaughter of the Christmas trees announced the onset of December's snow. I cherished Stew's companionship and the comfort of sleeping with him, but I was not yet ready to admit to myself that, like the seasons, the essence of our relationship was changing.

Neither Stew nor I were prepared to battle a Catskill winter. In urban Toronto where I grew up, steam heat gushed from radiators. Stew grew up with similar radiators in Brooklyn. Our cabin lacked hot running water; our major heat source was a six-inch firebox located in that black kitchen stove which occupied one corner of our living room. I telephoned the gas company and had six slim metal tanks outside our cabin filled with natural gas so to supply my kitchen cook stove. Stew's beard grew bushy; he morphed into a mountain man in a gray striped cap and puffy green down jacket. My brown hair turned scraggly from infrequent washings in cold water; layer upon layer of clothing turned me into a rotund forest gnome. But a gnome who acted with Thoreauvian self-reliance, who learned the self-help skills of country living traditionally associated with men.

Then Lindequist, my blue VW Bug, died. I grieved my loss; I adored that car. Stew helped me push her into a grove of tall pine trees at the edge of our property. For me, Lindequist represented my Judy Gumbo past; I'd revisit her grave if I felt hemmed in by Stew or cabin fever. In sympathy, and perhaps in recognition that our former life was passing, Stew hung his favorite paisley shirt over Lindequist's front passenger seat where he always sat. I replaced her with a used Volvo I never named. This car was winter suitable but too large and heavy for me care about or handle with ease.

Next, our outdoor TV antenna froze in locked position. Our black and white set brought in only fuzzy PBS from Albany. I felt as if I'd been cut off from an addictive drug—PBS TV did not cut it for this former news junkie. Our summer visitors had mostly vanished, making me more grumpily dependent for companionship on Stew than I preferred. For me, cooking epitomized that traditional and oppressive job foisted overwhelmingly on women. One day, fed up, I went on strike. I refused to cook. I took my passive-aggressive anger out, unfairly, on Stew and my friend and former roommate Marian—a rare late fall visitor from Boston. For three days in a row, I served up dinners of green fettuccini noodles garnished only with ketchup. After which, guilty and hungry, I caved.

Next our cabin's cold-water pipes froze. As did the stream from which we drew our water. Our lack of hot running water became moot; all the cabin's faucets went dry. I melted snow for drinking water and washed our dishes in water laced with dish soap and resentment. The exercise Stew got splitting firewood, swinging his red-handled ax high above his curly hair as if he were a professional lumberjack, may have lowered his blood pressure, but his efforts did not compensate for the lack of heat coming from our six-inch firebox. Icy crystals had turned the pine trees that surrounded us into a carillon of tiny bells.

I was shocked to learn later from local residents that 1973 had been a mild winter.

Was Mother Nature saying that, if I chose, I could remake Stew's and my love for each other into the new relationship it deserved? I decided that She was. I was left with only one question: could—and would—Stew do it?

I wrapped myself inside my pink electric blanket and inquired in a voice Stew interpreted as demanding, "Stew—if we become monogamous, how can I be sure you won't dominate me?"

The crinkle at the edges of Stew's eyes warned me he was starting to get defensive, but then he pulled back.

"Gumbo, I love you. You know I do. If we can be together, just the two of us, I'll do whatever you want."

Our first Catskill winter together turned out to be a purification ritual which cleansed me of the anger, the fury, and the rage I'd felt toward Stew. I'd taught myself through action to rise up and abandon the creeping meatballs of insecurity imposed on me by my family, a hostile world, and men in general. I'd seized the independence I craved by having fun. I'd gained perspective. Now I was ready.

As was Stew, who on occasion liked to call himself a "wounded faun." I found it odd when he'd say that; it didn't fit with my experience of Stew as a public figure. But I was touched by his emotional honesty and willingness to reveal himself—especially since I was, by then, familiar with Stew's empathy, his uncanny ability to identify with and comfort those in pain. Including me. If he could put himself in my place, I realized I had to put myself in his.

To shelter in place with Stew from a Catskill winter forced me to re-think what I once considered Stew's most egregious sin—him not treating me as an equal. I'd left him. Now I was back. With the exception of what we'd call our pussycat fights—hiss, hiss meow, stalk off, get over it, snuggle up—I felt content to be with Stew 24-7. I chose to trust his promise that he and I could re-engage without me losing the freedom to be myself. The inequality between us that I'd once experienced as insurmountable, that icy contradiction between our egalitarian ideals and the Stew Albert with whom I now shared an isolated cabin, began to melt.

Stew also kept his word. We started to live out the complexities of treating each other as equals. We ended our affairs. Friends told me they looked on our relationship as a model of emotional honesty. Stew became our family cook. I quit smoking cigarettes—except, occasionally those containing cannabis.

I still believe it was us being apart for two years—at my initiation—that gave me the confidence and self-knowledge to get back together with Stew.

* * *

CATSKILL ISOLATION ALLOWED ME TO RECONCILE not just with Stew but with the demands of time. And profession. I discovered that a mere two months remained before the University of Toronto's deadline to complete my Ph.D. I re-enrolled long-distance using snail-mail. I typed my thesis on a beige IBM Selectric typewriter that I'd set on a piece of knotty plywood on top of a black metal treadle from an antique sewing machine. I pedaled as I wrote. I argued against Francis Fitzgerald, a Pulitzer Prize winning author, to say that the social equilibrium of French-occupied Vietnam could be upended not just, as Fitzgerald claimed, by a shift in the Mandate of Heaven from one ruler to another, but equally by the will of common people. The Mandate of Heaven did not grant the Vietnamese people a right to rebel, but could, I claimed, be overturned by people's rebellion.

On April 29, 1975, my thesis was proven right. I heard the clatter of helicopter blades blare out of our black and white TV set. American invaders and South Vietnamese fled to the U.S. Embassy in Saigon. On April 30, Saigon was renamed Ho Chi Minh City. The Vietnam War was over. The anti-war movement I had so passionately supported had helped North and South Vietnamese liberation forces win the peace. To mark our common success, I sewed a six-foot-long NLF flag of red, yellow, and blue diaphanous material and hung it from the branches of a pine tree. Only one visitor to our cabin noticed.

By then I worked as an Assistant Professor at nearby SUNY New Paltz. To celebrate the victory, I handed out to each of my students a sprig of yellow mimosa, a flower traditionally given to women in socialist countries to observe International Women's Day. I announced the victory of what I considered "our" side. Thirty pairs of eyes stared back me as if I was from Mars. I did not hear from Oanh.

One day I picked up an envelope at the Hurley Post Office. It was brown, lightweight, and oversized, with a Hanoi return address. Instead of the handwritten message I still hoped, for I found a sheet of glossy white paper adorned on its left side by that famous black and white head shot of Vietnam's President Ho Chi Minh. On the right, handwritten in cursive was To: Mrs. Judy Klavier. Initially, I was perplexed. Who was Mrs. Judy Clavir anyway? "Mrs." was way too traditional to be me. Then I noticed a signature in Vietnamese from The Committee for Solidarity with the American People—Oanh's organization. Words handwritten in English followed.

With the most sincere gratitude of the Vietnamese people for your precious support and assistance to our just struggle for a peaceful, reunified, independent, democratic and prosperous Vietnam.

The inscription bowled me over, as if Ho Chi Minh himself was addressing me from the spirit world of charming revolutionaries. I framed the document in red and gold as if it was an award of merit and hung it on the wall of every place I've lived, until it found a permanent home at the Labadie Collection of Social Protest at the University of Michigan.

It is the most momentous thank you note I've ever received.

CHAPTER 23:
. . . DOESN'T MEAN THEY AREN'T WATCHING YOU

FROM, Director, FBI
Clarence M. Kelley

TO, The Attorney General
December 18, 1975
STEWART EDWARD ALBERT
SUBVERSIVE MATTER

JUDITH LEE HEMBLEN
SUBVERSIVE MATTER

INFORMATION MEMORANDUM

Albert and Hemblen have been subjects of security investigations for a number of years because of their numerous subversive activities. They are both suspects in the Weather Underground (WU) claimed bombings of the U.S. Capitol Building in March, 1971 and the Pentagon Building in May, 1972. They reside in a rural location north of New York City and have in the past few years been in continuous contact with individuals known to sympathize with the WU or are considered to be part of the above-ground support apparatus of the WU.

I'd hoped to leave FBI surveillance behind when Stew and I left New York City for the Catskill mountains that summer of 1973. But the FBI decided Stew and I had moved to our isolated cabin to set up a training ground for terrorists.

FBI Director J. Edgar Hoover had died of a heart attack on May 2, 1972. Six months after Hoover's death, the FBI, now directed by Nixon henchperson L. Patrick Gray, conducted their first break-in of my cabin.

> *SPECIAL AGENT JAMES (JIMMY) VERMEERSCH, NEW YORK OFFICE: When we got word from an informant that Hemblen and Albert were away, we decided to go up there and get a typing sample. Hemblen and Albert were suspects in bombings, and we thought Weather Underground (WU) communiqués were being typed there.*

> *SPECIAL AGENT ROBERT (BOB) THETFORD NEW YORK OFFICE: There was no need to pick a lock since the cabin was not locked.*

We lived in rural isolation. I saw no need to lock the cabin.

> *SPECIAL AGENT FRANCIS JARRETT NEW YORK OFFICE: The place was a pigpen and had plenty of cats in it.*

OK, OK, I confess—even by my hippie standards, yeah, my cabin was a mess. Not quite a pigpen but certainly cluttered. Having no hot running water helped. Plus, I hate housework. Did then, still do today. The chaos of my cabin had a positive yet unintended outcome—I never noticed anything out of place after an illegal FBI entry.

By mid-January 1974, Stew and I had acquired two cats, both black and white. I named my female cat Tarot so she could act as Mme. Gumbo's familiar. I named our male cat Kabbalah for the

Kabbalistic system of mystical Jewish insight. But cats, even highly domesticated cats, are predators. They protect their territory. Cats are also anarchists. They act however they want whenever they want.

> SPECIAL AGENT ROBERT (BOB) THETFORD NEW
> YORK OFFICE: A cat knocked over the copy
> box of the camera.

> SPECIAL AGENT CASSIDY NEW YORK OFFICE: One
> cat jumped on Jimmy Vermeersch.

My cats engaged in the only act I can think of which could be labelled "terrorist" that I, Stew, or our pussycats ever committed. In addition, unable to figure out how to use my Selectric III typewriter, Special Agent Jimmy Vermeersch—leader of the FBI's black bag team who burglarized my cabin—must have been humiliated. FBI files reveal Vermeersch had to ask a younger agent to switch my typewriter on, so he could obtain a typing sample. Attacked by my cats and embarrassed by not being able to turn on my typewriter, he left with this conclusion:

> The typewriters used were not used in the
> preparation of Communique #14 in the above
> captioned (ITT) case or the questioned
> typewriting in PENBOM.

Absence of evidence of wrongdoing did not deter the intrepid FBI. Like the Mounties of my native land, they had to get their man—or in my case woman. FBI agents continued to surveil me.

> SPECIAL AGENT JACK ALDRIDGE, NEW YORK
> OFFICE: Vermeersch and I took Enright and
> Kelly to show them the cabin and to explain
> the problems we were having in following
> Hemblen.

> HEMBLEN, who in every surveillance situa-
> tion encountered to date is the person who

> *drives when the subjects leave their resi-*
> *dence, is known to drive at speeds in excess*
> *of 80 miles per hour on roads which are*
> *sometimes devoid of any other traffic. This*
> *also makes surveillance very difficult.*

I confess to this too—I do like to drive fast. But I'm not *nuts.* Neither I nor my battered Volvo dared do anything close to 80 mph on those winding Catskill roads.

* * *

IN FEBRUARY 1974, I OBSERVED A camper truck drive, unannounced, over a light snowfall, up our dirt road, and park beside our cabin. I recognized the driver. If the cartoon character Yosemite Sam wore overalls, was bald under his cowboy hat, and had been a member of the American Communist Party who now claimed to be a courier for the Weather Underground, that would be the driver—Clayton Van Lydegraf. I could not turn Van away. To do so would have violated protest movement ethics: despite political disagreement, you maintain solidarity with your comrades.

But after two days in the cabin with Stew and Van, I seethed. Like arguments in my communist parents' home minus the alcohol, I hated the intensity of Van's disagreements with Stew over Marxist-Leninist theory. In purity peril lies; I found more empathy in the old stone walls outside our cabin than I got from Van and his ultra-ideological stances. Even Stew succumbed to partisanship. I despised having to live in our small space surrounded by intense male voices—the hallmark of political hard-liners. Van's complete lack of humor, combined with him treating me as if I existed only to cook, infuriated me. But on the third day Van surprised me.

He declared, his tone still clipped and strong: "I'm a plumber. I'll go get you guys a water heater. I'll hook up your shower in the bathroom. I'll insulate your pipes. You don't have to live this way."

I was dumbfounded. A dogmatic Stalinist with a heart? Van

drove to the nearby town of Kingston, where we paid for and he bought a new water heater. He installed it in our cabin's basement. I felt so grateful to have a shower with hot running water instead of having to sponge myself clean out of a pot with water heated on my decrepit and often broken kitchen stove, I let go of my hostility. Oanh was right to advise me that friends, both good and bad, go with you on the long road to revolution. I didn't consider Van a friend and his revolution was not mine—still, I hugged him when he left.

Van left us with a stack of paperback books bound in red with beveled edges and a request that we distribute these books clandestinely to friends in Woodstock. Van's books were first editions of *Prairie Fire*, a political manifesto of the Weather Underground, who'd decided (mostly) to renounce bombing property and go into publishing. I felt privileged to help distribute the original editions of *Prairie Fire*. To do so meant Stew and I could put into practice what by then seemed like an ancient trope—to unite hippie counter-culture with New Left politics.

THROUGHOUT THESE SURVEILLANCES, NEW YORK OFFICE PERSONNEL NOT ONLY IDENTIFIED MANY ASSOCIATES BUT WERE ABLE TO ASCERTAIN THAT NO RADICAL FUGITIVES WERE RESIDING AT THIS ISOLATED CABIN.

The FBI agents spoke truth to power here. Although they identified our many visitors as friends of Stew and me, they discovered not a single underground radical fugitive at our cabin. Because there were none.

* * *

THAT SPRING OF 1974, ABBIE DISAPPEARED underground to escape a drug charge. FBI agents took advantage—they switched their justification for surveillances of Stew and me from the Weather Underground to Abbie.

> *The purpose of the trip was to apprehend Abbie Hoffman, however, the decision was made prior to the trip to bag the place in the event that Hoffman was not there.*

A "bag job" or to "bag the place" is FBI parlance for making an illegal entry to obtain photographs and documents or plant a listening device.

> *Shortly thereafter we concluded that (Abbie) Hoffman was not at the cabin and the bag job was conducted.*

Excuse me? Abbie was *not* in our cabin, so FBI agents burglarized it?

Between February and November of 1974, according to my files, FBI agents made at least six more surveillance trips to Hurley. Some lasted a week or two. A few agents totaled four or five trips each.

I've convinced myself New York FBI agents actually enjoyed coming up to Hurley to surveil me, since, by burglarizing my cabin, they could justify to their superiors their need to take hunting trips outside the city and eat the famous steak at the Skytop Motel near Kingston on Route 28. The FBI also took the opportunity to check in with my local bank to gather information (from an informant) about the magnitude of my assets:

> Contact with (BLACKED OUT) determined that JUDITH L. CLAVIR continues to maintain a checking account at the Stone Ridge, New York Branch and as of 11/20/74 had a balance of $333.80. (BLACKED OUT) stated he further learned CLAVIR also maintains a savings account at the Hurley New York bank and as off 11/15/74 had a balance of $495.18.

Even with seven illegal burglaries, FBI agents discovered nothing except my low bank balance. In December 1975, they claimed to have stopped invading my cabin.

SPECIAL AGENT JACK ALDRIDGE: It was then decided to terminate the bag jobs because they were unproductive.

Instead they decided to track my car:

SPECIAL AGENT NEW YORK OFFICE: I was upstate twice. The first time I slipped on the ice and dislocated my shoulder. The second time was when the beeper was put on the car.

RESIDENT AGENT KINGSTON OFFICE: I conducted four surveillances . . . also two more in connection with the beeper that was installed on the car.

SPECIAL AGENT NEW YORK OFFICE: I made a fifth trip up to Hurley to install the beeper on Gumbo's car.

As it turned out, installing tracking devices was in fact a lesser evil. The following exchange appears in my FBI files:

SPECIAL AGENT FRANCIS JARRETT: I heard that a cheap microphone was purchased to be used in the residence of Judy Gumbo in Hurley, New York, and was actually installed.

SPECIAL AGENT JIMMY VERMEERSCH: We went up intending to put the mike in and stay for several weeks. It was monitored outside in the woods at night.

SPECIAL AGENT JACK ALDRIDGE: During the period the microphone was in place, we obtained very little of value.

It turned out that FBI higher-ups didn't want to know—officially—about illegalities that were taking place, so agents kept their machinations secret.

SPECIAL AGENT NEW YORK OFFICE: Kelley had gone drinking with ASAC Enright . . . .

> *Kelley said something like, "I told Enright*
> *you guys were doing something more than*
> *meets the eye. Enright said: I don't want*
> *to know the details but I know you guys*
> *are doing a great job.*

Of all the warrantless break-ins committed by the FBI against me, this one takes the cake—installation of a microphone that broadcast for ten days from my table lamp. When I first found this out, I wanted to put on my white karate-gi and pound the agents senseless. They had penetrated my cabin, skulked around in my woods at night, and listened in while Stew and I argued or made love. I fantasized that I'd ask my sisters from the Yippie coven of the Women's International Terrorist Conspiracy from Hell to put a curse on them. But when I read that agents had used the mic to overhear our book group discussing Stanley Aronowitz's book *False Promises,* I had to laugh. FBI agents had sent a memo to every FBI office in the United States—including far reaching Butte, Montana—to inquire if this book about the working class was code for a terrorist act. I embarrassed Stanley when I told him this. He could not believe the FBI had never heard of his book.

* * *

MUCH AS I'D LIKE TO, I cannot in good conscience blame the FBI for preventing me from attending my Ph.D. graduation. I can and do blame my dysfunctional relationship with my mother. I knew for certain Harriet would do her best to combine her jealousy of me with any praise for my achievement she'd manage to concoct. The ceremony was scheduled for early December 1975 at the University of Toronto. I chose avoidance. I'd celebrate instead in friendlier climes. I drove with Stew to New York City to visit Yippie lawyer Bill Kunstler, who I'd last seen at the Chicago 8 Conspiracy Trial, and Margaret Kunstler , a gifted attorney, also my friend, and Bill's spouse.

I parked our Volvo close by Margie and Bill's home in Greenwich Village. I could not put my finger on it exactly, but the air around me seemed charged with ions of suspicion. I spotted— or so I thought—a man in a trench coat and fedora lurking in the shadows of a nearby stairwell. I ignored him.

"This is New York." I told myself. "Everybody lurks in New York." I was wrong.

> Upon arriving in New York City Hemblen and Albert, in the company of an unidentified female, proceeded to 42 Perry Street. All proceeded on foot to 36 Grove Street where they entered. No further activity was observed on this date.

Stew and I stayed overnight at Bill and Margie's. Early in the morning of December 13, 1975, we returned our car. Again, I saw a man. This time his trench coat was black. I watched him scurry down the sidewalk like a rat exposed to daylight.

Then, in an act of spontaneous Yippie theater for which I am forever grateful, I chose to walk around my car's perimeter, looking for I knew not what. This is exactly when I saw it—a smear in the middle of my rear bumper, as if some employee at a car wash had wiped away the dirt I'd accumulated on my trip down-state. In the center of the smear, I glimpsed a six-inch long black wire hanging down—a wire which I knew did not belong. I squatted in the gutter, avoiding its stream of gray ice water as best I could, and contemplated the wire. The curiosity I've had my entire life trumped any foreboding. I called Stew over.

"Whaddaya think this is?" I asked him.

Stew looked at the wire, stroked his beard, shook his head, but made no comment. He knew nothing about cars. Born and raised in Brooklyn, Stew had never learned to drive. I'd tried to teach him once on an empty Catskill road, but cut my lesson short after he'd growled his way through two stop signs without stopping.

Still, I needed Stew's assurance. Three weeks earlier, in a fit of know-it-all feminist machismo, I'd installed a new battery in my Volvo by myself—reversing its poles and sending my car's electrical system up in smoke.

I told myself that if the wire I saw came from a bomb placed underneath my car by the FBI or some God Knows Who right-winger, to go out in a flaming blaze of glory would be a quintessential Yippie act. Such a death might at least attract the media.

"You wait on the sidewalk." I turned to Stew, commanding in my best General Gumbo voice, "I'm going to turn the engine on and see if it starts."

Stew refused. He sat down heavily in his usual place in the passenger seat. Stew told me later he did not want to see a headline that read *Sexist Survives.*

I decided the odds were good there was no bomb, but I'm enough of a romantic to feel overjoyed that Stew would choose to die with me. And, of course, to share in the media glory that martyrdom by FBI would bring.

Both entered Hemblen's vehicle, which was parked at 13th Street and Seventh Avenue.

I turned the Volvo's key. No click. And no explosion. The Volvo's engine kicked in. My breath rushed out from my lungs as if I was being released from prison. I returned to the rear of the car and knelt once again in that dirty, freezing slush. I did not doubt; I did not hesitate. I reached my hand up as far as I could behind my NO NUKES bumper sticker. My fingers touched an object I knew did not belong. I tugged. Nothing happened. I gave the foreign object a stronger tug and found myself clutching a size C battery attached to a piece of three-quarters inch black electrical tape.

No sane person, I told myself, has a battery attached to their rear bumper. Now paranoid with good reason, Stew and I spoke in one voice.

"Let's get the fuck outta here!"

> And proceeded to drive in a very circu-
> itous route, making several obvious
> attempts to lose any surveilling vehicles.
> The device appeared most effective,
> enabling agents to follow HEMBLEN at a
> discreet distance with better results than
> have been obtained in the past.

This FBI statement has got to be a cover-up. How could their tracking device produce better results with only a single battery?

The more I navigated 79th Street through Central Park, the more I observed four navy blue late model American cars following me. A horse-drawn carriage brought up the rear of this procession. I sped through an orange light and headed up Madison Avenue past store windows decked in peaceful holly and sparkling Christmas lights. The Wild West horse and buggy posse that trailed The Outlaw Judy Gumbo vanished; the late model cars maintained their ground, clearly visible in my rear-view mirror. I headed back across 86th Street to the Upper West Side, driving as if to save my life. All this time, my new best friends stayed close, a car chase in slow motion, never out of visual range. Without a working tracking device, the FBI made no attempt at concealment.

"Time to go for Chinese!" I managed to get the words out. Stew agreed instantly. Chinese food is comfort food for Jews of my generation.

I turned left down Broadway then spotted a Comidas/Chinois sign blinking in neon red and gold. I felt grateful to find an empty parking spot nearby. As I recall I shook so hard I dropped my quarter for the meter into a pile of slush and lost it.

> After parking on Broadway at 85th Street,
> Hemblen and Albert entered several stores
> within a five-block area.

Several stores in five blocks? Nope—just another FBI exaggeration. Stew and I sought comfort, not commodities.

Stew headed toward the restaurant, his face ashen under his blond curls. At our table, an indifferent waiter plopped down two bowls in which floated barbequed pork and shards of white tofu. The soup tasted like fear would, if fear came coated in tamarind and chili oil. The soup must have freed Stew's brain to strategize.

"Back to Bill and Margie's!" he declared.

If you think you're in trouble with the law, the best place to be is with your lawyers.

```
After re-entering their vehicle, Hemblen
and Albert drove by a circuitous route
back to 36 Grove Street where they parked
and entered. No further activity was
observed on this date.
```

No further activity beyond getting back to Bill and Margie's? Puh-leeze! This FBI memo is yet another a cover-up masquerading as news. Here is what actually happened:

With longer arms and stronger fingers than I could ever dream of, Bill Kunstler reached down under my Volvo's bumper and pulled out an object. It was a box. Made of rectangular black metal, 6" long by 4" wide. It had a number—107—scratched on one side. The wire I'd seen hang off one corner of the box was attached to it with a putty-like substance—clearly, an antenna. One size-C battery was secured to each end of the box with black electrical tape. And all batteries were intact.

As decades passed, I've asked myself which of us—me or the FBI—was the bigger schmuck? I was foolish enough to abandon my Volvo in front of that Chinese restaurant; I gave the FBI a terrific opportunity to do whatever they wished to my car. But I have no idea whether FBI agents only replaced the battery I'd disabled or substituted a second, fully functional tracking device. I do, however, recall what Bill said after daylighting my device.

"I believe this might be the first time in my experience that one of these was actually found by someone."

* * *

In May 2020, Arthur Eckstein—a professor and expert researcher on the FBI, and by then my fourth husband—discovered an FBI memo I'd inadvertently overlooked.

> *FROM: The Attorney General*
> *TO; DIRECTOR FBI*
>
> *Because of extensive activities of Albert and Hemblen, and their many contacts with known subversives and individuals suspected of or known to be involved in terrorist activities, it was approved at FBI Headquarters on June 22, 1975, that an electronic "beeper" be placed on the 1968 Volvo mentioned previously. This device was installed by our New York Office on August 26, 1975 . . .*

I appreciated in that instant—and for the first time—that FBI agents had planted not one but *two* separate tracking devices on my car—the first at the end of August 1975, and the one I found three months later. Art discovered this astounding FBI memo in 2020, just as the first round of Covid-19 pandemic was peaking. Already vulnerable from fear of virus, I went into shock: my reaction was intense but thankfully much more short-lived than Covid. Those damning FBI files were the only evidence of that first beeper.

Forty-five years earlier, in mid-December 1974, I'd handed what I thought was my one and only FBI tracking device to Margaret Kunstler. She put it inside their kitchen freezer. So that, Margie insisted, any transmission the beeper emitted would be blocked.

The next day, to keep it safe, Bill put my tracking device into a small safe located in the New York City office of the

Center for Constitutional Rights. Shortly afterwards, the Center was burglarized. The only item stolen was the safe containing my beeper.

Yippies all, Stew, Bill, and I also informed the media:

> An article in the December 15, 1975 issue of the "New York Post" states that Stewart Albert and Judy Gumbo, whose true name is Judith Lee Hemblen, located an electronic device on December 13, 1975 attached to the inside of a bumper on a 1968 Volvo registered to Hemblen while they were houseguests of well-known attorney William Kunstler. Kunstler, in an interview with newspaper reports, stated he did not know who was responsible for placing this device on Albert's and Gumbo's automobile "but there's no doubt it's a governmental source." Both Albert and Gumbo stated they believed they were under surveillance by unknown individuals.

The *New York Post* promoted my Yippie myth by publishing a photo of Bill, Stew, and me with the tracking device. Bill stands behind my Volvo, elation and resignation in his eyes. I crouch next to Stew, dressed in my favorite striped Guatemalan vest for maximum protester effect. Stew and I cradle the device in our hands. For public consumption, I put on a serious and disapproving non-Yippie face. Inside I was ecstatic. I'd listened to my inner feminist. I'd paid attention to her voice. For that, I'd won the greatest prize of all—proof positive that Stew and I were under surveillance. This fun-loving Yippie could not believe her luck.

* * *

MERE HOURS AFTER WE MET THE press, paranoia set in. I couldn't help twisting my neck to see if I was being followed. Even my calm, phlegmatic Stew looked rattled. Rather than return to

Catskill isolation, we decided to hide out in the anonymity of New York City. I suggested the apartment of a friend, a member of an anti-draft group, the Oakland 7, at whose rally on the Cal campus in early 1968 I'd first met Stew. I assumed that Stew and I could appeal to the compassion of a protest movement comrade. I rang the man's doorbell. I heard one two, three, four locks un-click. A gray metal door opened a mere six inches, entry to the apartment was clearly barred by a thick brass chain. Courage does not in every instance go hand in hand with comradeship; the man slammed his door in my face. For my fear-filled friend, my now public discovery of that tracking device was not a victory over evil. It made me a pariah in his eyes.

Stew came up with a solution: he and I would hide out with Al Goldstein, his buddy from Pace College. Stew had introduced me to Al in 1968. Al was a pioneer of hard-core, anti-feminist porn, producer of the X-rated hit movie *Flesh Gordon,* and founder and editor of *Screw,* a best-selling pornographic magazine for men. When I'd first met Al, he fit my Victorian (and anti-Semitic) stereotype of a lascivious Jew. *Screw*'s graphics made the sex ads I'd coordinated at the *Berkeley Barb* look G-rated. In 1968, I'd forbidden Stew, under threat of leaving him, to have anything to do with "that man." But in 1975, having just discovered that tracking device, my fear defeated my feminism. All I could do was mutter, "I'd rather be dead than hide out with Al!"

"Which is what we both will be if we don't find a place to hide," Stew retorted.

I walked upstairs inside Al's building—to be greeted by Al's jovial voice and an appalling guantlet. Penis candles lined both sides of Al's stairwell—fake erections made of white and yellow wax, many with red, white, and blue stripes. Some erections had balls, some were ball-less, some were circumcised, others not. A white wick sprouted from the center of each candle—a stream of cotton semen. I had no choice. Since I could not imagine any straight-laced

FBI agent making their way up that penis infested staircase, with great reluctance, I compromised. I placed myself under the protection of a Porn King and his penis candle collection.

Well-fed and entertained, Stew and I stayed overnight in Al's Temple of Male Members, until next day, our confidence restored, we felt secure enough to travel.

I will never forget those penis candles. And I'm still ashamed that Al Goldstein, porn king, demonstrated far greater willingness to risk his personal safety for the sake of friendship than my former friend, a dedicated anti-war activist.

* * *

I WAS LOOKING FOR A CEASEFIRE with the FBI, but I got one better. By discovering the second tracking device, which the FBI had nicknamed "bloodhound," I'd forced the FBI to stop surveilling me. On July 7, 1976, the FBI surrendered.

> *This matter is being placed in a pending inactive status. It is felt that any further active investigation of the subjects at this time would serve little purpose except to cause an embarrassing situation should it be detected.*

I had embarrassed the Bureau—an unpardonable sin in FBI World. I also got the last laugh. In an FBI report that does justice to Franz Kafka, agents had informed their superiors that:

> *Stew Albert and Judy Gumbo are difficult to surveil because of the extreme paranoia which pervades their thinking about being surveilled.*

* * *

IN 1978, THE U.S. DEPARTMENT OF Justice indicted former Acting FBI Director L. Patrick Gray for authorizing warrantless break-ins on more than a dozen people who were relatives or friends of the Weather Underground. Including Stew and me. Also indicted was Mark Felt, the FBI's key decision-maker on domestic spying. Felt turned out to be Deep Throat, the source who spilled the beans about the Watergate burglary that ultimately led to the resignation of President Richard Nixon. Both Felt and his henchperson Ed Miller were convicted in Federal Court—then pardoned by a new President named Ronald Reagan.

In retaliation for the break-ins, in the fall of 1979, Stew and I took the U.S. Government to court. I reveled in the grandiose title of my lawsuit: *CLAVIR VS. THE UNITED STATES OF AMERICA*. My lawyers' list of complaints included:

```
Illegal entry into plaintiff's premises
Electronic surveillance
Mail cover and mail openings
Interference with plaintiffs' employment
Interrogation
Physical surveillance
Speech monitoring
Car stops
Trailing
Use of bumper-beepers
COINTELPRO
Use of informers
Spreading of false rumors and allegations
of criminal charges
Spying on plaintiffs financial records
Photographing
Taking property belong to plaintiffs
```

Three years later, Stew and I settled our lawsuit for $20,000—a $75,000 value in 2020, and twenty-five times more than we survived on in 1979. In addition, I received a $5,000 settlement from the bank who'd passed my records on to local agents. For such an amount, I decided I could relinquish my anger at the Kingston Trust—but never at the FBI. Their sins were too pronounced.

I used a portion of our settlement to compensate our lawyers at the Center for Constitutional Rights and donate to the ACLU. I also purchased my first-ever, brand-new, beautiful but as it turned out notoriously unreliable car: an Audi. As a Yippie send-up for those few who recognized it, I acquired a vanity license plate that spelled out CAPBOM, the FBI acronym for the Capitol bombing. No one noticed until a customs official at the Canadian border demanded to know what CAPBOM stood for. Taken off guard, I fudged. It's a joke, I muttered. A bewildered customs official shook his head and let me pass.

I also discovered the following tag line affixed to my ten pounds of FBI files. This headline is written in boldface, capitalized, underlined, and typed or stamped from an ink pad.

ALL INDIVIDUALS INVOLVED IN NEW LEFT EXTREMIST ACTIVITY SHOULD BE CONSIDERED DANGEROUS BECAUSE OF THEIR KNOWN ADVOCACY AND USE OF EXPLOSIVES, REPORTED ACQUISITION OF FIREARMS AND INCENDIARY DEVICES AND KNOWN PROPENSITY FOR VIOLENCE.

This tag line explains it all. I may or may not hold an individual record for FBI surveillance by means of illegal burglaries, but today it's common knowledge that the FBI engaged in similar, often lethal acts against untold numbers of my compatriots—especially my compatriots of color. Unlike us fun-loving Yippies, the FBI was always deadly serious. I use the word deadly with intent: Black Panthers, resisters, radicals, political dissents and very often innocents were, and continue to be, imprisoned and murdered by agents of the U.S. government.

CHAPTER 24:
THE '60S EVENT OF THE '70S

IN THE SUMMER OF 1976, I still refused to give up my commitment to Yippie feminism on which my personal politics depended, but I also felt discouraged by the downward spiral of 1960s radical protest. To compensate, I chose another focus for my passions. If asked, I'd vehemently deny I wanted to be a mother, given how horrendous my own mother was. My friends disagreed, claiming they knew one day I would become one.

I took LSD for the third and final time in my life that summer. Inspired by the artist Judy Chicago, who in her work "The Dinner Party" created plates to represent vaginas of thirty-nine heroic women, I jumped naked into a Catskill stream, freed by hallucinogens from all constraints. The rushing water bumped and scraped me through a narrow canal of rocks and rapids. I gave birth to myself, a woman who now felt able, in her turn, to give birth to another being. By Stew's 37th birthday, December 4, 1976, I was three months along.

Like any woman who hesitates at first to reveal her pregnancy so as not to jinx it, I felt uncomfortable speaking about mine to anyone apart from Stew—until I wrote once again to Oanh. I was delighted with his quick response. Oanh wrote back with enthusiasm, expressing his love for me while yielding primacy in relationship to Stew.

> *I wish you every happiness, and hope the road before you two*
> *and the child will be that of flowers, songs and glories. Stewart,*
> *I guess, will be proud of being the happiest man in the world.*

Delighted at the prospect of a grandchild, Stew's mother Raizel gave us enough money to add a living room made from knotty pine that expanded our cabin's footprint by one third. Leo and Harriet paid for a washer and dryer from Sears. I watched as Stew, with a little help from our friends, painted the outside of our cabin in high-gloss red enamel. Our cabin glowed among the pine trees like a cherry tree of revolution to welcome our new baby.

To personalize my unrelenting nausea, I named my fetus "Bletch." I'd drive home after teaching Sociology at New Paltz to our cabin, bouncing at what was for me a moderate 50 miles an hour over rutted roads. To quell my nausea, I munched Nabisco saltines. Stew's hug on my return eased my distress. At the time Stew and I owned a dog named Oobie, bestowed on us by his former owner, a New York City friend with good intentions—to provide Oobie with a country home more suited to his half-mad personality. Oobie was large, black and curly-haired, a cocka-doodle—poodle/cocker spaniel mix. He was loyal to a fault but also fiercely paranoid—he'd claim any piece of food dropped on the floor as his and sink his teeth into your hand if you reached down for it. He did not discriminate. I could be the person Oobie lunged at, or Stew, or even Brian Flanagan—a former Weatherperson. Once, on my way home from teaching, Oobie deposited a half-gnawed deer carcass at my feet. It stained the white snow red. I saw this as his doggie way of saying, "You are home now, pregnant lady. Have a bite to eat."

After I obtained evidence our cabin had been burglarized, Oobie's previously unprovoked fits of nighttime barking made sense. We'd put Oobie in a kennel when we travelled to New York City When we returned after I found the second beeper, the kennel owners informed me, their faces grim, that Oobie had disappeared. But with what I heard as relief in their apologetic voices, Oobie had, they claimed, "chawed through two walls and escaped." Oobie was never found. To his credit, Oobie became a fugitive. I grieved my doggie's loss, but I empathized with his commitment to make that dash to freedom.

For exercise, I'd walk my favorite trail. From our cabin, I'd head upstream up the mountain, to end my hike at a birch tree whose single base had been split, I guessed by lightning, into two main trunks, each reaching skyward, as if to replicate my changing life. I'd walk back to the cabin where my trail turned into a U-shaped dirt road which ran past Mae and Ted Heath's trailer, then intersected with Hurley Mountain Road, a two-lane asphalt highway. Hurley Mountain Road arrived at the city of Kingston, where it transformed into the New York State Thruway and ran across the George Washington Bridge to end in cosmopolitan New York City. Being pregnant made me reflect on the interconnectedness of all things, and especially on how a trail that ran from bifurcated mountain tree to city skyscraper illuminated the bond I now had that joined my Yippie past to my procreating present.

* * *

STEW AND I DECIDED TO GET married. I did not need a ceremony to reach happily ever after. At this time, marriage was a right denied to LGBTQ+ folks but available to me. Since I saw marriage as an institution that kept women in our place, I decided I'd use my pregnancy to buck that trend—I'd wear a wedding gown that celebrated my pregnancy. Still, in 1977, I found no wedding outfit for this hugely pregnant bride at the only women's clothing store in nearby Kingston Plaza. I did manage to locate patterns for maternity clothes on a rack in a fabric store next to the plaza's Safeway. As if to make the point more obvious, maternity patterns were located immediately *after* bridal gowns. To me this mainstream message was clear—in Kingston New York and most of white America, pregnancy must follow marriage. A Yippie, feminist, and now a contrarian, I happily ignored that hint.

Hearing of my dilemma, a woman friend of Greg Mitchell, senior editor at *Crawdaddy* magazine, volunteered to sew a dress for me. The woman created a masterpiece. I wore a gown with puffy see-through cranberry-colored sleeves, eight-inch lace cuffs with faux-pearl buttons, and silky off-white rayon that fell in folds over my distended belly. As best I can recall I picked up my dress from the *Crawdaddy* editor; I know I never saw his woman friend again, nor do I recall her name. I acknowledge her and thank her now.

Stew and I married to placate Stew's mother and to ensure that our child had an easy, un-hyphenated last name. When women marry, we either keep our father's last name, take our husband's name, use both men's names (connected or not connected with a hyphen) or invent a new name of our own. My friends do all of these. I've used Clavir, Hemblen, Gumbo, Albert, and Gumbo Albert— with and without a hyphen. I've never used the last name Dobkin, the man I married after Stew, or, as I write this, the last name of my current husband, Eckstein. But I made my reputation as the Yippie feminist activist Judy Gumbo and did my best not to live my life dragging a patriarchal chain of names behind me like Marley's Ghost. I applaud anyone who creates a non-binary, non-patriarchal last name for themselves.

When Stew and I married, I faced an unusual quandary: what do I do about my Gumbo name?

In November 1975, Eldridge had returned to the United States from Paris, where he'd hung out with France's bon-vivant president Valerie Giscard d'Estaing. Rumors abounded: Eldridge had become a Moonie. Eldridge was promoting men's pants with giant, sock-like codpieces in between the legs. Were these rumors true, false, disinformation or government propaganda? What about Kathleen? The stories I'd heard and read bore such little resemblance to the Eldridge I knew that I began to question Stew—had Eldridge struck a deal with the Justice Department to allow him to return? Was Eldridge's timing suspicious—did the date of his return connect to the FBI installing our two tracking devices? Was Eldridge the reason the FBI escalated their surveillance of Stew and me? Being an informant topped my list of unforgivable sins. Yet for evidence I had only an assertion from a former FBI agent, an agent reputed to have come over to our side, that the space occupied by a name (blacked out) in one of my FBI files fit the number of letters in the word Cleaver.

I checked in with Kathleen. She vehemently denied the agent's story. She pointed out that the former agent was, as I'd later verify, an expert in fake news. I've since learned that after exile Eldridge had become emotionally unpredictable, but even so, Kathleen assured me, Eldridge was no informant. I trusted Kathleen Cleaver's word far more than any renegade FBI agent.

Still, what last name could I print on our wedding invitation without betraying my feminist principles?

I refused to give up the freewheeling Judy Gumbo or reject the adventures I'd had in her name. I put my last name Gumbo on our invitation. Then, perhaps feeling guilty about not being at peace with my birth family, after Gumbo I tacked on Clavir. My reasoning was faulty. Gumbo-Clavir left me cold. Only after I received our invitation, printed on card stock colored red for revolution with an illustrated border of dancing Vietnamese, did I feel like the invitation represented the person I'd become. Images of dancing revolutionaries—not the printed word—came closest to who I felt I was.

You are invited
to celebrate the wedding of
Judy Gumbo Clavir
and
Stewart Edward Albert
on May Day (Sunday, May 1), 1977
Beaverland Estate
Willow, New York

But my quandary over Gumbo revived a deeper ambivalence—would I lose my independence after I married and became a mother? I was resting my belly on a stack of gray mattresses, each no more than three inches thick, that I'd piled in a corner of our cabin. The mattresses gave my belly about as much support as the princess who slept on a pea.

I said bitterly to Stew, "I'll tell you one thing, Stewie, I will never be Mrs. Albert. I am not your mother."

Stew looked at me in sympathy and shrugged his shoulders.

With the exception of a hugely pregnant bride, our ceremony at Susan and Marty Carey's commune in Willow, just west of Woodstock, followed traditional wedding protocol. We held our rehearsal dinner in that same restaurant FBI agents had frequented when they surveilled us. Our wedding had the usual wedding glitches. By mistake I omitted Bob Fass, a beloved, burly night-time DJ on New York City's WBAI radio, from our invitation list—but he forgave me. Ignoring Oanh's advice and still angry at the interpersonal conflicts that defined Miami, Stew and I did not invite the Zippies.

I stood with Stew in all my pregnant glory in front of 150 people, beside a gurgling stream, framed by boughs of yellow forsythia in full bloom, under a chuppah made from tie-dye red, yellow, orange, blue, and purple fabric. Our wedding had its high points and its contradictions. Our wedding day dawned sunny and warm. The next day torrential spring rains fell. We had no indoor Plan B. Stew wore bright blue sneakers and a white pirate shirt with puffy sleeves, I dressed in my off-white haute couture hippie pregnancy gown. Around my hat I wore a lei of flowers given to me by Fay Stender, a white attorney friend who had travelled across country from Berkeley to attend our wedding. Two years later, Fay, a well-known prison rights activist, was shot and paralyzed by a member of a self-described revolutionary prison group, the Black Guerilla Family, who claimed that Fay had betrayed them. Fay subsequently committed suicide.

People rose to the occasion: My mother Harriet kept both her drinking and her patronizing attitudes in check. My father Leo charmed Stew's mother Raizel. My sister Miriam was my maid of honor; Jerry Rubin was Stew's best man. Bill Kunstler emceed as if his true profession was a Catskill comedian. A local Kingston rabbi in tallit, yarmulke, and Hollywood sunglasses officiated, as did our friend Cinnamon, a Universal Life Church minister whose name matched her hair. After the ceremony, the rabbi told Stew that Raizel, Stew's mother, had requested the rabbi insert the word "obey" in Hebrew into the ceremony. Since I don't speak Hebrew, I have no knowledge if he actually did. No matter, I never obeyed. Bill Schaap, and his partner Ellen Ray revealed to me they too were married but had kept their wedding in the closet in order not to appear politically impure. Our wedding ceremony was both a vanguard and a party. Shortly afterward "smash monogamy" got smashed into oblivion—even among us radicals.

I had not thought ahead to ask a wedding planner to help me cut our wedding cake—a homemade concoction so heavy with three layers of cake, cream, and fresh spring strawberries that it listed, appropriately, to the left. I cut the cake myself on aching feet as I shared with our close friends and community the sweetness of our love.

Even with marriage and a baby on the way, I included in the vows I made—not in public but to myself—that I'd follow my Yippie path: to be provocative, theatrical, oppositional, and, as much as I could, neither paranoid nor serious. And so began the first day of the rest of my life.

Stew turned out to be the person rabbis call a "beshert"—that half soul who unites with yours to create a whole. Our daughter was born five weeks after our wedding. My labor was short but excruciating. I screamed every combination of fuck I had in my vocabulary. My physician—a last minute substitute—used forceps to deliver her. Without asking, Kingston Hospital nurses put my baby in a section for white newborns, not the separate section they maintained for Black babies. At the cabin, I placed our new daughter in her bassinet and discovered that our cat Tarot had deposited underneath it a tiny gray bird with a black crown, quite dead—a congratulatory offering from one mother to another.

We named our baby Jessica Pearl—Jessica for Lady Jessica, a legendary prophet in Frank Herbert's sci-fi novel *Dune;* Pearl for my grandmother Ida Pearl and my favorite Janis Joplin album. Had Jessica been a boy, we'd have named her Malcolm for the Black revolutionary Malcolm X and Ernesto for the Cuban revolutionary Ernesto "Che" Guevara, resulting in a doubling down of revolutionary names—Malcolm Ernesto Gumbo Albert. Luckily for Jessica, she did not need to kill her parents, in real life or symbolically, to live up to such a lofty name. Stew and I were determined to raise our daughter exactly opposite to how we'd both been raised. We revived an old SDS slogan so Jessica could—within the bounds of safety—control the decisions that affected her life.

More forgiving than I was, *High Times Magazine*, run by Zippies, reported on our wedding in the "High Society" section of their magazine. They termed our wedding *"The Sixties Event of the Seventies."* And it was. There were, *High Times* reported, "nine lawyers to every ordinary person." Still, at the FBI's request, as if to re-enact a scene out of the Academy Award winning 1972 movie *The Godfather*, local Kingston police put up a roadblock and stopped cars of guests who left our hippie wedding, searching for Abbie.

* * *

In 2021, To honor Stew's and my 44th wedding anniversary, Jessica put up this piece on her Facebook page:

> *Have you ever heard the story of how my parents met?*
>
> *Once upon a time, a long, long, extremely long time ago, a young feminist Canadian found her very WASP-y husband in bed with another woman.*
>
> *So, she did what any heartbroken young Canadian feminist would do, she told Toronto to suck it (or whatever they said way back when) and headed to the bright sunshine of Berkeley CA. THE place to be at that time was, of course, Sproul Plaza on the UC Berkeley campus.*
>
> *One day, not long after she arrived, the young Canadian feminist spotted two rather attractive sun-kissed paisley clad blond men lounging around the fountain.*
>
> *So, she straightened her miniskirt, got her best saunter on with her knee-high boots (because you can be a feminist and rock a miniskirt and knee-high boots), and went over to these two blond men.*
>
> *My dad looked up at my mom, took his pinkie and touched her gently on her nose. The rest, as they say, is history.*
>
> *Happy 44th wedding anniversary, Judy and Stew.*

CHAPTER 25:
PORTLAND, OREGON 2006
"MY POLITICS SHALL NOT CHANGE"

REALLY LOVED

Judy is my old wife,
My best friend and lover,
And the wisest woman I ever knew.
I don't think life is fair.
Mostly we get cheated out of necessity
But Judy is so good she might cheat fate,
She might get justice, get what she deserves,
Get recognition, get appreciation.
Whatever happens,
At least Judy will know one true thing.
Judy will know
She was really loved

.

Stew Albert, 1992

I REMEMBER THAT SATURDAY. **STEW** SAT in my office on the second floor of our two-story blue bungalow that had been our home for twenty-two years. He sat on our sea-blue futon couch with its natural pine arms; I was at my pine computer desk with its single center drawer that opened on both sides. The previous day, an oncologist had diagnosed Stew with inoperable liver cancer. The doctor gave Stew six months. All I could do was sob and search endlessly on my computer for a cure that did not exist.

I had no way to know that two days later Stew would be dead.

"Write this down for me," I remember Stew asking. "And tell my friends I said this: My politics have not changed."

Our friends had shoved our king-size bed to one side, so I could lie next to Stew as he died, him in his hospice bed, me clutching our forest green velvet bedspread as if it was a baby blanket and breathing in his sweet and sour Stewie smell. In the chaos of the shoving, our friends had gouged a three-foot strip out of our bedroom wall—they might as well have taken another little piece of my heart out, baby, like Janis Joplin says. Stew insisted on standing up. Friends held him upright, one under each arm, so he could take that final piss erect, my macho man, his long ballerina legs bare, topped by a burly chest. Stew lay back down into the sterility of his hospice bed, eyes open, yellow curls framing his face on a white pillow. A sleepy golden storm, as in the Leonard Cohen song I'd have played at Stew's funeral.

At 3:20 a.m. Stew took a breath. Followed by an absence. A no-breath. Another inhalation. Silent time. Breath followed no-breath as if he welcomed the silence inside his body. Our daughter Jessica and I waited, listened, also silent. Then no more breaths. Just the finality of no-thing. I got up. I closed Stew's eyelids over those famous blue eyes of his, so piercing people quaked at their ferocity. I found scissors, clipped a lock of his curls, and placed it in a glass box with Mexican brass fittings like a mini mausoleum. I put them into the turquoise vinyl carrying case from the 1950s in which I store my keepsakes. How far gone in grief was I? I swear I saw a white puff of soul leave Stew's body.

Stew died on Monday, January 30, 2006, upstairs in our bedroom at 5204 Wistaria Avenue in Northeast Portland. He was 66 years old.

I planted poppies that year, that first year of excruciating pain, when I'd visit Stew every week to sit on the still-bare earth six feet above him, bawling my eyes out, yelling Stewie, Stewie, Stewie, pounding the unforgiving earth with my fist, trying to wake him up. To bring him back. To forgive him for dying. I was a wreck; alone in our bed at night I'd howl like a wolf, then wake up every morning into an endless grey fog.

Two weeks after Stew died, I was on the phone to our friend Naomi Kaufman. I looked down at my left hand and saw that my wedding ring was gone. Poof. Disappeared. My half of the set Susan Carey had made out of hammered silver for Stew and me when we married on Mayday 1977 at Susan and Marty's place near Woodstock, with forsythia in bright yellow bloom and me eight months pregnant. My ring had vanished. Transported into another dimension. I panicked, searched everywhere, re-traced every step, cried even more.

"*Don't worry, it'll turn up*," my friends said.

But I knew better. Loss begets loss.

To ease my distress, I needed to assign blame, so I talked out loud to Stew blaming him for his own death, for accepting that needle of heroin one night in deepest Brooklyn, well before I met him. Stew Albert, 21 year-old humanitarian, a social worker for New York City's welfare department, empathizer with the downtrodden, who had joined his client in an angry fix. Stew assured me he'd shot up only once, but, just as a single act of unprotected sex can leave a woman pregnant, that act passed Hepatitis C and the liver cancer that accompanied it on to Stew fifty years after the fact.

Less than a month after Stew died, I received an e-mail from Julie Herrada, Curator of the Labadie Collection of Social Protest at the University of Michigan.

> *Dear Mrs. Albert: Your husband was a role model. What will you do with his archives?*

I admired Julie for her rapid response to Stew's death. I understood why she looked at Stew as a role model. I even forgave her for calling me Mrs. Albert.

But I had to ask Jessica: "Archives? What does she mean by archives—the shit in the closet?"

Grieving is not linear. Everyone grieves in their own way; grief comes and goes without advance notice or control. But as twenty-four boxes of "shit in the closet" departed for the University Michigan, I felt the burden of my anger lift. I could acknowledge I was furious at Stew for dying but I managed to tiptoe forward. Then, in a back drawer of my office closet, I discovered our round aluminum cookie tin from the 1940s, with shooting rockets embossed on its lid. Inside, I found two ancient tabs of LSD that I remembered Timothy Leary had given Stew—along with perhaps a half-pound of shriveled psychedelic mushrooms and a few desiccated marijuana seeds. By then, to preserve my brain cells, I no longer smoked pot, or took mushrooms or LSD; neither—to my knowledge—did Jessica. Julie understandably declined to have such artifacts in her collection at University of Michigan. I know, I asked.

What to do? Jessica and I made a special visit to Stew's grave with its still raw earth. We dug a hole and planted our collection on top of Stew. I like to think some LSD filtered down for Stew to enjoy. And that perhaps the mushrooms or the pot seeds would sprout as a treat for any Yippie who visited Stew's grave.

One year later the time arrived, as is the Jewish way, to install Stew's headstone. By then I had become a sadder but more accepting version of myself. The poppies I'd planted had sprouted into green-brown fronds that leaned over Stew's grave just like the curls that Hubert, a right-wing preacher on the University of California campus, once claimed Stew wore in "calculated disarray."

Our friends chipped in to help me buy a slab of granite for Stew's tombstone. It came with a polished pink surface that sparkled from quartz crystals. I'd thought at first, I wanted the word "Yippie!"

engraved into his stone to mark his life, but after I saw the mock-up it was clear that wasn't appropriate for a gravestone. Yippie celebrates life; the mock-up looked like I was saying Yippie! You're dead.

STEW ALBERT
Husband and Father
Mentor and Friend
Scholar and Poet
Revolutionary and Rabbinic Inspiration
DECEMBER 4, 1939—JANUARY 30, 2006

I buried Stew in Jones Pioneer Cemetery in Southwest Portland. Stew's is the only gravestone I know of that has the word "revolutionary" on it. Wikipedia identifies Stew as "Stew Albert, Poet."

Nine months after Stew died, even though widows aren't supposed to make big decisions that first year, I sold our Portland house and moved back to the Bay Area, where Jessica and so many of my long-time friends lived. I just couldn't stay in our large and lonely former house anymore. Before I left, I held a yard sale and promoted its last day as the "Abbie Hoffman Memorial Free Store." Portlanders of all ages helped themselves to free stuff. Leaving Portland was the right decision. As I drove with Jessica across the Oregon/California border I saw in my rear-view mirror those familiar grey Oregon clouds, but straight ahead of me in all its glory shone that golden California sun.

* * *

WE WHO LIVE TO CHANGE THE WORLD
By Kathleen Cleaver, undated,
sent to me by Kathleen on 1/28/22

We who live by faith
Buffeted by winds of hate
And gusts of love
Believing what we do

Can change the world,
Even if that change comes
After our death.
We who loved the struggle
We who challenged evil, racism and hate
We who cry when our loved ones are killed
We who celebrate small victories of love
Still seek justice
Still stand against the wind
Never giving up our hopes and dreams
That we will change the world

* * *

PHIL OCHS TELEPHONED ONE RAINY DAY in June 1975. We still lived in our Catskill cabin. Phil wanted to come visit. His request was unusual—and out of the blue. I picked Phil up at the Kingston bus stop. His black hair was mussed, his suit jacket wrinkled.

"How are ya?" I inquired, unaware that to ask a person who is suffering how they are doing is a question they are least able to answer.

"Fine," Phil replied in a monosyllable.

At our cabin, Phil refused to go outside. He warmed himself by our new, top-of-the line Ashley stove with its gigantic firebox. He called himself John Train. John Train was, Phil said, a CIA agent.

"Are you commie scum?" John Train demanded.

Helpless, Stew and I communicated in whispers.

Next morning, Phil reversed himself, complaining that he was being "watched" by a CIA agent named John Train. Shortly after that, a semi-lucid Phil asked in his polite voice if I'd drive him to a bar. I took a back route, hoping the blue waters of the reservoir might calm him. No one in our Yippie circle understood that those who suffer from schizophrenia will mute their inner voices with alcohol.

At Phil's request we stopped on the way at a favorite antiques store of mine, located in a red barn at the corner of Shokan Road and Highway 28. Stew and I wandered its musty aisles while Phil purchased a gold-plated compact and postcards from the 1920s—four kittens in a brown and yellow wicker basket flew high above the Catskills, a male hand beckoned a flirtatious flapper in a pink dress to make her way through a giant gold wedding ring. *Won't you let me change your name?* the card inquired. I wondered why these postcards appealed to Phil in his current state and whether the images of kittens and romantic marriage helped him grasp that he had not entirely become John Train.

I dropped Phil at a local cowboy bar. He stayed for hours. A stranger drove him to our hill. Late next afternoon, I returned Phil to the Kingston bus station, only to find those three post-cards abandoned in our cabin. I still have them.

"Is anybody doing anything for Phil?" I asked as I drove Stew home another night. Stew said Jerry had tried to get Phil help, but to no avail. Nine months later, Phil hung himself from a shower rod in his sister's bathroom. I grieved, both for our collective helplessness and for Phil.

Patriot without a flag, sit by my stove just one more time, Stew wrote. Phil Ochs died on April 9, 1976. He was 35 years old.

Seven weeks after Phil's death, our telephone rang. I couldn't mistake that guttural voice. It was **Abbie**. Abbie's friends, including Stew and me, had heard that Abbie, now living underground on the St. Lawrence River, was in deep trouble. Two years earlier Abbie had fled the United States to escape a drug charge. Stew and I had heard reports—Abbie had become emotionally unstable, manic, a man whose neediness verged on desperation. He was now dependent on the kindness of friends, yet friends found him so difficult to deal with that they were always on the brink of abandoning him. On the phone, Abbie insisted Stew come visit! He must leave that day! Right now! Alone! I felt such sympathy for Abbie that I did not object.

Stew took a train to a ski town outside Montreal. Abbie the fugitive by turns insisted, cajoled, and demanded Stew be his

bodyguard so Abbie could attend, in disguise, a memorial for
Phil at the Felt Forum in New York City scheduled for May 28,
1976. Stew, 5'10" and muscular from chopping wood, had often
served as a bodyguard for Jerry. Despite my empathy for Abbie, I
was concerned that Stew would willingly take such a risk, one I
felt jeopardized our Catskill life. I was also not surprised at
Stew's decision; one of the many reasons I loved him was his
loyalty to friends. I agreed reluctantly, but I worried. After I
learned that Abbie had made it to Phil's memorial, I felt better.
Stew had done his job; he'd guarded Abbie all the way from
Montreal to New York City. Only when Stew, his guard duties
complete, put his arms around me and kissed me did I relax.

The day after Stew and I returned to our cabin, our telephone
rang. Again. Now it was our friend Susan Carey, a local Woodstock
jeweler. Susan and her artist husband Marty, longtime friends of
Abbie's, and at whose commune Stew and I had married, was on
the line. Abbie was at *The Bear*, a bar in Woodstock owned by
Albert Grossman, Bob Dylan's former manager. Abbie was yelling
at the customers that he was the fugitive Abbie Hoffman. Susan
and Marty would bring Abbie to a safe place, a motel on Highway
28A. Would Stew and I meet them there? To help? Right now?
Again, we could not ignore this request.

I found Abbie circling an unmade bed in a motel room whose
light brown fake wood walls allowed any argument, lovemaking, or
TV show to penetrate. Abbie's yells were punctuated by a laugh so
hyena-like it made me certain someone would call a manager. But
no manager appeared in that cheap motel. I watched Abbie extract
a hunting knife from his belt. The stress of this occasion may have
exaggerated my memory, but I recall Abbie's knife being about
one foot long, its blade affixed to a brown and white handle. Abbie
clutched the knife between his teeth, then jumped up and down
on the bed glaring at us as if daring us—plus any nearby cop—to
intervene. Abbie—a little boy pirate gone berserk.

"This isn't Yippie theater anymore, Abs," I muttered. Had the FBI been paying attention, each of us would have been arrested then prosecuted for harboring a federal fugitive—or being one. Luckily for us all, the FBI had given up surveilling me. Tough luck for them.

Next day, Marty ferried Abbie back to Montreal. After Marty returned, I organized a barbecue of welcome at our cabin. The charismatic Abbie Hoffman had become what with great sadness my friends and I began to call an energy vampire, who, through no fault of his own, sucked his friends dry.

When he died, Abbie was living in New Hope, Pennsylvania, in a turkey barn upgraded to a tiny home with whitewashed walls, indoor plumbing, and a roof three feet from the ground, eight feet tall at its peak. Abbie hated to be alone. He'd complained to his physician that Lithium, his anti-manic depression meds, had flattened him, siphoning off his precious energy. Abbie's doctor had taken him off Lithium, and instead prescribed Prozac. But Prozac is known to exacerbate suicidal tendencies.

Abbie Hoffman committed suicide on April 12, 1989. He was 52 years old.

The Abbie I'd experienced had so embodied life that I found it difficult to accept his death.

Less than six years later, on November 14, 1994, **Jerry** was hit by a car in front of his apartment as he crossed Los Angeles' busy Wilshire Boulevard. I recall friends saying that Jerry too had committed suicide, that he'd deliberately walked out into traffic, but then hesitated and was hit. I also heard that Fred Branfman, an LA friend of Jerry's who'd exposed the U.S. secret bombing of Laos, had yelled out, "Be careful!" Jerry stopped, turned and, or so the story I heard goes, looked back.

I chose not to believe either scenario since, the week before he died, Stew and I had a long phone conversation with Jerry. Jerry told us he had inoperable lung cancer. And that he'd been attending, uninvited, funerals of people he didn't know—he claimed for the food and entertainment. I did believe this since, given his diagnosis, it would be very Jerry-like to try and find out beforehand what a celebrity funeral was like.

In that final phone call, Jerry had invited Stew and me to come down to Los Angeles to spend Thanksgiving with him. We declined, most likely not to leave our by then 17-year-old daughter on her own, but I still regret not recognizing the urgency in Jerry's voice.

It was not the Jerry way for Jerry to commit suicide. The Jerry who was Stew's best friend could be fastidious and occasionally fearful, but his trademark was being impatient to get things done. Stew and I agreed that Jerry often acted on impulse—including to cross a busy street.

According to popular wisdom Jerry became a greedy stock-broker. This is a myth. Yes, Jerry did work on Wall Street but he advised clients to ensure they invested in companies with ecological and non-discriminatory practices. Such practices are widespread today as socially-responsible investing.

Jerry Rubin died on November 28, 1994. He was 56 years old.

Bill Kunstler died suddenly of heart failure in 1995, less than a year after Jerry. His diagnosis did not surprise me: Bill's heart was bigger than almost everyone else I knew. My last memory of Bill is him lying full length, stretched out on a hospital gurney. His memorial at St. John's Cathedral in New York attracted over 1,000 people, including Jessica. Bill was 76 years old.

Stew, Jessica, and I last met up with **Eldridge Cleaver** at Jerry's funeral. We talked one-on-one for the first time since Eldridge had returned from overseas. Despite the rumors surrounding Eldridge, ours was a warm and heartfelt reunion. Together we threw earth on Jerry's grave. Eldridge told us that he'd talked his way into Jerry's room at UCLA Medical Center when Jerry was in a coma. Initially, the nurses were skeptical—only relatives were allowed to visit. Eldridge obviously, was Black, Jerry, white.

"Same mother, different fathers," Eldridge had explained. He'd emerged from Jerry's room in tears.

By the time Eldridge died, he and Kathleen had been separated for ten years. Stew and I were no longer in touch with him, while Kathleen and I talk warmly to this day. "Eldridge loved the Yippies because they were so free," Kathleen told me recently. Kathleen is quoted in Eldridge's *New York Times* obituary saying that Eldridge had come back from Cuba, Algiers, and Europe, "a very unhealthy person, unhealthy mentally, and I don't think he's ever quite recovered. He became a profoundly disappointed and ultimately disoriented person." From a distance, I agreed.

I have a personal charisma meter in my mind. It measures an individual's moral righteousness, political effectiveness, humanistic vision, and articulation of a key message of resistance. To which I add being a genuinely nice person. Kathleen Cleaver, Bobby Seale, Emory Douglas, Big Man, and many members of the Black Panther Party score at or near the top. Not so for Eldridge. I ask myself: how do I justify my former enthusiasm for a man I considered a friend, a visionary Black leader for whom Black lives truly mattered yet who advocated rape and was unfaithful to Kathleen? Eldridge often repeated this quote he said came from the Quran:

And the Devil said, though I had no authority over you, I called you and you came.

As I believe Eldridge Cleaver did.

In the early 1980s, I went with Stew to hear Eldridge speak. He had returned to the Berkeley campus where he'd once attempted to teach his famous 139X course on racism and revolution. Now he'd arrived in the guise of a repentant born-again Christian. I recall a white man rising up from his seat in anger to confront Eldridge, faulting him for selling out the Panthers and the Revolution. Eldridge lost his cool.

"Yo mama's a whore, sucker!" Eldridge yelled at his accuser.

Stew and I repeated this story again and again to our friends in the presence of our then four-year-old daughter Jessica. One morning Jessica was playing outdoors in our front yard at the same time as Stew was trying to coax her to get ready for pre-school. Jessica, with exquisite four-year-old intransigence, refused.

"Your mama's a horse, sucker!" Jessica yelled at Stew, who fell to the ground laughing. From whore to horse, so went the Yippie/ Panther revolution.

I believe Malcolm X coined, and I know Eldridge popularized, the slogan, "You're either part of the solution or part of the problem"—a defining binary of my generation. The man I knew as Eldridge Cleaver embodied both.

Eldridge Cleaver died on Mayday, 1998. He was 62 years old.

I last saw **Anita Hoffman** that winter of 1998. The movie star Winona Ryder had loaned Anita her Pacific Heights home with its spectacular view of the San Francisco Bay. By then Anita's breast cancer had metastasized. She'd refused what she called the violence of radiation, her cancer had spread to her bones. Anita was paralyzed from the waist down; her nights were filled with nausea and pain. And her pain pills no longer worked.

She told me, "I always thought I would be an old lady, but I won't."

I'd brought Anita a gift of a tiny menorah which she accepted gladly; I then offered her a tallit which she angrily rejected. I guess a tallit felt too extreme in Jewish identification for Anita. I did not take her rejection personally. Anita's love and beauty, truth and decency gave her good cause for anger—at her impending death, at those she did not name but felt had in some way betrayed her, as well as those who loved her. Stew caught Anita's mood when he wrote:

"Good-bye" she said when we departed,
"See you in the next world."
I kissed her hand and face
And looked into her bottomless eyes

And wasn't so sure
It would be a better world.

Anita Hoffman died on December 27, 1998. She was 56 years old.

I met **Rosemary Leary** for the first time at Anita's bedside. She was supplying Anita with Mendocino County marijuana grown specifically to combat cancer. She followed Anita in death in 2002. Rosemary Leary was 66.

Tim Leary died in 1996 at age 75, of cancer. Stew visited him before he died. Leary's ashes were shot into space.

In 2021, I received a letter from my sister Miriam. It was from my mother **Harriet Clavir**. She'd dated it Wednesday, April 16— but without a year. The words "never sent" appear in her handwriting. In this letter, Harriet claims she intends to enter an in-patient alcoholism treatment program. She acknowledges that 30 or 40 years previously she'd been an inpatient in that same treatment program. On first read, I experienced my mother's letter as a litany of denial and self-centered complaints:

"Lectures do not tell me anything I do not already know."

"I truly don't care to be part of a group with whom I have little, or nothing, in common—except for addiction."

"I am maybe too old."

"They have no pool."

Harriet's letter gave me a new insight—my mother understood fully that she was addicted to alcohol.

"I found myself in the middle of the afternoon looking at an empty one-liter bottle of wine while I phoned the worker at the clinic to quote my favorite poem—

I stand beside my grave
Confused with my life
Which is commonplace and solitary

"My drinking," my mother's letter continues, "has gotten out of hand in a time sense. I have a real need for alcohol in the day-times—from anywhere to 11 a.m. to 6–8 p.m. This results in a nothing life. I should also tell you that I am not vicious in my daytime drinking, verbally or otherwise."

My mother never sent this letter. I'm not surprised—it's too honest.

Harriet Clavir died on June 30, 1999. She was 85 years old. Never able to control her drinking, she suffered a lonely death in a Toronto nursing home. I regret that I was not with my mother when she died, nor was my sister Miriam—only a former helper and impersonal caregivers heard her announce to anyone willing to listen: "I'm dying, I'm dying."

My father **Leo Clavir** was the true believer, my mother was the emotional extremist. Long after Russian President Khrushchev had exposed Stalinist atrocities, my father continued to defend the ideals of Soviet communism. And keep its secrets.

In the mid-1980s, Leo, Harriet, Stew, and I attended a musical recital in Portland, Oregon, where Stew and I then lived. Anxious and excited at the end of the concert, my father insisted that we go up onto the tiny stage so he could introduce himself to the older, grey-haired pianist. But the name that popped out of my father's mouth was not Leo but Allan. My father's business card read A.L Clavir, but never in my life had I heard him use the name Allan.

"What name is that?" I asked as I watched my mother scowl.

"My other name," my father replied. "But just forget I said that, understand?"

His "other" name? A secret name I'd never learned? My Red Diaper colleagues in the United States had learned to keep their parent's secrets; I was never a party to them. For all his life, my father had functioned under levels of secrecy I had no idea existed.

Leo Clavir died in 1989, ten years before Harriet. Leo was 77 years old.

Do Xuan Oanh was not just the go-to person for visiting international peace activists; he was a celebrity songwriter and artist, well known in Vietnam for composing a patriotic song titled "August 19." Oanh wrote and published poetry in the romantic Vietnamese/French style, painted watercolors, and translated into Vietnamese Mark Twain's *Huck Finn*—as well as two works by the best-selling popular author Jacqueline Suzanne. Oanh never wanted me to call him a "diplomat"—he insisted his title was "emissary." I decided Oanh was being modest, since during the time I knew him he was secretary to Xuan Thuy, the Foreign Minister of the DRV and signer of the 1973 Paris Peace Accords.

When Oanh gave me permission, forty years after our affair and shortly before he died, to "write about anything we shared in the past," I felt free to disclose that we were lovers. Oanh's youngest son validated my decision when I visited Hanoi in 2013. In front of Oanh's family, he proudly named me, "The American Girlfriend."

I emailed Oanh when he was close to death asking to visit him in Vietnam. Oanh refused, wanting me to remember him as the younger, vibrant man with whom I fell in love. On January 1, 2010, I received Oanh's final email.

Your message brings a bit of life and significance to my seclusion. I suddenly remember a proverb of my native place that may express what it means: Giving birth to me are my parents, understanding me is Judy. That also is a way to express how telepathy works.

Do Xuan Oanh died in Hanoi on March 27, 2010. He was 87 years old.

Paul Krassner died on January 21, 2019, also at age 87. I regret again I did not manage to visit Paul before he died, but he lived a full, productive Yippie life well beyond that of many of his pals. Including helping women obtain abortion care when it was still illegal. Paul's friends have put together a functioning list of all his friends—we e-mail each other with anecdotes and updates to memorialize Paul's humor and the Yippie politics Paul embodied during his life.

My first husband **David Hugh Milner Hemblen** died on November 16, 2020. By then I no longer cared about his infidelity and I'd long since ceased to be bothered by the FBI's ongoing use of what once was a hateful name. In fact, I am grateful to Hemblen, in the same way I'm grateful to the FBI. Had I not discovered Hemblen's infidelity and left him in Toronto, I'd never have led my Yippie life. Hemblen was 79 years old.

And **Pigasus**, our Yippie candidate for president, has long been in hog heaven.

RIPigasus.

EVERY REVOLUTION HAS ITS CASUALTIES

Let me raise a cup to my fallen pals,
The empty chairs and tables
At the Yippie Café
To Jerry Rubin, Abbie Hoffman, Phil Ochs and all the others.

In dreams they come for me.
And say they love me, miss me, want me.
OK, someday I'll be coming
But not just yet.

I've got a few more poems up my sleeve
And a few more Bushies to burn.

Stew Albert, 12/4/2002

THE END

AUTHOR'S NOTE

OF ALL THE QUESTIONS I FACED writing *Yippie Girl*, I agonized most over how much information to disclose.

"Cover your ass," a Black Panther archivist advised.

"Tell the truth," one friend, at the time an editor at a major university press, said.

I've done both in *Yippie Girl*. But how could I decide what to reveal and what not—let alone what is truth? I have a duty to history; but I feel even more strongly that I not betray the confidence of friends. I write about events as I experienced them directly but, unless I obtained explicit permission, I've left any reveal of toxic personal experience up to the person violated, raped, injured, abused, harmed, harassed, wronged, or implicated. Such a reveal is theirs to make, not mine.

Given my unusual cast of characters, I realized early on that the only way to tell my story was as a work of narrative or creative non-fiction—facts told as story. I also freely use the words "woman" and "man"—descriptors from the bygone era about which I write. *Yippie Girl* is my story of how I travelled out of girlhood into womanhood.

I regret any material in *Yippie Girl* that you, my reader, consider that I have mis-stateted, misremembered or misquoted. I alone am responsible for what is written here.

My final section, "Every Revolution Has Its Casualties," contains only names of major characters who died before 2022—I didn't want to hex anyone by including names of those who, as I write this in late 2021, are still alive. I also gave my major characters an opportunity to review and comment. That turned out to be a wise decision. Kathleen Cleaver, an early reader of my MS, appeared to care little that I'd revealed Eldridge's infidelities, but she got incensed when I intimated Eldridge might have been an FBI informant. He was not. I'd wasted my agony on the wrong sin.

Bizarre as it still feels, the FBI tops my list of those I need to thank. Had FBI agents not followed me with such dogged determination, I would not have been able to write this book. I now possess ten pounds of precise and detailed records of the times, dates, and places the FBI surveilled me. All quotations I've reproduced from my FBI files are verbatim. They appear as they do in my files: in *italics*, **bold**, CAPITAL LETTERS and `Courier New` font—for typewriters.

I'm indebted above all to my late husband Stew Albert. Stewie—I did my best to do justice to your extraordinary compassion, tolerance, and love for me—and to your story. I'm also grateful to my late husband David Dobkin, who founded Berkeley Cohousing where I live. Our time together was too short. I'm even grateful to Hemblen, my cheating first husband, without whose infidelity I might never have left Canada for the United States. And I'm especially indebted to my current husband Art Eckstein, without whose loving help and dedicated discipline as a Distinguished Professor, editor, and researcher of FBI files I'd never have completed this manuscript. I love you Artie! Above all, I'm truly grateful to my daughter Jessica Albert Epstein, who has supported the *Yippie Girl* endeavor from the day she was born and uses her extraordinary skills today as my truly dedicated adviser and publicist.

I'm indebted also to the amazing publishing team of Peter Carlaftes, Kat Georges, and Mary Rose Manspeaker of Three Rooms Press, who took a chance on me and published *Yippie Girl*. Their confidence and expertise inspire me. I'm also indebted to my extraordinary group of friends, writers, and advisors who assisted me along the way. Ann Hasse, Jane Brunner, Roxanne Schwartz, Louise Yelin, Kelley Leathers, Jonah Raskin, Mike Pincus, and the late Betsy Benford gave valuable comments and re-writes on early drafts. My friend Susan Faludi was my role model as a writer. Deborah Lichtman, Michael Denneny, and Steve Wasserman brought me out of composing fundraising letters to writing memoir. My sister Miriam Clavir provided valuable (and painful) documents and information from my childhood. Laura Foner and Dana Biberman provided details about Abby Kaplan's beating and death. Larry Roberts encouraged me by telling a portion of my story in his excellent book *Mayday 1971*; Noreen Banks publicized *Yippie Girl* to the Mayday list. Pat Thomas, author of *Jerry Rubin: From Yippie to Yuppie* hooked me up with Three Rooms Press, and heartily promoted *Yippie Girl*. John Jekabson donated copies of the *Barb* and *Tribe* from his collection. Benjamin Seashore-Hobson helped type the final draft. And Tom Dalzell helped me copy-edit. I thank you all.

I'm especially grateful to my long-time friends and comrades from the Black Panther Party. Kathleen Cleaver, Bobby Seale, Emory Douglas, and Bill Jennings (Billy X) who shared their expertise with me but more importantly, devoted their lives to combatting racism. For me the Chicago 7 was and will always be the Chicago 8. Power to the People, Panther Power to the Vanguard!

To my readers: If I encountered you along the way but inadvertently omitted your name from *Yippie Girl*, please know I consider myself beholden to you—and to all of us who took to the streets back in the day and who continue, each in our own way, to overturn racism, destroy misogyny, and protest war—on our environment and around the planet.

Everyone has their own 1960s. *Yippie Girl* is mine.

Judy Gumbo
www.yippiegirl.com
2022

RECENT AND FORTHCOMING BOOKS FROM THREE ROOMS PRESS

FICTION

Lucy Jane Bledsoe
No Stopping Us Now

Rishab Borah
The Door to Inferno

Meagan Brothers
Weird Girl and What's His Name

Christopher Chambers
Scavenger
Standalone

Ebele Chizea
Aquarian Dawn

Ron Dakron
Hello Devilfish!

Robert Duncan
Loudmouth

Michael T. Fournier
Hidden Wheel
Swing State

Aaron Hamburger
Nirvana Is Here

William Least Heat-Moon
Celestial Mechanics

Aimee Herman
Everything Grows

Kelly Ann Jacobson
Tink and Wendy

Jethro K. Lieberman
Everything Is Jake

Eamon Loingsigh
Light of the Diddicoy
Exile on Bridge Street

John Marshall
The Greenfather

Aram Saroyan
Still Night in L.A.

Robert Silverberg
The Face of the Waters

Stephen Spotte
Animal Wrongs

Richard Vetere
The Writers Afterlife
Champagne and Cocaine

Julia Watts
Quiver
Needlework

Gina Yates
Narcissus Nobody

MEMOIR & BIOGRAPHY

Nassrine Azimi and Michel Wasserman
Last Boat to Yokohama: The Life and Legacy of Beate Sirota Gordon

William S. Burroughs & Allen Ginsberg
Don't Hide the Madness:
William S. Burroughs in Conversation with Allen Ginsberg
edited by Steven Taylor

James Carr
BAD: The Autobiography of James Carr

Judy Gumbo
Yippie Girl: Exploits in Protest and Defeating the FBI

Judith Malina
Full Moon Stages:
Personal Notes from 50 Years of The Living Theatre

Phil Marcade
Punk Avenue: Inside the New York City Underground, 1972–1982

Jillian Marshall
Japanthem: Counter-Cultural Experiences; Cross-Cultural Remixes

Alvin Orloff
Disasterama! Adventures in the Queer Underground 1977–1997

Nicca Ray
Ray by Ray: A Daughter's Take on the Legend of Nicholas Ray

Stephen Spotte
My Watery Self:
Memoirs of a Marine Scientist

PHOTOGRAPHY-MEMOIR

Mike Watt
On & Off Bass

SHORT STORY ANTHOLOGIES

SINGLE AUTHOR

The Alien Archives: Stories
by Robert Silverberg

First-Person Singularities: Stories
by Robert Silverberg
with an introduction by John Scalzi

Tales from the Eternal Café: Stories
by Janet Hamill, with an introduction
by Patti Smith

Time and Time Again:
Sixteen Trips in Time
by Robert Silverberg

Voyagers:
Twelve Journeys in Space and Time
by Robert Silverberg

MULTI-AUTHOR

Crime + Music: Twenty Stories of Music-Themed Noir
edited by Jim Fusilli

Dark City Lights: New York Stories
edited by Lawrence Block

The Faking of the President: Twenty Stories of White House Noir
edited by Peter Carlaftes

Florida Happens:
Bouchercon 2018 Anthology
edited by Greg Herren

Have a NYC I, II & III:
New York Short Stories;
edited by Peter Carlaftes
& Kat Georges

Songs of My Selfie:
An Anthology of Millennial Stories
edited by Constance Renfrow

The Obama Inheritance:
15 Stories of Conspiracy Noir
edited by Gary Phillips

This Way to the End Times:
Classic and New Stories of the Apocalypse
edited by Robert Silverberg

MIXED MEDIA

John S. Paul
Sign Language: A Painter's Notebook
(photography, poetry and prose)

DADA

Maintenant: A Journal of Contemporary Dada Writing & Art
(Annual, since 2008)

HUMOR

Peter Carlaftes
A Year on Facebook

FILM & PLAYS

Israel Horovitz
My Old Lady: Complete Stage Play and Screenplay with an Essay on Adaptation

Peter Carlaftes
Triumph For Rent (3 Plays)
Teatrophy (3 More Plays)

Kat Georges
Three Somebodies: Plays about Notorious Dissidents

TRANSLATIONS

Thomas Bernhard
On Earth and in Hell
(poems of Thomas Bernhard with English translations by Peter Waugh)

Patrizia Gattaceca
Isula d'Anima / Soul Island
(poems by the author in Corsican with English translations)

César Vallejo | Gerard Malanga
Malanga Chasing Vallejo
(selected poems of César Vallejo with English translations and additional notes by Gerard Malanga)

George Wallace
EOS: Abductor of Men
(selected poems in Greek & English)

ESSAYS

Richard Katrovas
Raising Girls in Bohemia:
Meditations of an American Father

Far Away From Close to Home
Vanessa Baden Kelly

Womentality: Thirteen Empowering Stories by Everyday Women Who Said Goodbye to the Workplace and Hello to Their Lives
edited by Erin Wildermuth

POETRY COLLECTIONS

Hala Alyan
Atrium

Peter Carlaftes
DrunkYard Dog
I Fold with the Hand I Was Dealt

Thomas Fucaloro
It Starts from the Belly and Blooms

Kat Georges
Our Lady of the Hunger

Robert Gibbons
Close to the Tree

Israel Horovitz
Heaven and Other Poems

David Lawton
Sharp Blue Stream

Jane LeCroy
Signature Play

Philip Meersman
This Is Belgian Chocolate

Jane Ormerod
Recreational Vehicles on Fire
Welcome to the Museum of Cattle

Lisa Panepinto
On This Borrowed Bike

George Wallace
Poppin' Johnny

Three Rooms Press | New York, NY | Current Catalog: www.threeroomspress.com
Three Rooms Press books are distributed by Publishers Group West: www.pgw.com

31901068772567

CPSIA information can be obtained
at www.ICGtesting.com
Printed in the USA
JSHW021626270222
23406JS00003B/3

9 781953 103185